BORN TO RUN 2

THE ULTIMATE TRAINING GUIDE

CHRISTOPHER McDOUGALL
& ERIC ORTON

BORN TO RUN 2
THE ULTIMATE TRAINING GUIDE

2

SOUVENIR
PRESS

CONTENTS

Part 1:
BORN TO RUN

The Run Free Feeling

Ever since *Born to Run* came out, I've gotten messages from all over the world, many saying the same thing:

'Thank you! You changed my life.'

To which I reply:

'I know exactly what you mean.'

Because I was in their shoes. I'm *still* in their shoes – even when I'm not wearing any. *Born to Run* may come across as a rock'm-sock'm adventure story, because let's face it; that's what you get when a mysterious loner called *Caballo Blanco*, the White Horse, holds a fifty-mile footrace against a legendary tribe right under the nose of two murderous drug cartels.

But at its heart, *Born to Run* is something very different. It's a story of transformation, of the climb from defeat, to hope, and finally, to power. Real, life-changing power. The power to step outside and explore the world on your own two feet, running wherever you want, for as long as you want, whenever you feel like it.

To really appreciate what a superpower that is, you have to either try it once, or lose it forever. Those are the people I hear from most: ex-runners who are overjoyed to discover they have another chance, and beginners who finally received the inspiration they need to get started.

In its own rollicking way, *Born to Run* showed that no matter what age you are, no matter the shape you're in or the kind of injuries and discouragement you've suffered in the past, your best days of running are still ahead. 'You don't stop running because you get old,' as Jack Kirk, the 94-year-old trail runner known as the 'Dipsea Demon', liked to say. 'You get old because you stop running.'

But no one becomes a Demon overnight. Running is a dance, and it takes a while to learn the steps. That's why many of the thank-yous I receive end with this plea:

I can't wait to begin. Where do I start?

To that, I had no answer.

For years, I couldn't say for sure what to do next, because I was in the middle of finding out for myself. I felt like I'd won the lottery, but I couldn't believe the money was mine. By that point, it had been more than a decade since Eric Orton had trained me for the wild escapade in Mexico's remote Copper Canyons that would become *Born to Run*. We'd seen the book ignite a worldwide boom in barefoot running, and ultramarathons, and the Rarámuri superfood, chia seeds.

To me, that proved we were on to something important. People didn't just want to run; they wanted to *like* running. They were searching for that same sense of joy that we *Más Locos* had experienced during a long, dangerous race under a blazing sun at the bottom of a canyon.

Rarámuri youngsters use the *rarájipari* ball-chase game to perfect their running form.

'Run free!' the White Horse liked to declare, and that two-word battle cry sums it up perfectly. *Free* isn't the same as *wild*, although it's close. Caballo Blanco meant free from injuries. Free from stress. Free from overpriced shoes and gear and race fees. Run free, like a kid busting out the door for recess … or a grouchy loner who left the modern world behind for a tiny hut and a strange but loving family among the Rarámuri.

But I wasn't sure I'd found it myself.

I had complete faith in Eric's approach: his version of the Run Free system never failed me, not for race after race, year after year, adventure after weird adventure. What I didn't have was faith in myself. In the back of my mind, I could still hear those doctors warning me that running was bad for the human body, especially bodies like mine. I couldn't shake the feeling that running wasn't meant for a guy like me. Maybe I was getting away with it for now, but one of these days, I'd pay the price.

And then, on a surprisingly hot morning in late September, a different day arrived. I was at my favourite event, our local Bird-in-Hand Half Marathon. It's hosted by my Amish neighbours every year to raise money for the firefighters and first responders who raced to help the children who'd been shot in an Amish schoolhouse massacre in 2006.

The Bird-in-Hand course is breathtaking and utterly serene. There's no blaring music, just the soft singing of a Mennonite family on their front porch at Mile 2. Amish children are the aid station volunteers, offering cups outside their family farms while calling, '*Vater! Vater! Vater!*' Runners wind their way through the green hills of the Valley of No Wires, so named because none of the homes have phones or electricity.

But one of those hills, I'm here to tell you, is a beast. Every year I know it's coming and every year, it's worse than I remember. First of all, it's just mean. Red Lane Hill catches you just past Mile 10, right when you think you're on the home stretch. And it's sneaky. One moment you're looking at a gentle ribbon of road, the next you're veering onto a hidden dirt lane knifing skyward through a corn field. Plus, it's *hot hot hot*. There isn't a tree in sight, so the full force of the mid-morning sun smacks you right in the face. And

> **" I HAD COMPLETE FAITH IN ERIC'S APPROACH: HIS VERSION OF THE RUN FREE SYSTEM NEVER FAILED ME, NOT FOR RACE AFTER RACE, YEAR AFTER YEAR, ADVENTURE AFTER WEIRD ADVENTURE. "**

finally, for us barefoot runners, Red Lane Hill is where we rediscover how many jabby little rocks a dirt road can hide.

When I reached the top, an older guy ahead of me stopped dead in his tracks. He was pouring sweat and huffing like a dying locomotive. Suddenly, he threw his arms in the air like he'd just won Olympic gold.

'Yeah!' he gasped. 'Aren't we lucky?'

Of all the things I was feeling at that moment – thirsty, tired, cranky, footsore – 'lucky' was nowhere on the list. At least not until I stopped, and looked around, and got what he meant. That morning, we'd all gathered in a hayfield to watch the sun rise. Then we'd surged off on our own two legs to run as fast, as far and as freely as we felt like. We'd climbed that hill under our own power, and we were about to feel the rush of flying back down again.

That's an amazing gift. That's a superpower. And that's what Eric was offering when we first met in a public park in the middle of Denver. It took a lot of miles to silence my doubts, but standing at the top of Red Lane Hill, it finally hit me. Eric never meant to train me for a race.

He was training me for a lifetime.

I'd begun this journey as an average jogger who'd been injured so often that doctors told me, repeatedly, that the only thing in my future if I continued to run was a nifty pair of knee replacements.

Before journeying down to the Copper Canyons, I'd gotten fed up with chasing new approaches to an old problem. I'd never been much of a runner in the first place, just a few-miles-a-day guy who occasionally tried to ramp up for a half-marathon, but I could never go more than a few months without getting hurt. When I asked a leading sports-medicine physician why I was constantly injured, he looked at me like I was brain-dead. 'Didn't we go over this?' he asked, as he prepared to inject my foot with cortisone for the third time that year. 'All that pounding is bad for the body.' Especially bodies that look like Shrek's, he implied, in case I'd forgotten I was 6'4" and 240 pounds.

But what was I meant to do? You're supposed to run to get in shape. Except if you're not in shape, you're not supposed to run. And it's not just me; it's all of us. The injury rate among runners is crazy high, somewhere north of 70 per cent a year, and it's been that way for decades. New shoe models are rolled out constantly, and not one – *ever* – has been shown to reduce injuries.

Ironically, I was writing for *Runner's World* at the time, so it wasn't as if I were lacking for injury-prevention and training advice. I'd tried every tip you'll find in a running magazine – stretching, cross-training, heat-moulded custom insoles, soaking in ice, replacing my $150 shoes every four months with a fresh pair – but no matter what, it was only a matter of months before fiery twinges began shooting out from my heels, hamstrings or Achilles tendons.

The only thing I hadn't tried was changing my running form, because why would I? I wasn't crazy.

You're never supposed to tinker with your form. Never, never, never. Running pundits may disagree about a lot, but when it comes to this point, they're a church choir.

'Everyone has a unique running style,' is the way Dr Reed Ferber, head of the Running Injury Clinic at the University of Calgary, explains his argument. 'There is no right way to run, nor is there a wrong way to run.' The authors of the very popular *Advanced Marathoning* guide agree: 'Because everyone has a unique physical make-up, there is no ideal or perfect form.'

Amby Burfoot, the long-time *Runner's World* editor and columnist, likes to repeat a quote he got from another scientist of the sport, Dr George Sheehan: 'We are all an experiment of one.'

But isn't that the *opposite* of science? Running, according to this thinking, is the only activity that is utterly free from the laws of physics. Dancing, swimming, swinging a bat,

Christopher McDougall and Iman Wilkerson practise Skipping for Height, a Coach Eric favourite.

strumming a guitar, eating with chopsticks – every other movement your body can perform has styles you can improve through practice.

But not running. The running establishment would like you to believe there is no right or wrong – except when it comes to shoes, its $130-billion-a-year cure-all. Because that's all we're ever told to change. Not our form, only our footwear. Don't learn, in other words – just buy.

Then the White Horse opened my eyes.

If you've read *Born to Run*, you'll remember my long search through the Copper Canyons and the moment I finally cornered the wary, hungry, sun-baked drifter known as Caballo Blanco. He was a strange sight, all dusty from the trail and geared up in battered sandals and a straw cowboy hat, but on closer inspection, we had more in common than I thought. Caballo was my same height, my same shoe size and my same age when he, like me, first set off to Mexico in hope of discovering the secrets of the legendary Rarámuri distance runners.

Caballo was in Leadville, Colorado, back in the mid-90s when a band of Rarámuri turned up at the starting line of the Leadville Trail 100 – a one-hundred-mile footrace across the top of the Rockies – and proceeded to destroy the field, capturing eight of the top ten places. The following year, the Rarámuri repeated their astonishing performance … and then disappeared back down to the canyons, never to return.

Caballo followed, intent on learning how the Rarámuri could run long distances wearing only the simplest sandals and continue well into old age without suffering the same injuries, discouragement and physical breakdowns as the rest of us. If running is bad for our knees, he wondered, why wasn't it bad for *their* knees? How come the Rarámuri didn't need fancy shoes and orthotics?

I thought I'd gotten a glimpse of the answer myself, but I needed the White Horse to confirm. By the time I found him, he'd been in the canyons for more than a decade, living in a little hut he'd built himself with stones he'd hauled up from the river by hand.

He heard me out, then shook his head.

" THE BIRD-IN-HAND COURSE IS BREATHTAKING AND UTTERLY SERENE. THERE'S NO BLARING MUSIC, JUST THE SOFT SINGING OF A MENNONITE FAMILY ON THEIR FRONT PORCH AT MILE 2. "

Micah True – aka Caballo Blanco, the wandering White Horse of the Sierra Tarahumara.

I'd never get the right answer, he said, because I was asking the wrong question. Forget about why the Rarámuri are so different than us, he explained. Focus on why they're so much like each other.

That was it. That was the moment I finally understood what I'd seen. A few days earlier, I'd watched a group of Rarámuri kids running back and forth along a dirt trail, flicking a wooden ball to each other off the toe of their sandals. I was struck by one odd detail:

The kids all ran the same way.

Some were fast and some slower, but when it came to style, the Rarámuri kids were nearly identical. If you think that's no big deal, try watching a local 10k some time. For every hundred racers who stream past, you're guaranteed to see a hundred interpretative dances: some runners landing on their heels, others on their toes, many hunched forward, a few ramrod straight, all with arms and legs and heads swinging to a rhythm only they can hear. If you're looking for experiments of one, you can't beat the average road race.

'Maybe these kids are on to something,' I'd thought to myself as I watched them run. I was convinced of it later that morning, when Rarámuri grown-ups appeared on the trail, all of them trotting with the same light-footed, knee-driving style as the kids.

That was the secret that lured Caballo down there. 'Ya wanna learn?' he finally grunted. 'I'll show you.'

At dawn the next morning, Caballo led me towards a dirt trail winding into the pine woods. As I fell in behind him, he uttered the six words that would upend my life:

'Stick tight. Do what I do.'

He broke into a trot. I followed a few yards back.

'Closer,' he ordered.

I pulled up so tight, his heels were nearly kicking my knees.

'Right there,' he said.

For a tall guy, his stride was weirdly short and almost bouncy, kind of *pop-pop-popping* along. He landed as gently as a dancer, which made sense because instead of cushioned running shoes, he wore battered Teva sandals.

'Now, think "Easy",' Caballo called back. 'You start with Easy, because if that's all you get, that ain't so bad. Then

work on Light. Make it effortless, like you don't give a shit how high the hill is or how far you've got to go. When you've practised that so long that you forget you're practising, work on making it *Smoooooth*. You won't have to worry about the last one – get those three, and you'll be fast.'

I kept my eyes on Caballo, trying to duplicate his pitty-pat steps, his straight back, his driving knees. I watched him so intently, I didn't even notice at first when we left the forest.

'Wow!' I exclaimed.

The sun was just rising over the Sierras. Far ahead, giant standing stones like Easter Island statues reared from the mesa floor, with snow-dusted mountains in the background.

'How far did we go?' I asked, breathless but ecstatic.

''Bout four miles.'

I couldn't believe it. 'Really? It felt so—'

'Easy?'

'Exactly.'

'Told ya,' Caballo gloated.

Chasing Wobbles

2

So how do we find our way back to that Run Free feeling? Luckily, it's easier, faster and more fun than you think. You don't have to go Full Caballo and live on beans and chia at the bottom of a canyon. You don't even have to run in sandals. But just like any other puzzle, the first step to solving it is seeing the whole picture. If you don't know where you're going, be careful of how you begin.

'If there are twenty-eight million runners in the country, twenty-seven-point-something are just winging it,' Eric says. We like to rely on our strengths and ignore our weaknesses. Parts of us get stronger, putting more stress on the parts that are weaker.

Until …

'C'mere!' Eric called. 'Quick.'

I hurried over to where Eric was guiding Challis Popkey through a simple wall squat. On a Friday afternoon in November 2021, Eric and I gathered a dozen runners – including Batman the Adventure Dog – at a park in Colton, California. We were planning to shoot a bunch of action photos. But our plan quickly changed once we saw what was going on.

Challis is everyone's image of The Perfect Athlete. She's strong and fast, and at age twenty-nine, just hitting her peak. She recently crushed the field in a one-hundred-kilometre mountain race, beating the man in second place by a jaw-dropping ninety minutes. Challis has a great attitude, a great coach, and exceptional talent.

She also, at this moment, has her hand on her hip.

'See that?' Eric says.

Challis yanked her hand away. 'Is that bad?'

Eric put her through the exercise again. Challis braced her right hand on the wall and lifted her right foot off the ground. As she lowered her left leg into a squat, her left hand instantly shot back up to her hip.

'Wow,' I said.

'Am I doing it wrong?' Challis asked.

'Yup,' Eric said. 'But that's good. Doing it wrong means you're doing it right.'

The funny thing about these movements is how easy they are to learn. The amazing part is what they reveal. Take Challis: one look at her and you'd think she'd rip through fifty of those wall squats without a sweat. And she could – except her hand keeps flying up to support her hip. A few minutes earlier, Iman and Jenna were chatting casually in the middle of sideways leg lifts, while right beside them, Emmanuel – whom I've seen jump so high he could nearly clear a car –

Marcus Rentie and his rescue pup, Batman the Adventure Dog.

was grimacing in pain. Three equally fit athletes; one simple move; two wildly different reactions.

'Where you feel it,' Eric says, 'that's where you need it.'

And everyone here needs something. With the possible exception of Batman the Adventure Dog, who seems to grasp running on a level we can only achieve in our dreams, the rest of us are finding hidden hot spots we never suspected we had.

Eric is the only one who's not surprised. He's been watching the same shock of discovery flash across the faces of athletes of all ages and skill levels for years. 'Strengths are fun,' he explains. 'They feel good, and for a long time they can compensate for any weak links in our chain. But the second your secret weakness comes under stress, *wham!* The whole chain snaps apart.'

Margot Watters was pretty sure her chain was 100 per cent adamantium. She'd been a terrific field hockey and lacrosse player in college but drifted away from sports after she married and had the first of her five children. She was pretty happy with her life – until suddenly, and dangerously, she wasn't. Margot sank into postpartum depression so severe her doctor urged her to begin immediate medication. Margot decided to try another route.

'*Bam!*' she says. 'I started running and it saved me.' Margot thrives on goals, so she threw herself into causes, like fundraising for a friend's son with leukaemia, and quickly escalated from a tentative jogger into an Ironwoman on a mission. Even in her forties, Margot remained a speedy road racer who could win her age group in 10ks and podium in Olympic-distance triathlons. But the first few times she tried trail running, her Achilles screamed. The pain kept getting worse despite two years of medical consultations.

Finally, Eric spotted something the doctors had missed.

'Eric had me stand on a Bosu ball, and he noticed the way I struggled to balance,' Margot told me. 'He said, "I don't think it's your Achilles. I think it's something lower on the chain."' This time, a targeted MRI revealed that Margot's ankle still had torn ligaments from a field hockey injury she'd suffered twenty years earlier.

Surgery reattached the tissues, then Eric took the wheel.

'She was in a cast for two months, so this was a chance to start over from ground zero,' he said. Because Margot is

> **INSTEAD OF BIG MILES, THEY'D FOCUS ON SMALL REFINEMENTS. THE KARATE KID WAS ABOUT TO START PAINTING SOME FENCES.**

usually *Go! Go! Go!* all the time, Eric seized on her recovery as an opportunity for a full Run Free reboot. Instead of big miles, they'd focus on small refinements. The Karate Kid was about to start painting some fences.

'I was a typical orthotic-wearing, thick-running-shoe person before Eric,' Margot says. 'But what I was doing previously wasn't working, so I put my trust in him.'

Eric convinced Margot to forget how much and how fast she could run, and think exclusively about *how well*.

How light was her landing?

How balanced was her body?

How rhythmic was her cadence?

Put down the paint roller and pick up the brush; running was now calligraphy, a series of precise and tiny brush strokes.

Well, yeah – if you don't mind getting your butt kicked. But Margot was used to bringing home the hardware, so it was difficult to shake the feeling that Eric's artsy approach would make her look good but race poorly. Instead, within six months of her cast coming off, she was representing the United States at the triathlon world championships.

'We could address all kinds of imbalances and dial in her form for real strength and efficiency,' Eric says. 'All of those dormant muscles she'd been ignoring were now firing.'

So was Margot's mind.

That wonky ankle became Margot's version of my *ah ha!* lightning bolt down in the Copper Canyons. For years, she'd been spinning her wheels and never knew it. She thought she wasn't working hard enough, when the true problem was a wobble in her gait from that long-buried weakness.

'I got away with it for a long time because roads are so smooth and stable,' Margot adds. 'But once I got on trails, my ankle was all over the place.'

'She had no lateral stability at all,' Eric agrees. 'It was like she was running on one leg.'

Today, it's been ten years since Margot's Run Free reboot. Since then, a lot has changed. She's become a grandmother. She's completed seven Ironman triathlons and competed in two world championships. And she's turned into an absolute *terror* on the trails that once hobbled her, outracing runners half her age in ultra-ultramarathons of up to 200 miles.

Process that: Margot is now tearing off seven-plus marathons in a row, back to back to back, on wobble-free legs that never age.

'Having strong feet,' Margot says. 'Nothing like it.'

Here's the thing about wobbles: they don't always come from your feet. Or your legs. Or even your body.

A wobble may not present as an injury – yet – but it's in the same family. It can lock you into a cycle of low-grade frustration and nagging pain, and prevent you from reaching your health and performance goals. If your feet hurt when you get up in the morning, if your back is twingey, if every run feels like a slog and you never seem to get fitter or faster, guess what?

You've got a wobble.

Wobbles are hard to spot because they can come at you from any direction. Your shoes can be the culprit, or your meals, or the way you push your jog stroller, handle your dog or run with your buddies. Wobbles are master criminals, because unless you know what to look for, they're invisible. That's what makes them so tricky.

But luckily, wobbles always leave one clue. Caballo Blanco figured that out, and he made sure to pound it into my head the first time we ever ran together. Your running should feel Easy, Light, Smooth, and on fast days, Fast.

If it doesn't, you need to look under the hood.

Eric doesn't even need to search for the next wobble. This time, it jumps right out at him.

The odd part was, Eric and I didn't assemble our twelve runners in that California park because we thought they had

problems. We chose our recruits because we wanted a truly universal group, a rainbow of body types and backgrounds. As it turned out, they weren't just united by running. They were united by wobbles.

'Wait till you see this,' Eric calls, waving me over again.

He's standing with Jenna Crawford, a 30-year-old marathoner and backcountry racer who logs more than 2,000 training miles a year. Jenna is so fit, she's been featured as a model for Nike, New Balance and Asics, and so fast that less than two months after our session in the park, she'd win the Rose Bowl Half Marathon.

'She's probably the most solid runner here,' Eric notes. 'Good foot strike, good leg extension, really relaxed with good arms. Very dialled with everything, which speaks to her race performance trajectory and increase in distance.'

But as she dips into the same wall squat that challenged

The Born 2 'Original Cast'.
Top: Luis Escobar. Middle row, l–r: Eric Orton, Zach Friedley, Karma Park, Jenna Crawford, Christopher McDougall, Marcus Rentie. Front, l–r: Patrick Sweeney, Alejandra Santos, Iman Wilkerson, Challis Popkey, Emmanuel Runes. Sprawled: Batman the Adventure Dog.

“ IF YOU CAN CRANK OUT A CRISP SIX MILES ON A SUMMER DAY, THEN YOU, MY FRIEND, ARE A LETHAL WEAPON IN THE ANIMAL KINGDOM. ”

Challis, Jenna's left glute starts shaking like a paint mixer.

'That's not a strength issue,' Eric explains. 'It's neuromuscular, a disconnect between brain and body. Jenna has plenty of power, but it isn't being activated. That twitching is actually a good sign. It shows the muscle fibres are beginning to fire now.'

Eric continues working through the group, and one by one, we watch each runner discover their limitations. No one is immune: not Zach Friedley, an adaptive athlete whose leg prosthetic makes him extremely mindful of balance and form. Or Karma Park, who has run every day *for eight years* (!), exclusively in Rarámuri-style sandals. Or Marcus Rentie, a former rollerblade stunt skater who now cruises the woods with his rowdy rescue dog, Batman.

'What about Batman?' I ask. 'How's the pup looking?'

'Batman is *dialled*,' Eric notes, with as much envy as admiration. 'She has perfect paw strike that allows her to use her natural elastic energy and suspension system. She uses her front and rear legs beautifully in unison, allowing her entire body to work as one unit—'

'Hang on,' I interrupt. 'How come she's the only one without a wobble?'

Yes, Batman is female. And yes, I'm 100 per cent serious.

Sure, Batman is a dog. But humans are biological animals too, right? So if all of us have biomechanical problems, shouldn't she? We didn't just evolve to run with dogs – we evolved to run *better*. Humans are the greatest distance-running creatures on the planet. We have two special qualities that no other mammal can compete with, not a dog, not a horse, not a cheetah:

We're naked, and we sweat.

Humans vent heat by perspiration, not respiration. We don't have to pant to cool off, meaning on a steamy day, we can both breathe *and* keep our temps down. If Batman tries to keep up with Marcus on an August afternoon, she'll either stop to exhale her internal heat, or *clunk* – over she goes.

So when I ask what's so special about Batman, I'm not setting the bar too high. I'm aiming way low. Genetically, we're just as close to our wild ancestors as Batman is to hers. We descended from runners who weren't just good on their feet. They were unbeatable.

Remember all those tall tales about ancient heroes who could run down prey? Turns out, they weren't so tall after all. Those stories pop up in every culture in the world, from Native American legends to Norse myths, from the Hadza people of Tanzania to Greek gods and the Dreamtime of Australian Aborigines. It's not a coincidence. It's shared history.

Instead of a single hunter, though, it was the entire clan: men and women, old and young, fanning out together in a hunting pack, each using their individual skills – eager youngsters leading the chase, seasoned old-timers studying hoof prints, strongest adults held in reserve – as they chased their prey across the savannah until it overheated and collapsed.

And it doesn't even take that long.

The Kalahari Bushmen still engage in persistence hunts to this day. On a toasty morning, they'll trot along behind their quarry, staying just close enough to keep it on the move. After about ten or fifteen kilometres of constant running, the kudu will begin to slow … stagger … and fall in a heap. Which means if you can crank out a crisp six miles on a summer day, then you, my friend, are a lethal weapon in the animal kingdom.

'So if we're born to run,' I asked. 'Why are we so bad at it?'

On the receiving end of this question was the most qualified person in the world to answer it: Dr Dennis Bramble, the biologist at the University of Utah who, along with his junior colleague Dr David Carrier, made the discovery that our ability to run was the most important factor in human evolution. Long before we developed projectile weapons, we survived by using our fantastic distance running to chase prey into heat exhaustion.

So what went wrong?

'You and I know how good running feels because we've made a habit of it,' Dr Bramble replied. But lose the habit, and the loudest voice in your ear is your ancient survival instinct urging you to relax. That's the bitter irony: endurance gave our brain the food it needed to create extraordinary technology, but now that technology is undermining our endurance.

'We live in a culture that sees extreme exercise as crazy,' Dr Bramble said, 'because that's what our brain tells us:

> **YOUR RUNNING SHOULD FEEL EASY, LIGHT, SMOOTH, AND ON FAST DAYS, FAST.**

"Why fire up the machine if you don't have to?"'

Firing up Batman's machine, on the other hand, is what Batman's brain is all about. Dogs are the living rebuttal to Abraham Lincoln's comment that if he had six hours to cut down a tree, he'd spend the first four hours sharpening his axe. Your brain is constantly whirring in search of energy-saving shortcuts. That's how we're wired. A dog would just pee and start chopping.

Batman never persuaded herself it was a good idea to stare at a screen at night instead of going to sleep, or spend an afternoon watching others play games instead of jumping in herself. If you tried to rest Batman's feet by sticking them in cushioned shoes, she'd turn those shoes into lunch. It's not clear what kind of vocabulary Batman has, but 'Go easy' and 'Take a rest day' definitely aren't part of it. Throw a stick, and Batman won't tell you why Joe Rogan is against cardio.

Unlike us, Batman's brain didn't race into the future before her body had time to catch up. The next time you see a dog flash across a park, remember:

Everything you need to know about running was discovered 10,000 years ago. And the journey back is a lot shorter than you think.

Pre-run warm-ups, Run Free style.

Journey Back to the Beginning – in Ten Minutes

3

The easiest part of the entire Run Free programme is the one people worry about most:

Changing stuff.

We've been conditioned to believe that changing our habits is painful and tedious, like relearning to walk after coming out of a body cast. But here's the thing about running: if it were difficult and complicated, we'd be extinct. For humans to rely on running to survive, it had to be a skill we could learn as toddlers and count on as old-timers. It had to be as fun and freeing as the feeling a fish has when it's released back into water.

So if you think this will be tough, take heart. To reboot your running and follow in Caballo Blanco's footsteps, you just need to focus on these three goals:

- Flatten your Footwear.
- Quicken your Cadence.
- Find a Friend.

Smell a trick? Think it can't be that simple? Then go ahead and put it to the test. As a taste of what's to come, here's how hard it is to learn Run Free running form. First, you'd better clear your schedule, because this is going to require a time investment of approximately … ten minutes.

Here's what you do:

1. Pull up 'Rock Lobster' by the B-52s.
2. Stand with your back facing the wall, about one step away.
3. Blast the song.
4. Run in place to the beat.

That's it. That's all it takes to learn perfect running form.

You can't heel-strike or overstride when you run in place. You can't kick back or stray off balance when you're keeping your back near the wall. And thanks to the B-52s, you'll never have to guess how many footsteps per minute you should be doing.

Posture, foot strike, cadence: the three ingredients of perfect form, easy to learn and impossible to screw up.

Mastering it is another matter, but that's the fun part. Every time you head out the door, you get to feel that instant surge of joy whenever you get it just right. If swishing a jump shot or drilling a backhand were easy, basketball and tennis courts would be empty. What keeps us coming back is the challenge of making our dreams come true, of trying to match our movements to our imaginations.

That takes practice, and practice is what mastery is all about. But learning it? That part is easy.

Even now, more than a decade later, I'm still a little whiplashed by how quickly Eric Orton turned me around and built up not only my speed and mileage, but my confidence. Within a few weeks of my first Run Free workout, Eric was sending me off on two-hour jaunts that were so far beyond my perceived limits, I felt like I was on a manned mission to Mars. A few months after that, I was next to Caballo Blanco and the rest of the *Más Loco* crew in the back of a bus, heading to the bottom of a canyon for the race of a lifetime.

What makes Eric's system work so well, I discovered, are two key ingredients which make it foolproof.

Number 1 is *Feel*:

Eric doesn't teach you what to do; he teaches you how it should feel. That's the beauty of the Ten-Minute Rock Lobster Run Form Fix. You don't need to film yourself. You don't have to study a bunch of YouTube videos, or get a fitness tracker. After five minutes of listening to New Wave alternative rock, you'll instantly know the difference between good and poor form.

Likewise, every other aspect of the Run Free programme – from eating habits to overall fitness – will teach you to read your body. You'll learn how to dial in your eating, form, overall fitness and optimal cadence without chest straps or Fitbits. You'll become your body's own master mechanic, so if a wobble is coming on, you'll know how to course-correct and avoid it.

Number 2 is *The Free Seven*: the seven ancestral pillars of lifelong athleticism.

Running used to be a daily occupation. Now it's an interruption. Instead of weaving it into every part of

our lives, we shrink it down to a one-hour allotment of recreational exercise. That's perfectly reasonable, of course, since we no longer spend our days literally running for our lives. Except—

No one told your body.

Your body thinks it's still deep in the African savannah, racing to catch up with dinner before it disappears over the horizon, while checking that the kids are matching you stride-for-stride. Your body still believes that on any given day, it needs to run to find a mate, or fresh water, or a safe hideaway for the family before glowing eyes emerge from the dark.

And because running was life or death, you couldn't rely

on just one motor. You had to have multiple fuel cells, all of them uniting to make sure your body was powered up and ready to go at any time. What you ate, who you hung out with, what put a smile on your face – all those ancestral strands of your existence are also energy sources:

Good form = elastic leg recoil = *free energy*

Running together = shared workload = *free energy*

Proper footwear = good, stiff landing = *free energy*

Fitness and strength = reliable leg compression = *free energy*

Pull apart those strands, and the whole system weakens. Combine them, and the Free Seven work together to make your running easy, light, smooth and fast.

THE FREE SEVEN

1. Food: *Your fork is not your coach*
You can't outrun a bad diet. No matter how many miles you put in, you'll continue to store body fat as long as your eating causes your blood sugar to spike. That's why Step #1 in the Run Free reboot is to dial in your approach to food – not to starve off pounds, but to remove appetite from the equation and maximise your energy per bite.

2. Fitness: *Become the master mechanic*
Our ancestral need to survive on our feet left us with an extraordinary ability to bounce back from mistakes. You'll learn to assess any structural weaknesses – just the way Challis and Jenna learned to reactivate their dormant glutes – and reverse them with strengthening movements that are so easy, you can knock them out in the kitchen while your morning coffee is brewing.

3. Form: *The art of easy*
Too many runners make the mistake of thinking that if cushioned shoes ruined their form, then minimalist shoes can fix it. But changing footwear changes nothing, as their strained calves and aching heels would later attest.

What does work are a four-pack of deceptively easy exercises. As soon as you take them on the road, you'll feel decades of poor form disappearing from beneath your feet.

4. Focus: *Faster, farther and forever*
'Listen to your body' may be the only fitness advice more useless than 'We are all an experiment of one'. You and your body don't speak the same language. You have no idea what each other is saying. Remember, your instincts were formed in a time when food was scarce, physical energy had to be conserved at all costs, and freezing weather wasn't a hassle, it was your one-way ticket into the fossil record. Every natural impulse you inherited is urging you to never make a move unless survival depends on it.

Likewise, we've lost our mastery of hard and easy, fast and slow. Rather than using our full range of gears, we mostly schlump along in the middle, eventually burning out our transmission. Luckily, the soldiers of Ancient Rome created a simple trick that can teach you how to find your ideal pace for each effort. You'll build a big, Run Free engine with the right gear for every challenge.

5. Footwear: *First, do no harm*
Running shoes can't improve your form, but they can make it a lot worse. The more mush under your feet, the less you can feel the ground. Cushioning is a narcotic. It's a numbing agent. It deadens your feet to the sensations that can make

you a better, healthier runner. Think of the harm you'd do by Novocain-ing your hand and hitting it with a hammer, and you'll have a sense of what's going on every time you run in squishy shoes. And if you think 'gait analysis' is the answer, think again: studies have shown that runners who bought shoes based on gait analysis are up to *five times* more likely to suffer an injury.

6. Fun: *If it feels like work, you're working too hard*
'I'm not interested in the limits of what's painful,' my *Born to Run* adventure buddy Barefoot Ted explained, when I asked how he could race a hundred miles on just twenty-five miles a week of training. 'I'm exploring the limits of what's *pleasurable*.'

Scientifically, Barefoot Ted's Pleasure Principle makes perfect sense. Evolution doesn't reward pain; it rewards joy. Suffering limits your experience, instead of enhancing it. It creates tunnel-vision, disassociation, self-absorption and mistakes. Your head is down, your brain is starved for oxygen, your stress levels are jacked. Every cell in your body is warning you this can't be good. You're trying to block it out, not drink it in.

Fun, on the other hand, spikes awareness, confidence, stress-relief and competency. When you're having fun, you're focused. Why? Because your body approves and wants more. Your head is up. Your breathing is strong. Your range of vision and motion are at max function. Your ancestral brain is popping the cork on a magnum of endorphins, encouraging you to keep it up. You're in the flow state.

> **FUN SPIKES AWARENESS, CONFIDENCE, STRESS-RELIEF AND COMPETENCY.**

7. Family: *Those who sweat together soar together*
We evolved to encourage and assist each other, because the pack lived or died by mutual success. The more varied the minds and abilities on hand, the better the chance for success. Sharing your run is one of the best ways you can improve, because as social animals, many of our invisible mechanisms are synchronised: without a word being spoken, a running partner can help centre your heart rate, tighten your cadence and sharpen your form.

And a bonus:

Injuries: *Fixing your flat tires*
There is almost no dysfunction that can't be fixed with a little more function. If you're struggling with plantar fasciitis, tendinitis, achey IT bands or troublesome hip flexors, you'll learn some mobility and strengthening skills that will remove the obstruction and retrain the movement pattern.

Think of the Free Seven as a balanced meal, not a buffet. Each item is linked to the rest, so resist the temptation to pick a few and chuck the others. Together, they provide everything you need to locate your wobbles, correct them, and improve your strength and suppleness as you advance through the **90-Day Run Free programme** near the back of the book.

In the following chapters you'll learn how each of the Free Seven works and why they connect. You'll be introduced to new skills, like Movement Snacks, the Two-Week Test and the 100 Up. You'll discover a 2,000-year-old trick for gauging heart-rate zones, and learn the best way to choose footwear (hint: it's got nothing to do with 'gait analysis' or 'Stability').

Practise these skills as you go. Get comfortable with them, and be ready to put them to work when you begin the 90-Day Run Free programme. By the time you finish, your old habits will be gone, and your new ones will be locked in. You'll be ready to train for any race – or just head off on a whim, running as far as you want, whenever you want, for the rest of your life.

3.1
CABALLO'S GREATEST SECRET

'I felt this fire in me, this anger,' recalls Jordan Marie Brings Three White Horses Daniel, and that made up her mind. 'I got the red paint and let my fingers do the talking.'

Until then, Jordan's life as a professional road racer had been all about how she ran. Now, it was only about why.

Carefully, she painted a blood-red handprint across her face: a thumb on one cheek and fingers on the other, the palm covering her lips, a horribly lifelike depiction of the way so many Native American women have died – a hand clenched over their mouths, silencing them.

Jordan pinned on her bib and took her place among the elites at the starting line of the 2019 Boston Marathon. She kept her eyes straight ahead, even when spectators began to point and stare. 'HEY, NICE HANDPRINT,' someone shouted. How heartless do you have to be, she wondered, to think a blood-red hand covering a woman's mouth was a joke?

'But the Indigenous people who saw me, they understood,' Jordan says. 'They know about our girls.'

For Native American women, murder is epidemic. They're ten times more likely to die from violence than other Americans, victims of such widespread brutality that Amnesty International investigators issued a call for action. But even though nearly 6,000 Indigenous women are believed missing, barely more than a hundred are documented in the Department of Justice database. Who is speaking up for them? Why does the disappearance of

> " JORDAN COMES FROM SOUTH DAKOTA RUNNING ROYALTY. HER GRANDFATHER WAS FRIENDS AND RIVALS WITH OLYMPIC LEGEND BILLY MILLS, WHO BECAME HER MENTOR. "

a young blonde woman spark a national outcry, Jordan seethed, yet when an Indigenous woman is in danger, not even the FBI seems to care?

For Jordan, the threat hit close to home when her mother joined the search for a young woman who vanished near Jordan's family home on tribal land in South Dakota. The woman's body was discovered not far from where Jordan had grown up running alongside her grandfather. It could have been her, Jordan thought – until she realised it *was* her. Twice, she'd been the victim of violence in her relationships. By the time she was in college, she'd already gone to more than a dozen funerals of relatives and friends who'd died tragically.

Jordan was one of the lucky ones, though. Her legs gave her an opportunity that other women didn't have. Jordan comes from South Dakota running royalty. Her grandfather was friends and rivals with Olympic legend Billy Mills, who became her mentor. Jordan's mother was on course for the 1988 Olympics as a sprinter before she had Jordan instead, and Jordan herself had a stellar track career at the University of Maine before turning pro as a runner for New Balance and Altra.

'I always thought of running as a superpower,' she says. But when power is simply stored, it's useless. It needs to be used, conducted, applied to an engine of change. All the running that Jordan had done until then, all her victories and medals and pro sponsorships, were just bottling up her power. It was time to use it.

Before the starting gun in Boston, Jordan added four red letters down her legs: 'MMNW', for Missing and Murdered Native Women. She was going to pray for one woman every mile, and she was disheartened to discover how easy it was to come up with twenty-six names. 'I wanted this run to be for our stolen sisters,' Jordan says. 'It was my way to give these women a platform to be seen, heard and remembered.'

With her prayer run through the streets of Massachusetts, Jordan became a lightning rod, a conductor who transferred a powerful tradition from its place in the past towards a purpose in the present. From that day on, she's been devoted to Indigenous advocacy, and it's given her running an urgency and a sense of mission she'd never felt before.

'I'd always wanted to keep running as something for me,

for my own competitive goals,' she says. 'It was my identity, so I didn't want to bring any outside stress into that. But I realised I couldn't keep separating those things. I've been seeing so many other groups using running as a form of speech, and it's amazing to witness.'

Micah True went through a rebirth like that of his own when he became Caballo Blanco.

He'd been a formidable prizefighter and solid ultrarunner in his day, but technique was never his strength. He bulled ahead on raw drive until, over and over again, he collided head-on into the brick wall of overuse injury. Down in the Copper Canyons, he turned that around. He spent years immersing himself in the hows of running. He learned to patter down cliffside switchbacks like a billy goat, and transform a long, galumphing stride into the double-time quick step he'd learned by watching fleet Rarámuri older folks.

By his fifties, he'd reached the age when many runners from his past life were complaining about sore knees and creaky lumbars and giving up on running for good, but Caballo was just getting started. 'His range was huge,' I remember being told by Luis Escobar, the trail running legend who shot those iconic photos of Caballo's first Copper Canyon ultramarathon and remained close to him ever since. 'If he felt like it, he could turn twelve miles into thirty.'

The White Horse settled into a comfortable loner's life, spending his daylight hours rambling across the mesas and his evenings watching the sun set outside his little stone hut above the Batopilas river. Most likely he'd have finished out his years that way—

If he didn't get angry.

It wasn't just one murder that infuriated him. He was already getting hot before drug cartel thugs killed the son of one of his closest companions. By then, he'd seen some of his good friends, like Silvino Cubesare, being lured into trouble by the cartels, and he'd watched as the ancient artistry of Rarámuri runners was undermined by the persistent spread of the outside world into the canyons.

He began looking at running in a way he never had before. Not as a hobby or a sport, but a force. A power. He'd been lucky to meet Rarámuri friends who'd shared that power with him, and it changed his life. Now it was his turn.

If it had gone only that far – if Micah had just bottled up that power and kept it for himself – no one would ever have heard his story. Instead, he went beyond the how of running and threw himself into the why, creating something greater and more beloved than he could have imagined.

That's the true legacy of Micah True. His ultrarunning festival of fellowship down in the Canyons isn't a race. It's a reminder of how magnificent running can be when it's coupled, as it has been since the beginning of human history, with a purpose greater than ourselves.

Even on rocky trails, sandals are just fine if you've mastered good running form.

Getting Started

Most of us learn to run in reverse.

As beginners we go slow, thinking we'll get faster as we get better. But that's doing it backwards: first, we need to develop raw speed, and that will give us the strength and skill to run longer. Running fast is the secret to running easy.

That's how the Rarámuri teach their youngsters. Rarámuri schoolkids begin by racing each other in short ball games, charging up and down a short stretch of trail as fast as they can. The genius of the ball race is the way it includes everyone as an equal member of the team, from oldest and youngest to swiftest and slowest. If you're trailing behind when the leaders reach the turnaround point, the ball comes sailing back to you and suddenly you're the thrilled breakaway striker leading the attack while the rest of the pack sprint to catch up. Rarámuri kids don't practise slow. First they go fast; when they get good at fast, then they go long.

Speed is a terrific teacher. Speed encourages good running form: when you're in top gear, no one has to explain why you should land on your forefoot or pop your foot back off the ground. You just do it. Youth runners in the rest of the world follow a similar approach to the Rarámuri: in middle-school, you start by training for short races, and progress to longer distances as you get older. You first develop a foundation of speed and strength, then add stamina.

But a lot of us missed out on that crucial speed and strength phase. We began running later in life, usually for the same reason: we wanted to get back in shape and figured the best way was to train for something big, like a half-marathon or trail ultra. We focused on running longer, not better – and that's what gets us into trouble. We built our structure on a very narrow foundation, stacking up more and more miles, without learning to be adaptable and efficient. When the slightest wobble comes along, down we go.

The 90-Day Run Free reboot is designed to fix that. It's the small step back we need for a big leap forward. You'll become faster, stronger and more injury-resistant. You'll master skills that will make running a joy for the rest of your life.

You'll find Action Items at the end of each chapter. You'll start with Food, and progress through the Free Seven towards Fun and Family. Once you're familiar with those skills, you'll have all the tools you need to begin the 90-Day programme.

So when should you start? It depends on where you are right now. Are you a Beginner? A Dabbler? A Veteran? This guide will help you determine your Day One:

BEGINNERS

Prep phase before starting the 90-Day programme: 3–4 weeks

- Use this time to practise the Form, Fitness and Movement Snack exercises.
- Run gently three or four times a week, going easy and stopping when you still have a little extra in the tank. You should never finish one of these runs feeling sore or exhausted. The goal is ease and consistency.
- When you feel confident enough to run the One-Mile Test, you're ready to begin.

DABBLERS

Prep phase before starting the 90-Day programme: 2–3 weeks

- If you're a runner with experience but not a lot of consistency, sometimes going weeks or months without running regularly, get ready by practising the exercises and running three or four times a week.
- When you feel confident enough to run the One-Mile Test, you're ready to begin.

VETERANS

Prep phase before starting the 90-Day programme: 1 week

- If you're a consistent runner coming off a solid base of training, take a week of recovery to allow your body to rest.
- Use this one-week break to master the Form, Fitness and Movement Snack exercises.
- At the end of that week, you should be ready to complete your One-Mile Test and begin.

IF YOU'RE INJURED

- If you've got a nagging pain, something that feels like a heel or Achilles or shin splint issue, follow the remedies at the back of the book (see Injuries: Fixing Your Flat Tires, page 238).
- You should feel function and flexibility returning, and quickly begin to feel better.
- If you don't, you may have an injury that requires a visit with your doctor.
- As soon as you're pain-free, follow the Dabblers protocol.

Pre-Game: Movement Snacks

5

Prepare yourself. This is going to be an emotional journey.

Changing the way you run doesn't have to be difficult, but your brain may take some convincing. We instinctively pull back from new movements, because our Stone Age survival instinct is resistant to anything it hasn't tried before. That's why the high dive, which we *know* is safe, is so excruciating the first time and easy the second.

'You can make that process much easier on yourself if you soothe your nervous system first,' says Julie Angel, a Parkour and ancestral movement specialist. 'Your body is always trying to protect itself, which is why you feel such a flood of exhilaration when you accomplish something new.'

So to prep your mind and body for these unfamiliar Run Free movements, first begin with 'Movement Snacks': a series of bite-sized, mood-altering games which function as both playful warm-ups and easy range-of-motion assessments that let you identify any hidden trouble spots.

Julie and her coaching partner, Jared Tavasolian, created Movement Snacks after realising that the biggest impediment to mastering new skills wasn't strength or coordination, but confidence. Rather than battle that resistance, why not defuse it? 'The more you can move, the more emotionally safe you'll feel,' Jared explains. 'The safer you feel, the happier and less anxious you'll be.'

'In modern exercise we have this idea that things have to be big and "Sweat it out!", but what if it's something that's small?' Julie adds. 'Something that feels safe to do, that connects to your nervous system because it makes your body feel empowered?'

I became a Movement Snacks superfan by accident when I attended an all-women's Parkour session on the outskirts of London. I was there to mostly observe from the sidelines, but I had nowhere to hide when team leader Shirley Darlington called everyone in for their signature greeting: the group forms into a big circle, then everyone bear-crawls towards the centre, reaches out to shake hands

> **" THE MORE YOU CAN MOVE, THE MORE EMOTIONALLY SAFE YOU'LL FEEL. THE SAFER YOU FEEL, THE HAPPIER AND LESS ANXIOUS YOU'LL BE. "**

with someone else, then quadrupedally reverses to their starting point.

Balancing on one hand while bear-crawling in a crowd was tricky, and collisions were unavoidable – at least for me and anyone around me – but when I eventually popped back to my feet, I felt so much better than I had a minute earlier. Everything from my shoulders to my Achilles was stretched and loose, and that one silly exercise had transformed these strangers into teammates.

'One minute of movement has the power to change how you feel, how you think, and what you do next,' Julie says. 'Everyone has one minute to play during their day, and never think that minute doesn't have the power to unwind you, and release tension, and bring your energy back.'

Since my first Parkour greeting, I've used some variation of Movement Snacks nearly every time I've visited a running club or held a book talk. The reactions are amazing, which doesn't surprise Julie and Jared one bit.

'People think movement is muscles and physical, but your mind moves, your ego moves, your heart moves,' Julie says. 'A lot of coaches never talk about that. Movement is a transportation action. It's how we get through life. That's why, when you see some people run, they literally fight the ground beneath them. As much as it can be fun, it can also be paralysing, make you angry, make you anxious.'

You can play around with these Movement Snacks on your own, but you'll get the biggest bang for your snack if you team up with a buddy. For group bonding, they're unbeatable. Start right away. They only take a minute, they're super low impact so you can indulge in them as often as you like throughout the day, and everything that follows will feel better and easier.

DEADBUG BELLY BREATH

How to:

- Lie on your back with knees bent, feet in the air, so your shins are parallel to the ground (or as close as possible without straining).
- Extend your arms straight out past your head.
- Lift your head until your chin is tucked against your chest and you're looking in between the legs.
- Breathe in through your nose, feeling your belly expand and your lower back flatten against the ground.
- Breathe out through your nose, feeling your belly soften while maintaining position.

How many: 5 inhales and exhales.

Pay special attention to: Chin tucked in, looking between the legs, tongue on the roof of the mouth (you can find this position by swallowing), nose breathing with mouth closed. Make sure that the belly is expanding and contracting.

Purpose: How you breathe tells your body whether you're safe. By training your breathing, you can conserve energy and calm your nervous system.

QUICK FEET
WITH PARTNER

How to:

- Facing a partner, raise your hands and place your palms against theirs.
- While maintaining palm-to-palm contact, the 'lead' partner then tries to quickly step on the other person's toes.
- The following partner should dance away, doing everything possible to avoid foot contact while keeping palms connected.
- Switch.

How many: Just have fun with it and switch back and forth several times between leaders.

Pay special attention to: Never breaking hand contact.

Purpose: This is a fun group warm-up to get the heart rate up and stimulate the central nervous system with some multi-directional, quick movement with the feet.

DEEP SQUATS:
SOLO OR WITH PARTNER

How to:

SOLO

- Stand with your feet shoulder-width apart and pointed straight ahead.
- Squat down, sinking as deep as you can, while maintaining an activated core with a relaxed body.
- For beginners, feel free to use a sofa arm to ease down as far as is comfortable.
- Pause a moment or two, then rise back up to the start position.

WITH PARTNER

- Face your partner and grab each other's wrists.
- Support each other by pulling backwards, easing down into a squat at the same time.
- Pause a few beats, then pull each other back up.

How many: 10–12, with a focus on range of motion and controlled technique, rather than speed.

Pay special attention to: Focus on getting as deep as you can, with good form, keeping feet facing straight forward. Improve through time.

Purpose: Deep Squats can unlock your entire range of motion, everything from your neck to the soles of your feet, while loosening tight hips and Achilles and easing lower back tension.

WARM-UP SHIN BOX + ROCKING SHIN BOX

How to:

WARM-UP SHIN BOX

- Sit in what is called 'shin box', with both knees bent, the bottom of your left foot against your right thigh and your right knee bent a little more than 90 degrees. Sit tall with your gaze forward.
- Place your hands behind you for support, if needed.
- Look to the right, press both feet into the floor, and shift your knees to the right and into shin box with opposite leg positions.
- Repeat this sequence, so you are alternating sides/leg positions in shin box.
- Once you feel comfortable, bring your hands in front of you and practise that position.

ROCKING SHIN BOX

- Sit with your knees bent, feet on the floor.
- Place your left hand on the outside of your left knee, right hand on the outside of your right knee.
- Pull to extend your chest and sit upright.
- Round your spine and roll onto your back so your shoulder blades touch the floor.
- Reverse and roll back up to a sitting position.
- While continuing the same flow of motion, shift onto your right hip while swinging your feet to the left, ending in the shin box position.
- Rock back and alternate sides.

How many: 5 reps/rolls on each side.

Pay special attention to: Keep your eyes open when rocking back, mouth closed, tongue on the roof of the mouth, breathing softly in and out through the nose. Round your spine on the rocking section to keep the rocking motion smooth and pain-free.

Purpose: Increases mobility of the spine and the hips. The more we're able to both recruit and release tension when needed, the more supple, efficient and reactive we are in all of our movements.

BEAR CRAWLS

How to:

- Start on all fours with your hands under your shoulders, knees under hips, and head in a comfortable position, eyes looking at least 1–2 feet ahead of you, ideally straight ahead.
- Press evenly onto your palms, tuck your toes under and lift your knees to hover just off the floor.
- Push onto your left toes and right hand, stepping forward with the left hand and right foot.
- Continue forward in a nice fluid motion. Keep the hips stable and avoid overly swaying from side to side. Repeat the same opposite arm–opposite leg pattern to move forward. Throughout your movement, keep your focus on easy breathing through the nose.

How many: 20 steps (each time the right hand makes contact with the ground) to start, and build from there.

Pay special attention to: Keeping the knees 2–3 inches off the floor. Work on keeping the hips stable and avoid shifting from side to side. Rest as needed.

Purpose: Crawling builds full body strength and connects upper and lower body, as well as developing coordination. It's also a sneaky quad burn!

STRAIGHT LEG BEAR CRAWL

How to:

- Start on all fours with your hands under your shoulders, knees under hips. Raise the hips and straighten the legs.
- Keep your head and neck in a comfortable position, eyes looking down between the hands.
- Push onto your left toes and ball of the foot and right hand, stepping forward with the left hand and right foot.
- Continue forward in a nice fluid motion, moving opposite hand and foot. Lead with the hand and as you progress play with lifting the hand and foot at the same time. Throughout your movement, keep your focus on easy breathing through the nose.

How many: 20 steps (each time the right side makes contact with the ground) to start, and build from there.

Pay special attention to: Keep the knees soft when you start and don't force anything. Rest as needed.

Purpose: This crawl helps to unfold and open the hamstrings and shoulders, which get stuck from over-sitting in chairs. For runners especially, these movements create a more balanced kinetic chain rather than having dominant parts with weaker links.

THREE-POINT CRAB

How to:

- Start on all fours with your knees under your hips and hands under your shoulders (Bear Crawl position).
- Spread your fingers wide. Tuck your toes under and lift your knees an inch off the floor.
- Press into your right hand and left foot as you lift your left hand and bring your right knee forward and through.
- Place the right foot on the floor and bring your left hand to the floor behind you, ending up in a 'crab' position. Your chest should now be facing up.
- From the crab position, lift your right hand towards the sky. Push into the left hand and both feet to balance, squeeze your butt and engage your stomach to stabilise.
- Push your hips up in a straight line as high as possible.
- Hold for one breath, then lower your hand and hips back into your starting crab position.

How many: 3 on each side.

Pay special attention to: Make sure that you are on your palms and not your fingertips. From the crab position tuck your chin with a proud chest. Never work to failure; rest as needed.

Purpose: Opens your chest and strengthens your upper back and shoulders, which significantly aids breathing. Lengthens tight hip flexors that often tighten from sitting.

NINJA JUMPS

How to:

- Squat and leap forward, landing as softly and as quietly as you can.
- Focus on sticking with precision, allowing your knees to bend deeply to hold your position and soften your landing.

How many: 5 jumps in multi-directions.

Pay special attention to: Focus on relaxing, so you land with soft knees and good arm balance. Use your entire range of motion to absorb the landing. Don't rush; be as efficient as you can.

Purpose: Awakens explosive power and activates full-range kinetic chain.

Part 2:
THE FREE SEVEN

Running Free on Hawaii's Ohana Trail: (l–r) Danielle Kinch, Sienna Akimo, Kaimana Ramos, Sky Kikuchi and Daniel Gutowski.

Food: Your Fork Is Not Your Coach

6

'Do you know the healthiest diet in the world?' Phil Maffetone asked me.

'The Mediterranean?' I guessed.

'Right. Do you know where it's from?'

'Greece?'

'Close,' he said. 'Crete.'

'Wow. That's really …' I struggled for something smarter to say, but I was a little stunned. Of all the places in the world, Crete was the exact reason I'd shown up at Phil's door. 'Wow,' I repeated.

I'd come to see Phil at his home in too-apt-to-be-true Oracle, Arizona. The Greek oracles, you'll recall, are the hardcore truth-tellers whose wisdom was sought by the greatest leaders of their day, because it was said to come directly from Mother Earth. Without sledgehammering the metaphor too hard, I couldn't have invented a better place for a sports performance expert whose ancestral eating advice was revered by Ironman champions and rock musicians alike to hang his hat.

Phil began working with elite athletes in the early days of ultramarathons and triathlon, back when the demands of these new sports were uncharted territory. The marathon was still louted as 'the ultimate challenge', but suddenly, people were heading into the mountains to tackle four of them in a row at high altitude, or pre-gaming their 26.2-mile run with a 2.4-mile open-water swim and 112 miles of cycling.

Not surprisingly, top Ironman triathletes weren't just hitting the wall; they were smashing into it headfirst and knocking themselves out of training for months at a time. Athletes were constantly breaking down from stress fractures and tendon tears, and struggling to maintain energy levels and healthy body weight.

Was it even possible to prevent a human body from failing under such extreme challenges? Fuel and maintenance were the two big mysteries – until Phil Maffetone discovered they were actually the same thing. What you eat affects not only your strength and body weight, he realised, but your injury risk as well.

> **❝ WHAT YOU EAT AFFECTS NOT ONLY YOUR STRENGTH AND BODY WEIGHT, HE REALISED, BUT YOUR INJURY RISK AS WELL. ❞**

One of the first to adopt the Maffetone Method, as I would go on to describe in my book *Natural Born Heroes*, was elite ultrarunner Stu Mittleman. Stu had extraordinary stamina and speed whenever he was healthy, which was never. He'd race anyway, gritting his way through twenty-four-hour races and later discovering he'd had a dislodged bone in his foot the entire time. At their first session, Phil reset Stu's foot, but warned him worse trouble lay ahead unless he made some changes.

Stu was all ears. Sure. What's my problem – running technique? Weak arches?

Sugar.

Sug— really?

And not only sweets and sodas, Phil explained. Pasta, power bars, pancakes, pizza, orange juice, rice, bread, cereal, granola, oatmeal – all the processed carbohydrates that Stu had been told were the ideal runner's diet. They're just sugar in disguise, Phil believed. Humans are superb endurance athletes who've roamed farther across this planet than any other species, and we didn't do it on Red Bull and bagels. We did it by relying on a much richer and cleaner burning fuel: our own body fat.

'The point of your training isn't to see how fast you can get your feet to move,' Phil said. 'The point is to get your body to change the way it gets energy. You want it to burn more fat and less sugar.' And as it stood now, Stu's body was 'a sugar-burning, fat-storing monstrosity'.

Stu was baffled. Okay. But how does food hurt your foot?

Think of your body as a furnace, Phil explained. Fill it with slow-burning logs and it will run smooth and strong for hours. But fill it with paper and gas-soaked rags and it will burn hot, rattle the pipes, and die out until it's fed again.

That's what you did, Phil said. You shook yourself into an injury by stuffing your furnace with garbage. If you want to stay healthy and perform your best, you need to teach your body to use fat as fuel.

'We store only a very limited amount of carbohydrate in our bodies,' Phil explained. 'Compare this with a relatively unlimited supply of fat.' Carbs, in the form of glycogen, are a puddle; fat is the Pacific. At any time, your body has some 160,000 calories on tap: 2,500 in glycogen; roughly 65,000 in muscle protein; and the majority – nearly 90,000 calories – in stored fat.

'Even an athlete with only 6 per cent body fat will have enough fat to fuel exercise lasting for many hours,' Phil went on. 'When you use more fat, you generate more energy and your carbohydrate supply lasts longer. When you teach your body to rely on fat, your combustion of carbs goes down, and so does your craving for them.'

But there's no pussyfooting around. Your body loves fat; it's a treasure your system would rather hoard than burn, so if it senses there's any other fuel at hand, it will use that first and convert the leftovers into more fat. To free himself from the sugar-burn cycle, Stu would have to go cold turkey: he could stuff himself silly all day, but only on meat, fish, eggs, avocados, vegetables and nuts. No beans, no fruit, no grains. No soy, no wine, no beer. Whole dairy like sour cream and real cheese were in; low-fat milk was out.

To be honest, it wasn't Phil's logic that won Stu over; it was his foot. Pain relief is the ultimate persuader, so Stu decided to give the Maffetone Method a chance.

From then on, Stu was unstoppable. He began smashing records with such strength and style, it looked more like art than effort. In a display of 'virtually flawless footracing',

Sky Kikuchi and Danielle Kinch proving every run is a chance for Movement Snacks.

as one journalist put it, Stu defeated the reigning world champion in a thousand-mile showdown while running his second 500 miles faster than his first. Somehow, he got stronger as he got older; in his mid-forties, Stu set three American records, including a 577-miles in five days triumph that still stands today. 'No other American ultrarunner, male or female, has exhibited national class excellence at such a wide range of racing distances,' his American Ultrarunning Hall of Fame induction proclaimed.

And Stu wasn't even Phil's best student. When Mark Allen came to Phil in the late 80s, he was struggling to break out of a cycle of injuries and poor Ironman finishes. Mark's training partners were convinced he was washed up … until a few months later, when Mark went flying past.

'I had become an aerobic machine!' Mark exclaimed. 'I was now able to burn fat for fuel efficiently enough to hold a pace that a year before was red-lining my effort.' Mark went on an insane victory streak: for two years, he didn't lose any race, anywhere, at any distance. He won Ironman six times, including a stunning comeback victory at age thirty-seven, setting a record that wouldn't be broken for two decades.

'I was no longer feeling like I was ready for an injury the next run I went on,' he'd explain. 'And I was feeling fresh after my workouts instead of being totally wasted.'

Up-and-comer Mike Pigg was so impressed by Mark's comeback that he went to Phil as well. 'I feel very fortunate to have met him when I did,' Mike would say. After switching to the Maffetone Method, Mike won four triathlon national championships and continued competing for nearly twenty-five years. Before long, superstar musicians got wind of what Phil was doing and began calling as well. The Red Hot Chili Peppers, James Taylor, Johnny Cash – they all relied on the Maffetone Method to power them through gruelling studio sessions and concert tours. At age forty-eight, Peppers bassist Flea even ran a 3:52:59 marathon in a driving rainstorm and then returned the following year for an encore, finishing ten minutes faster.

'I have kind of an odd question,' I told the Oracle of Oracle. 'It's about a very different kind of running.'

I'd come across a story about a Greek shepherd who couriered messages for the Resistance on the island of Crete during the Second World War. The shepherd would scamper thirty miles through the woods to a Resistance hideout in the mountains, deliver the note, then turn around and run back again, all of it on a starvation diet and under threat of death.

And he wasn't alone. The more I looked into the Resistance, the more amazing stories I discovered – like the band of men and women who crossed a mountain range by dark, surprised a German outpost and stole their guns and food, then disappeared over the ridge with heavy sacks on their backs before the sun came up.

'How is this physically possible?' I asked Phil Maffetone. 'These are ordinary civilians pulling off incredible feats of endurance. They're running a backcountry marathon through the mountains, fighting for their lives, then running back again with packs on their backs. Olympic athletes couldn't pull that off.'

My question wasn't about courage or skill; it was about raw physical ability. The Resistance fighters on Crete weren't even soldiers; they were regular folks who took to the mountains after the German invasion and mobilised into guerrilla bands. They were constantly scaling cliffs and travelling long miles on foot. They only ate what they could scrounge, and energy slumps were fatal: lag behind on one of those missions, and you wouldn't live long enough to catch up.

'Yes, I'm sure it's possible,' Phil said.

'How?'

'Like this,' he replied, gesturing towards the lunch he and his wife had laid out for us. On the table was a platter of steak – sliced thin and blood rare – alongside a jumbled salad of torn greens, tomatoes, cucumbers and homemade goat-milk feta glistening with olive oil and sprinkled with fresh herbs.

Granted, it was a pretty upscale spread compared to the walnuts, dried mutton, dried figs and foraged forest greens the Cretans had to survive on, but broken down to its raw components, it's the same superfood that humans thrived on forever – or at least until farming took over and modern, easily grown grains knocked out traditional nutrition.

Every culture on the planet – north and south from Africa to Iceland, east and west from America to Mongolia – thrived for centuries on the same diet that fuelled those unbreakable Cretan Resistance fighters. If you're looking for diet advice, that's a hard role model to ignore. Physically, their lives were infinitely more demanding than ours, so their daily meals left zero margin for error. Maasai herders covered dozens of miles a day on foot, Inuit peoples hunted for days without rest, and Genghis Khan's warriors rampaged across 9 million square miles of Asia, all of them powering up each day on their own version of pemmican, the Native American energy bar made from equal parts animal fat and smoked meat, with some dried berries for sweetness.

Even the great Rarámuri runners, I suddenly recalled, had surprised me with their pre-race breakfast down in the Copper Canyons. Caballo Blanco and the rest of us went hard on Mamá Tita's pancakes, but Arnulfo and Silvino ignored the carbs and filled their bowls with *pozole*, a rich stew thick with bone broth and fatty pork chunks. Ordinarily, the Rarámuri are desert farmers who live, by necessity, on tough heritage corn, but given the chance to feast on goat or deer, they don't hesitate.

Today, there is no ethical argument that can be made in support of commercial meat production. We mistreat animals in service to our plates, and that can't be defended. But nutritionally, and historically, there is also no question about what we ate for strength and stamina.

'Those Resistance fighters couldn't have gotten their calories from starch and sugar, because it just wasn't available,' Phil explained. 'If they could only eat on the run, they needed food that would provide steady caloric energy all day.' Greek battlefields didn't have Powerade stations and orange slices. Fugitives couldn't detour in search of snacks. Survival depended on two things: choosing slow-burn food and adapting their bodies to use it.

'Food is only half the equation,' Phil went on. 'You can have the finest fuel in the world, but it's useless without the proper engine. It's two systems. It's input – what you eat – and output – how it's converted.'

Converting fat to fuel is a matter of training at low intensity so your body doesn't feel like it's under attack. The more mellow your base training, the more your body will rely on stored fat, rather than shifting into emergency mode and reaching for fast-burn sugars. Low-intensity training is a breeze to learn and a pleasure to practise. The trickier step, as we all know, is changing our approach to fast-burn foods.

'But here's the funny part,' Phil said. 'It's really, really, simple.'

'For anyone, or just seasoned athletes?'

'Anyone.'

'How long does it take to learn?'

'Two weeks. Two weeks and you can master it. Two weeks and you'll be running on fat like your Resistance fighters.'

I pushed my notebook towards him across the table.

Phil began scrawling notes. To give him time, I got up to help clear the table. Maybe I'd take a walk around until—

'Here you are,' Phil said, handing me back the notebook.

He couldn't have written more than a dozen sentences. I sat back down and started to read.

'Really? It's that easy?' I said.

'Of course,' he shrugged. 'Healthy ought to be easy.'

" THE RED HOT CHILI PEPPERS, JAMES TAYLOR, JOHNNY CASH – THEY ALL RELIED ON THE MAFFETONE METHOD TO POWER THEM THROUGH GRUELLING STUDIO SESSIONS AND CONCERT TOURS. "

6.1
THE TWO-WEEK TEST

Phil underlined '<u>Test</u>' to make sure I got the point: the Two-Week <u>Test</u> is emphatically <u>Not a Diet</u>.

Diets are a cruel joke. They're based on a sacrifice and guilt dynamic which has been proven, over and over, to fail. You don't gain weight because you're lazy, and you don't lose it because you're tough. That's not how the human animal works, or any other animal.

'It's baffling anyone still believes that, but they do,' Phil said. 'Even when it's so clearly, visibly, unnatural.'

Humans are hunter-gatherers; we're born to search for food all day, every day, and scarf it down once we find it. Eating is an intrinsic pleasure; it feels good because it *is* good. Going hungry is extrinsic; we only do it because we're told we're supposed to. Starving yourself is the opposite of everything we've evolved to do, and just like every other time we try to deny Mother Nature, it's doomed to fail.

So dig in! Eat all you want! Just reset your appetite so it craves the food we've always hunted and gathered, not the fake stuff we've created. That's what the Two-Week Test does: it restores your natural metabolism, like a factory pre-set, so you won't have to wonder whether something is good or bad for you, or has 'too many calories' – you'll know by how you feel when you eat it. You'll crave better foods because they'll make you feel good, instantly. You'll turn healthy eating back into an intrinsic pleasure.

Once you've gotten off the starch cycle and brought your body back to its natural metabolism, Phil says, you'll be free of hunger pangs and afternoon sugar crashes and midnight munchies. It only takes fourteen days, as long as you follow one rule of thumb: nothing high-glycaemic. Nothing that jacks your blood sugar, in other words, and causes insulin to start storing fat.

The toughest part is paying attention. Most processed foods are loaded with sugar and corn oil to give them more mouth appeal, making them softer and sweeter. Even the food you think is unprocessed, like raw turkey breast, is often injected with sugar. And those Subway sandwiches advertised as a healthy alternative to other fast foods? The rolls are so loaded with refined flour and sugar that in Ireland, they're classified as cake.

By the end of two weeks on the Test I should be a fresh slate, glycaemically speaking, and no longer cycling from sugar surge to sugar surge. Then, once the Test is over, I can gradually add processed carbs back to my meals and see what happens. If I eat a slice of bread and feel fine, okay. But if it makes me feel bloated, sluggish or sleepy, I'll know it's too much starch for my body to metabolise efficiently.

That's what the Two-Week Test is all about; it's designed to reactivate your natural diagnostic panel, so that instead of relying on some diet book to tell you what to eat, you'll get instant, accurate feedback from your own body.

'You'll actually know what it feels like to have normal insulin levels and optimal blood sugar,' Phil explains.

> ❝ YOU'LL CRAVE BETTER FOODS BECAUSE THEY'LL MAKE YOU FEEL GOOD, INSTANTLY. YOU'LL TURN HEALTHY EATING BACK INTO AN INTRINSIC PLEASURE. ❞

TWO-WEEK TEST 'YES' AND 'NO' FOODS*

'YES' FOODS

Plants
Squash
Carrots
Tomato
Leafy greens
Lemon and lime
Broccoli and cauliflower
Tree nuts (and nut butters)
Coconut
Mustard
Chia seeds
Avocado

Meat/Fish
Beef
Turkey
Lamb
Fish
Shellfish

Dairy & Eggs
Unprocessed hard cheeses
Unprocessed soft cheeses
Creams
Eggs

Fluids
Vegetable juice
Coffee and tea
Oils
Vinegar
Pure distilled spirits
Carbonated water
Dry red wines

'NO' FOODS

Plants & Plant-based Foods
All sugar products
Sweets and desserts
All non-caloric sweeteners (natural and non-natural)
Many canned and prepared veggies
Energy/protein bars (with or without added sugar)
Ketchup and other sauces
Refined flour
Crackers
Whole-grain bread
Whole-grain pasta
Corn
Rice
Quinoa
Potatoes
Berries
Sweet citrus
Banana
Melon
Honey

Meat
Processed meats
Many canned and prepared meats
Smoked products

Dairy
Milk
Half-and-half (milk and cream mix)
Full-fat yoghurt
Processed cheeses

Fluids
Dry white wines
Fruit juice
Carrot juice
All soda
All diet drinks
'Enhanced' beverages
Sports drinks

* Adapted from www.philmaffetone.com.

When I got home from my trip to Oracle, I hit the supermarket. I filled the cart with steak, fish, broccoli, avocados, canned squid, tuna, tomato juice, romaine lettuce, sour cream and walnuts – tubs of walnuts, because they'll be my go-to temptation snuffer. Also on the 'yes' list: eggs, cheese, whole cream, dry red wine, Scotch and salsa.

But no fruit, breads, rice, potatoes, pasta or honey. No beans, which means no tofu or soy of any stripe. No chips, no beer, no milk or yoghurt. No deli ham or roast beef, either, since they're often cured in sugar. Turkey was fine if you cooked it yourself, but even then you have to be careful. I thought I'd hit the perfect multi-meal solution when I came across a stack of turkey breasts in the frozen food section, and only as an afterthought did I check the label and discover they were sugar-injected.

'Garbanzos [chickpeas] are pretty moderate glycaemically,' I emailed Phil after I'd done a little research on my own. 'So I'd like to lobby for hummus.'

'Rule number one of Step number one,' he replied. 'No lobbying.'

Phil's science and expertise were impossible for me to challenge, so instead I went behind his back and asked someone else. And lost again.

Eric Orton is 100 per cent on board with both the Two-Week Test and Phil's Utterly Unfair Hummus Ruling. 'To me, the question of nutrition is more about mindset,' he says. 'With the commitment to living as an athlete comes the sense that you live with awareness. That includes awareness of what you put in your mouth. The key is to stop taking half measures and just do it right.'

Because once you start with Garbanzo Advocacy and half measures, you sabotage your mission. You're either retraining your appetite or you're not, same as kicking any other chemical dependence. If you don't do the job completely, you didn't do it at all.

The trick, I discovered, is solving one meal at a time. Breakfast was easy: by some whim I discovered that those $1.98 cans of squid from the Mexican food aisle are great in an omelette, so I'd fry up one of those, douse it with salsa, and be a happy man for the rest of the morning. I kept almonds and spicy meat-sticks on hand throughout the day as snacks, and learned to add a splash of whole cream to

> " IN TWO WEEKS, I LOST 11 POUNDS, TRIMMING BACK TO THE SAME WEIGHT I'D BEEN AS A COLLEGE ROWER NEARLY THIRTY YEARS EARLIER. I FELT MORE LIKE THAT TEENAGE ATHLETE AGAIN, TOO; NOT JUST SKINNIER BUT SPRINGIER, MORE REVVED AND RESTED. "

my coffee instead of half-and-half. Lunch and dinner were only borderline crises when I got distracted and let myself get ravenous before planning what to eat.

Phil Maffetone's website is a great resource for main-course meals, with recipes like his high-protein breakfast shake (blending soft-boiled eggs with leafy greens and a little fruit) and pasta-free eggplant [aubergine] parmigiana (sandwiching tomato sauce, mozzarella and ground beef between pan-seared eggplant).

By Day 4, I'd settled into a comfortable groove. I knew what I wanted to eat, and when, and had no trouble keeping myself fed and content. Most of the cravings I had on Days 1–3, I realised, were more about the idea than the actual food. I'd think, 'Man, I could *murder* a Shamrock Shake right now,' and then I only had to wait a beat or two for the impulse to fade.

Day 14 arrived quicker than I expected. So did the changes. In two weeks, I lost 11 pounds, trimming back to the same weight I'd been as a college rower nearly thirty years earlier. I felt more like that teenage athlete again, too; not just skinnier but springier, more revved and rested.

Even more surprising was the change that came over food: good old standbys like pizza, cheesesteaks and doughnuts now seemed untempting and kind of gross. About a week or so after I finished the Two-Week Test, I got a roast-beef sandwich and tried a test of my own. I ate half, waited a few minutes, and assessed: delicious, maybe a little light on tomato. I tucked into the other half, and—

Colin Lee blends running and surfing on his hometown streets of Oahu, Hawaii.

There it was. The sensation was old but also weirdly brand new, because for the first time I knew where it came from. My eyelids began drooping as the post-lunch, pre-caffeine brain fog took over, and it hit me that I hadn't felt it since I'd started the Two-Week Test. That second piece of bread was my trigger point; I could handle a single piece without a problem, but add one more, and up go my blood sugars. It was like spending half your life with a sore foot and suddenly discovering a pebble in your shoe. Shake it out, and suddenly, you're feeling better than you have in years, maybe ever.

For me, it's now been more than five years since I ejected that rock. Plenty of times since then it's slipped back in, but when it does, I recognise the chemical reaction for what it is. I can keep eating that other half of the sandwich, but I'll know how I'll feel if I do.

That's the goal of the Two-Week Test: not to ban any foods or turn you into a zealot, but to simplify the conversation between your brain and your belly. You'll know exactly the foods you need to eat to meet your goals, and if you have any doubts, within a few bites your body will tell you.

6.2 AID STATION: THE TWO-WEEK TEST CALLIE STYLE

Callie Vinson was twenty-three years old, nearly 400 pounds, and gasping for air when she invented her own Two-Week Test.

Callie was supposed to meet friends for brunch that day near her apartment in Chicago, but after a few blocks, she realised the walk was too much for her. 'I couldn't breathe, my feet hurt, everything just hurt,' she recalls. 'And I thought, "This isn't right. I'm staring down the barrel of an early death and I'm barely in my twenties."'

The weird thing was, it all seemed to happen so fast. In high school in Orlando, Florida, she was recruited for the crew team because of her height, and proved to be such a natural talent that she helped power her boat to a national championship. She was recruited by college coaches, but four years of pulling an oar left her so burnt out that she decided to quit rowing and attend Savannah College of Art and Design instead.

Callie comes from a family with no money and a lot of tough breaks, so she had to hustle. She worked at both a restaurant and a coffee shop to pay her way through school, but that kind of easy access to treats maybe wasn't the best environment for a college kid who'd also begun to smoke and party. By graduation, she was already heavy, and things got worse when she moved to Chicago to begin a copywriting job with an ad agency. She worked long hours, but also had money in her pocket and a city full of Italian beef sandwiches and Portillo's hot dogs right outside her door.

Within four years, the national champion rower had more than doubled in size. Callie has addiction in her family, but also the kind of stress and heartache that makes comfort food feel like medicine. Callie's mother barely survived a family shooting when her stepfather murdered her mother in front of her eyes, then shot himself. Callie's mom had to raise her siblings on her own, and became a single mother after her husband – Callie's dad – left her with two daughters as he slid into alcoholism. Callie's older sister ran away from home as a teenager and somehow turned up in Mexico. She sank into meth abuse and died mysteriously, leaving behind three children for Callie's mother to care for, including one with autism and one who'd been sexually abused by Callie's brother-in-law, who's now in prison.

So, yeah. Callie was dealing with a lot. Food helped her cope, until the morning she realised it was killing her. She didn't grasp how much her world had shrunk until the moment she discovered that a walk to meet friends for brunch was now impossible. Callie knew she was facing a soul-crushing challenge: losing 200 pounds, safely and healthfully, could take two long years.

Luckily, Callie is kind of a genius: she handled the problem by forgetting about it.

Not entirely. Just the two years part. Callie formulated her own two-week test – not Phil Maffetone's, exactly, but considering she was making it up on the fly, it was pretty close. There's some kind of magical reprogramming that happens when you do something for fourteen days, she discovered, like turning off your computer for ten seconds.

'I decided to start small,' Callie says. 'I began packing my lunch every day. I did that for two weeks until it became a habit.' She stuck to the outer edges of the supermarket, where all the fresh stuff and real foods are, and steered clear of those dangerous middle aisles with all the jars and boxes.

> **I PRETENDED I HAD MY OWN FOOD SHOW, TALKING OUT LOUD TO THE 'AUDIENCE' ABOUT ALL THE HEALTHY INGREDIENTS WE'D BE USING WHILE I WAS COOKING.**

She didn't have any real eating plan at first, other than assembling big salads and loading up on veggies which left little room on the plate for grains or potatoes.

'Then I decided to make my own dinners.' She began looking into the Paleo diet, because she liked the idea of eating single-ingredient whole foods and getting closer to the source of where they came from. 'I did that every day for two weeks, and that became a habit. I pretended I had my own food show, talking out loud to the "audience" about all the healthy ingredients we'd be using while I was cooking.'

Like I said – kind of a genius. Callie got ready to begin running by acting as if she already were. She treated her new approach to eating like the opening miles of an ultramarathon: taking it slow, savouring the fun parts, focusing only on the next aid station, not the finish line. But my favourite part of Callie's approach is the way she became her own sideline cheerleader and reference library, committing her new recipes to memory by reciting them out loud in her fantasy Beat Bobby Flay routine.

'I began to learn so much about food, people started calling *me* – the 300-plus pound woman – for tips,' she marvels. 'My mom learned to keep a bag of carrots and almond butter in the fridge for when I'm there. They're a good sustained fat and protein. I also figured out how to make something like pemmican: mostly oats, almond butter, shaved ginger and turmeric. *Perfect!*'

After a month of semi-simulating the act of running in her kitchen, Callie was ready to try the real thing.

Sort of.

'I didn't start exercise until I had a good system for eating,' she says. 'Week before my first run, I was so embarrassed I was going to look dumb. *What does a stride look like, how do I swing my arms, what shoes should I get …?*' She randomly selected a pair of lime-green Nike Pegasus at her local Fleet Feet, 'did a half-ass jog around the store' and ventured outside to begin her journey.

> ## " MAN, IF YOU EVER WANT TO SEE TRUE LOVE IN SOMEONE'S EYES, VOLUNTEER AT A RACE. "

'Forward movement creates ideas,' Callie realised, and her next step in this adventure was as brilliant as her first: she found a way to minimise self-consciousness and make every run foolproof. Callie is Choctaw, and she remembered that her people looked at running as a prayer, not a punishment.

'You get up and run east to meet the sun, and I've been doing that,' Callie told me. It's a time to think about the land you're on and the people who travelled it before you, and the magnificent privilege of sharing that timeless ritual of flowing towards the centre of warmth and light on your own two legs. Those early-morning prayer runs are a chance for Callie to reflect on the people she loves and the pain they're enduring, which sure as heck puts her little side-stitch in perspective. She feels relaxed, less anxious, as if each frosty Chicago morning run is the chance for a one-way telepathic phone call to her mom and nephews and niece back home.

After a year of steady progress, Callie felt she'd been good long enough. It was time to get stupid. She decided to run a half-marathon, the only stipulation being that nobody else could be there. She had never run with anyone else, ever, and she wasn't going to start by tackling a distance that she had no idea if she could finish. So she mapped out a route and set off before dawn, covering mile after mile by herself, within herself, for herself.

When she came to a stop in front of her apartment 13.1 miles later, something cracked inside her. 'I was so ecstatic to reach a place where my body could match the adventures in my mind,' she says. 'I always dreamed of this adventurous lifestyle, and now I had a body that could do it. My inner self finally matched my outer self, and that connection just makes me so happy.'

Now, looking back, it seems bizarre that all that Callie Vinson joyfulness was hidden in secret for so long during her solitary runs in the dark. Today, she's a voice for Native Women Running, which helps First People return to their ancestral running tradition. Her ad agency job lets her work from the road with a laptop and a hot spot, so whenever a friend calls with an invitation, she now takes that all-terrain vehicle of a body she created and points it towards anything that seems like a bad idea:

Can you be my one-woman crew for three months as I run across the US?

Absolutely.

Want to race 100k?

When is it?

This weekend.

Cool. I'm in.

How about a 240-miler a few months later?

Sure.

And then a 250-mile race, then crew at Badwater, then—

Yup, yup, and whatever the last one is, also yup.

Somehow, Callie still finds time between races for her new favourite side hustle: turning up for ones she's not even running.

'Man, if you ever want to see true love in someone's eyes, volunteer at a race,' she says. 'I was handing out finishers' medals at the Javelina 100, and it was like proposing to 5,000 people in a row. You have this thing people trained hundreds and hundreds of hours to achieve, and when they cross the finish line, all bent over and exhausted, and they look up and you have this buckle for them ... the look in their eyes ... wow.'

Callie isn't superstitious or self-impressed. She's happy with what she's accomplished but still talks about losing 200 pounds and turning herself from a one-block walker into an unstoppable ultramarathoner as No Big Deal. But even she was struck by the weird beauty the universe cooked up to pat her on the back. Last winter, she drove through ice storms to move from Chicago to her new home in Arizona.

She slept a few hours, then pulled herself out of bed before dawn to greet the sun. She headed east into the foothills, and as she climbed, a strange sound drifted down. She pushed higher, finally summiting a peak she never could have reached before, to find a lone stranger playing a drum and singing an ancient song.

Welcoming her home.

6.3
ON THE RUN RECIPES

The real danger zone for healthy eating isn't your kitchen. It's everywhere else.

Planning breakfast, lunch and dinner isn't hard, especially after you've completed the Two-Week Test. By that point, it's a matter of choice: you'll know what you should eat and how you'll feel if you don't, and recipes for your major meals are easy to find and quick to master.

But when you're rushing out the door in the morning, or grabbing lunch at your desk, or craving a quick bite in the car on the way to your kid's soccer game – that's when a tasty, On the Run snack can come to the rescue.

All of these recipes are easy to prepare, and many are perfect for stashing in your pocket. They were created by athletes who've learned that no matter how busy your day or how long your run, with a little prep you'll always have food you won't regret.

Note: Some of these recipes aren't suitable for the Two-Week Test because they contain oats or fruit. But the Two-Week Test is designed to reset your food awareness, not set lifetime restrictions. Once the Test is over, these On the Run recipes are ideal for mid-run or daytime snacks. Nearly all the ingredients are relatively low-glycaemic.

Callie's Adventure Blobs (vegan)

Since moving to Arizona, Callie Vinson is out nearly every weekend exploring the desert. She never knows what she'll find to eat on the drive, or how long she'll trek between meals, so she pre-games by filling her pockets with her own easy-to-make energy blobs.

INGREDIENTS

1 cup/80 g rolled oats

½ cup/50 g coconut flakes, unsweetened

½ cup/70 g ground flaxseed

½ cup/75 g nuts, chopped or pieces

1 tbsp chia seeds

½ cup/240 g nut butter

⅓ cup/80 ml agave

1 tsp vanilla extract

TIP:
Add a couple tablespoons of grated turmeric or ginger root for extra anti-inflammatory goodness.

INSTRUCTIONS

- Mix all dry ingredients together, then combine with remaining wet ingredients.
- Roll into 1.5-inch/4-cm balls (roughly 6) with both hands, squeezing as you roll.
- Store in the fridge up to a week for a quick snack to take on all your adventures!

ALYX AND BILLY'S SUPERFOOD KITCHEN

Surprisingly, one of the best sources for trail-tested recipes turned out to be none other than the original *Born to Run* cover boy himself: the skateboarder-turned-surfer-turned-ultrarunning-wildman, Billy 'Bonehead' Barnett.

Looking back now, I can see why Billy was the perfect cover model for *Born to Run* even beyond his good looks. We were all tickled as we watched Caballo Blanco and Billy become buds, even though Caballo was twice his age and could barely tolerate the rest of us. At the time, I thought they got along because Caballo was Billy's role model, only realising later it was the other way around: Caballo wished he liked anyone as much as Billy likes everyone, and enjoy anything as much as Billy enjoys whatever weirdness he wanders into. Billy, amazingly, is now thirty-seven years old, but just as fit and fast as ever. He's still besties with Jenn Shelton, his ferociously fast ex-girlfriend who went toe-to-toe with the Rarámuri in both the race and the after-party, although their instinct for extreme choices now extends to their zip codes: Jenn is homesteading with her new baby on the Alaskan frontier, while Billy lives in Hawaii with his wife, Alyx, the only human on earth besides Jenn who can keep up with him.

'Nothing jacks your adrenaline like knowing you're about to get punched in the face,' Alyx told me soon after we met, before going on to describe her cyclone of a life as an MMA cage fighter, national champion equestrian, Las Vegas-stage bodybuilder, professional fitness model, Ironman triathlete – and now, a naturopath healer and endurance coach.

Billy was already a skilled home baker before marrying Alyx, and together, they've combined into a dream team who use their own appetites and long workouts to test their recipes for both tastiness and all-day energy.

Alyx's Chia Breakfast Pudding

Alyx created this recipe for a coaching client who's a mother of three, a full-time school principal and a military spouse, whose husband is often away on deployment. The client is also an aspiring triathlete with gluten and egg allergies, so finding healthy meals that she and her kids can grab-and-go is both a priority and a challenge.

'I recommend using a mason or similar wide-mouth jar for breakfast or snacks, so you can prep once a week and grab any time you are in a pinch,' Alyx says. 'Dessert for breakfast? Who doesn't like that?'

INGREDIENTS

1 cup/250 ml coconut, cashew, almond or soy milk (full-fat coconut milk for a denser, higher-calorie meal)

4 tbsp chia seeds

A sweetener such as sugar, honey or stevia

Fancy toppings such as hemp hearts, fresh fruit, nuts, coconut shreds or even granola

INSTRUCTIONS

- Mix the milk with the chia seeds, and allow time for the chia to swell.
- Stir a second time after a few minutes to make sure it's not clumpy.
- Add sweetener of choice. Alyx likes honey since she's a beekeeper, but stevia or monk fruit are also great options.
- Chill until it thickens, then enjoy with fruit and any fancy toppings you like.

Carrot-Top Pesto

Alyx: 'This tangy recipe is a great way to reduce produce waste and has become a household favourite. It stores easily in the fridge for weeks and is great in wraps for long-run refuelling, as a topping on all dinner meals, and as one of our son Cosmo's favourite first meals.'

INGREDIENTS

1 entire bunch of carrot leaf tops (2 carrot bunches' worth if the greens are looking scrawny)

½–1 cup/125–250 ml lemon juice or the juice of 3–5 lemons (adjust amount for your preferred texture)

1 cup/150 g raw walnuts or nuts of choice (pine nuts and macadamia nuts are other top picks in our household)

A healthy amount of raw garlic ('I use a ton,' Alyx says. 'But tamer palates may prefer just one or two cloves.')

2–4 tbsp olive oil for texture and healthy fat

Handful (approximately ½ cup/30g) of mint leaves (optional)

Raw honey or stevia, to balance the flavour (optional)

Salt and pepper to taste

INSTRUCTIONS

• Blend or purée in a food processor.

Berry Date Energy Gel

Perfect for a pre-run snack, or for an energy boost in the middle of a speed workout. Commercial gels are thick and dehydrating, whereas this is both refreshing and easy to digest.

INGREDIENTS

1 tbsp chia seeds

10–12 pitted dates

8–10 strawberries or 20–25 raspberries

1 tbsp lemon juice

Salt to taste (we use Himalayan salt, but kosher or sea salt is fine)

3–4 tbsp water, as minimal as you can while not breaking the blender. Add slowly, checking for your preferred consistency

Agave or honey (optional)

INSTRUCTIONS

- Soak the chia seeds in 2–3 tablespoons of water until swollen.
- Combine all the ingredients in a blender. Mix slowly, drizzling in additional water as needed.
- Pour into reusable gel flasks and chill.

Billy's Mid-Run Pancakes

Alyx: 'Billy wanted a lower glycaemic energy option he could rely on before hitting the trails or snacking in the middle of a long run. These pancakes keep well in a ziplock and can sit in a car or backpack pocket all day without refrigeration.'

INGREDIENTS

¼ cup/25 g almond flour

2 eggs

2 tbsp cream cheese

1 tbsp coconut oil

Cinnamon, chopped banana, berries or other fruits of choice (optional)

Peanut or almond butter, honey or maple syrup (optional)

INSTRUCTIONS

- Mix the flour, eggs and cream cheese, pour into a frying pan with a light coat of coconut oil and fry on both sides until golden.
- Serve topped with cinnamon, fruit, nut butter, honey or maple syrup.

Billy's Long-Run Muffin

When we were in the Copper Canyons, we all learned a hard lesson during our first run in the backcountry. After two hours of steady climbing, we slid under a tree for a break. Some of us were smart enough to bring granola bars. None of us were as smart as Scott Jurek, who unzipped a pocket on his hydration pack and pulled out tortilla wraps filled with hummus and adzuki bean paste.

Since that lesson, Billy has been bringing his home-cooking A-game to challenge the seven-time Western States 100 champ by crafting his own pocket-ready trail muffins.

INGREDIENTS

1 cup/120 g white or whole wheat flour

½ cup/40 g rolled oats

Honey to taste

Cinnamon to taste

¾ tsp baking soda (bicarbonate of soda)

1 tsp baking powder

¼ tsp salt

2 eggs (can be substituted with yoghurt)

1 cup/120 g grated carrot (1 large carrot)

½ cup/150 g mashed overripe banana (1 medium banana)

¾ cup/180 ml apple sauce

1 cup/185 g cooked quinoa

1 tsp vanilla extract

¼ cup/40 g raisins

¼ cup/40 g chopped nuts: cashews or almonds work great!

¼ cup/40 g dried figs

Goat cheese (optional)

INSTRUCTIONS

- Preheat the oven to 350°F/180°C.
- Liberally spray a 12-hole muffin tin with cooking spray.
- In a large bowl, combine all the dry ingredients.
- In a medium bowl, combine the wet ingredients (eggs through vanilla).
- Pour the wet into the dry and stir until smooth. Fold in the raisins, nuts and figs.
- Spoon the batter into the muffin tin.
- Make balls with the cheese and push halfway down into the batter until the cheese is submerged.
- Bake for about 25 minutes.

Margot's Salmon Jerky – Three Ways

Margot Watters is not only a world-class endurance athlete, but also an inventive home cook who creates her own performance foods. We wanted a tasty alternative to sugar-loaded energy bars, so we tasked her with creating a dried jerky that's easy enough for anyone to prepare. Margot came back with a masterpiece.

Note: There are cooking options for oven, dehydrator or smoker, depending on what you have at home.

INGREDIENTS

1¼ pound/500–600 g side of skin or skinless salmon

½ cup/125 ml soy sauce

1 tsp molasses

1 tbsp lemon juice (freshly squeezed)

2 tsp fresh ground black pepper

1 tsp liquid smoke (only for Oven and Dehydrator method below)

(Liquid smoke can be found in bottle form in the BBQ section of most grocery stores – it is basically the vapour produced by a wood fire that has been condensed, filtered of its impurities and distilled, prior to bottling.)

INSTRUCTIONS

- Place the salmon in the freezer for 30 minutes to make slicing easier.
- Mix the soy sauce, molasses, lemon, pepper and liquid smoke (if using) together in a bowl. Set aside.
- Remove the salmon from the freezer and cut into ¼-inch/5-mm-thick slices lengthwise. Then slice the lengths into 3–4-inch/8–10-cm-long pieces.
- Place the salmon in a large ziplock bag and pour the marinade over the salmon. Mix well and refrigerate for 4 hours or overnight if time permits
- Strain the salmon well in a colander. Pat dry with a paper towel.
- For all three methods you are dehydrating the salmon, *not cooking it*. Try to keep each piece separate so air can move around it and remove when dry and chewy, not crunchy. Each method will vary in time so it's always best to monitor progress just to make sure you do not end up with an overly dehydrated, crunchy jerky.
- Dehydrator: 145°F/60°C for 3–4 hours (or follow manufacturer instructions).
- Smoker: Try to set and maintain a temperature around 200°F/90°C until dried, but still chewy, 3–4 hours (no need to add liquid smoke to the marinade if dehydrating with smoker).
- Oven: Set to lowest setting (170–200°F/80–90°C), place on a baking sheet lined with parchment paper or a silicone pad. Dehydrate for 3–4 hours, flipping once during the process.
- Store in an airtight container for up to a few weeks.

This recipe was adapted from Alton Brown from the Food Network

Vegan Pemmican

Keep these tasty pemmican balls on hand for snacking at home or on the go, and stash in your pockets as a long-run snack.

INGREDIENTS

½ cup/80 g almond meal or cornmeal

⅛ cup/15 g ground flaxseed

½ cup/40 g rolled oats

¼ cup/40 g total dried fruit (e.g. blueberries, figs, cherries, cranberries, raisins. Mix it up and experiment.)

1 egg

3 tbsp warmed coconut oil

2 tbsp liquid sweetener: honey, agave, maple syrup

INSTRUCTIONS

- Preheat the oven to 325°F/165°C.
- Combine the dry and wet ingredients.
- Fill the holes of a 12-hole muffin tin halfway.
- Bake for 15–20 minutes.

> NOTE:
> Don't worry if they seem crumbly while warm. They firm as they cool.

Margot's Power Dates

The 'Fruit of Kings' is rich in fibre and has double the potassium of bananas. Dates are also high in fructose, which makes them an ideal boost in the middle of a high-intensity workout. On long trail runs, the walnut filler is the richest source of omega-3 fatty acids you can find in a shell.

INGREDIENTS

Whole dates

Halved pieces of walnuts

INSTRUCTIONS

- Slice open one side of the dates, lengthwise.
- Stuff a walnut piece inside.
- Stash in plastic baggies.

LUCY BARTHOLOMEW'S 'PANTRY OF POTENTIAL'

Australia's Lucy Bartholomew burst into ultrarunning at the insanely young age of fifteen, mostly because she was tired of waiting around for her dad. Lucy was crewing her dad's first 100k, but instead of catching a ride between aid stations, she took off running, cutting through the woods to stay ahead of him.

'I'd have all his stuff laid out and he'd come in saying, "Oh, Luce, there was this hill and these stairs",' she recalls. 'And I'm like, "Yeah, I just did it."' Meanwhile, the race director was asking people, 'Who's this little blonde girl who keeps popping up all over the place?'

Lucy was soon charging through the ranks of the world's best ultrarunners, becoming a sponsored pro for Salomon while still a teenager and finishing third in her first attempt at the sport's crown jewel, the Western States 100. But secretly, her fame and drive were taking a toll. Her Western States performance attracted legions of new fans, many of whom felt it was their business to let Lucy know what they thought of her body. What they didn't know was that Lucy had battled an eating disorder at age twelve, and the barrage of online scrutiny helped trigger another episode.

'If you're a female athlete, people can see you at a dangerously low weight and go, *You look great!*' Lucy told me. 'Suddenly you have 50,000 people writing about you – writing *to* you! – commenting on your appearance, saying you look chubbier, connecting dots between your times and your weight, saying what you should eat and look like.'

Lucy was in a dangerous spiral; one she broke out of by accidentally signing up for a five-day retreat in Nepal she didn't realise was silent. 'Classic Lucy,' she says. 'I thought I was going to have a great time running the Himalayas, but as soon as I arrive, they take my gear and hand me this Buddhist robe and plop me on a mat.'

Sitting alone with her thoughts was brutal. 'Your mind comes up with all kinds of stories about who you are, and it's just like reading online comments.'

But gradually, she began to see another side. 'I came out of it realising I'm more than just running,' she says. 'In ultras, we learn to smile and fake it till it changes. But that approach was putting me in a position of poor health. People are always telling me, *You're living the dream!* Well, let me tell you about this dream …'

Today, Lucy looks at food as a source of power. When she inspects her pantry, she sees potential, because the better you eat, the more you can do and the farther you can go. Lucy now cooks for pleasure and eats for adventure. She's compiled her recipes in a downloadable cookbook called *Sustain Your Ability*, and even though she's vegan, she includes this advice for Lucy-style cooking – and living:

'I want to help you thrive and be happy. If you want to make additions, go for it. You do you. I can't say this enough.'

During ultramarathons, Lucy Bartholomew prefers real food over sugary gels.

Sweet Potato Date Slice

'This is the first trail snack I ever made,' Lucy says. 'I love that it isn't crazy sweet but fills you up with sweet potato, nuts and seeds. The turmeric is great for inflammation, the black pepper helps you absorb it, and the ginger helps settle your tummy on the run.'

INGREDIENTS

½ medium sweet potato, steamed, skin removed

½ cup/70 g cashews

½ cup/70 g almonds

4 dates

¼ cup/40 g chopped dried fruits (Lucy: 'I like cranberries and dried ginger chunks.')

1 tsp salt

2 tbsp warmed coconut oil

2 tbsp cacao powder

2 tbsp chia seeds, soaked till softened

2 tsp ground ginger and/or cinnamon

1 tsp turmeric powder

Crack of black pepper

INSTRUCTIONS

- Blitz all the ingredients in a food processor until combined.
- Line a baking tray and press the mixture into it.
- Place in the freezer for up to 12 hours.
- Cut into slices and place in individual ziplock baggies.

NOTE:
This slice is best eaten cold. If you take it running in warmer weather, the coconut oil will turn back into a liquid and the bar will become a delicious mush.

Arnulfo's Pre-Race *Pozole* with Roast Kale

Tragically, I only came home from the Copper Canyons with Mamá Tita's pancake recipe when I really should have been focused on her *pozole*. After a few years of trying to recreate it from memory, I'm satisfied that this version I came up with is a worthy substitute. It's a perfect slow-cooker dish that you can assemble on Sunday morning and have waiting when you return from a long run Sunday afternoon.

For a meat-free version, substitute roasted eggplant [aubergine] and/or portobello mushrooms, vegetable broth instead of beef.

INGREDIENTS

Bone-in pork butt, about 5 lbs/2.3 kg

Chipotle peppers in adobo

12 oz/350 ml dark beer, or cheap red wine

1 large can crushed tomatoes

1 large sweet onion, chopped

Fair amount of chopped garlic

12 oz/350 ml beef broth

Salt and pepper to taste

Sugar-free BBQ sauce, bottled or homemade

1 can Mexican-style hominy (you can use regular canned hominy, but the kernels are smaller)

TO GARNISH

Shredded kale

Lime wedges

Cilantro [coriander]

Sour cream

INSTRUCTIONS

Pork version:

- Place the pork butt in the biggest slow cooker you can get your hands on.
- Add all other ingredients EXCEPT the BBQ sauce and hominy.
- Set the slow cooker to high and cook for 3 hours, or until the meat is ready to fall off from the bone.
- Remove the pork from the broth and place in a large bowl. Using two forks, remove the bone and discard.
- Shred the pork. Using a slotted spoon, position the bowl over the slow cooker and drain as much meat broth out of the pork as possible while keeping the pork in the bowl.
- Get your oven broiler [grill] cranking to high.
- Mix the shredded pork with the BBQ sauce. Spread the BBQ-covered pork on a baking tray and slide under the broiler for about 5 minutes, just till it gets a little char.
- While the pork is crisping, add the hominy to the slow cooker and give it a good stir.
- Turn the slow cooker down to LOW.
- Check your pork. When you feel it's a little charred but not dry, remove it from the broiler BUT KEEP THE BROILER ON.
- Return the pork to the slow cooker. Let it simmer for another 30 minutes, or until you're ready to eat.
- On the same baking tray used for the pork, scatter the shredded kale and place under the broiler for 2–4 minutes, until crisp.
- Remove the kale and put aside in a bowl.
- Ladle the *pozole* into bowls, and garnish with any combo of lime, cilantro, sour cream and roast kale.

Vegetarian style:

- Half-fill a large slow cooker with all the non-meat ingredients except the hominy. Substitute vegetable broth for beef.
- Set the slow cooker to HIGH and let the ingredients simmer.
- Preheat the oven to 400°F/200°C.
- Chop two eggplants [aubergines], or one large eggplant and a bunch of portobello caps, and scatter across one or two baking trays.
- Bake the veggies for approximately 15 minutes. Remove from the oven and add to the slow cooker.
- Stir in the hominy and let simmer for another 30 minutes.
- On the same baking tray, scatter the shredded kale and place under the broiler [grill] for 2–4 minutes, until crisp.
- Remove the kale and put aside in a bowl.
- Ladle the *pozole* into bowls, and garnish with any combo of lime, cilantro, sour cream and roast kale.

Pinole Energy Bars

I had no idea what I was tasting when I arrived at Arnulfo's home at the bottom of the Copper Canyons and he offered me a cup of milky brew he'd scooped from a five-gallon paint bucket. It took a few sips before I realised it was pinole, the heritage corn concoction which has powered Rarámuri champions for centuries.

Caballo Blanco was a convert before he even got there, because he'd had his mind blown at the Leadville Trail 100 in 1994 as he watched Rarámuri runners storm through the Rockies while fuelling themselves on little handfuls of pinole from bags on their belts. Caballo began following their lead after moving to the Rarámuri homeland, stuffing a satchel of pinole into his pocket whenever he set off on his epic rambles through the canyons.

So what's pinole all about? It's basically just toasted cornmeal, but here's the key: when made from low-glycaemic heritage kernels, pinole is a complex-carb combo platter, hitting that sweet spot between instant fuel and slow-burn nutrition. Our go-to is Pinole Blue, mostly because it's made traditionally from Old World kernels with the same health benefits as blueberries, but partly because founder Eddie Sandoval grew up drinking pinole in Kansas with his dad, a Mexican road-crew worker, and got his first sack of blue kernels from a cousin who drove it up from Chihuahua.

We adapted this terrific bar from a recipe by Andrew Olson, a trail runner known as 'The One Ingredient Chef'.

INGREDIENTS

2 tsp chia seeds, soaked in 4 tsp of water

2 cups/320 g Original Blue Corn Pinole (Andrew prefers to make his own pinole by skillet-roasting masa harina)

½ cup/115 g chopped dates

½ cup/125 ml water

3 tbsp honey (Andrew prefers brown rice syrup)

A dash of cinnamon

INSTRUCTIONS

- Preheat the oven to 350°F/180°C.
- Soak the chia seeds for a few minutes. When soft, combine all the ingredients in a food processor or blender.
- Pulse into a thick paste, adding water or pinole if needed.
- Form the paste into 4–5 cookie-style rounds.
- Bake on a nonstick tray for about 10–12 minutes until the outside browns into a crackly crust.
- Remove and let cool.
- From Andrew: 'I like to cut these into half-moons and eat half before I go running and the other when I get back. Or, if it's a long workout, I'll take the other half (in plastic wrap) with me and eat it along the way. When eating at home, I highly recommend topping with peanut butter for extra awesomeness.'

Atole de Pinole, the Post-Run Power Drink

Food scientists recently discovered something that Mexican farmers and French cyclists figured out a long time ago: coffee helps muscle recovery. That's why multi-day bikers used to finish each stage with a steaming *café au lait* loaded with sugar: coffee bioactives boost glucose metabolism, speeding fuel into your tank for the next day's workout. In Chihuahua, the drink of choice before and after a hard day's work is *atole*, a pinole-based brew that's delicious either iced or hot. Traditionally, *atole* is made with Nescafé and condensed milk, but our version swaps in espresso, turmeric, honey and almond mylk, which cuts sugar, reduces inflammation and really complements the nutty pinole flavor.

INGREDIENTS

2 cups/500 ml water

2 tsp Original Blue Corn Pinole (or pinole of choice)

1 tsp ground turmeric

Honey to taste

1 cup/250 ml almond mylk (check out Lucy Bartholomew's homemade almond mylk, p. 81)

2 shots espresso (or coffee of choice)

INSTRUCTIONS

- Heat the water in a medium-sized pot.
- While waiting for it to boil, mix the pinole in a bowl with a little cool water and whisk into a smooth paste.
- Add the pinole paste to the boiling water, whisking well.
- Reduce to a simmer. Continue whisking until the pinole has mostly dissolved and the water is reduced by half.
- Add turmeric and honey, whisking continually, then almond mylk and espresso.
- Simmer a few moments to blend.
- Pour into a mug or over ice, and enjoy.

Chia Fresca, or *Iskiate*

I was first offered *iskiate* at the Rarámuri schoolhouse just before beginning our long, hot climb back out of the canyons. Secretly, I was planning to dump the dented tin mug I was handed behind a cactus first chance I got, because there was no way I was drinking that crazy-looking goop.

Back then, chia seeds were only known to the outside world as the gag gift you got when the Secret Santa limit was five bucks. Nobody ate them – nobody, that is, except the Rarámuri, who'd been using them for centuries to make their own super drink. Luckily, I figured out what kind of treasure I had in my hand just before ditching my mug.

I remembered that back in the 1800s, an adventurer named Carl Lumholtz found himself in my same situation I was in. 'I arrived late one afternoon at a cave where a woman was just making this drink,' Lumholtz wrote. 'I was very tired and at a loss how to climb the mountain-side to my camp, some 2,000 feet above. But after having satisfied my hunger and thirst with some *iskiate*,' he went on, 'I at once felt new strength, and, to my own astonishment, climbed the great height without much effort. After this I always found *iskiate* a friend in need, so strengthening and refreshing that I may almost claim it as a discovery.'

As tiny as chia seeds are, they're super-packed with nutritional amino acids and antioxidants. Aztec runners used to down a dose of chia before heading into battle, as did Hopis as they set off on epic runs from Arizona to the Pacific. Nothing will fuel you up better with as little fuss as a cold, citrusy cup of *chia fresca*.

INGREDIENTS

2 tbsp chia seeds

2 cups/500 ml water

1 lime, juiced

1 tbsp honey

INSTRUCTIONS

- Soak the chia seeds in a little water for a few minutes.
- Add the water with a healthy squirt of lime and a drizzle of honey.
- Stir, chill and enjoy.
- Perfect for reusable gel flasks.

SWITCHEL, THE AMISH GUT-BUILDING (AND GUT-BUSTING) SPORTS BREW

I felt a little burst of local pride when I heard that soon after Scott Jurek crossed into my home state of Pennsylvania during his record-breaking run along the Appalachian Trail, an old farmer greeted him at the trailhead with a weird-looking jug of home brew and urged him to drink up.

Scott had never heard of switchel, but neither has just about anyone else who uses electricity and zippers. My Amish neighbours in Peach Bottom have been drinking it for centuries to perk them up and quench their thirst while working in the fields. Scott considered it 'wildly reckless' to drink anything from an unmarked jar that a stranger handed him in the woods, but he's way too Minnesota to hurt an old farmer's feelings, so he took a polite sip – and fell in love.

'The switchel was crazy-good, gingery and vinegary, and it really hit the spot after a long hot day,' Scott raved. Besides the great zesty flavour, Scott also knew that ginger root and apple cider vinegar are terrific anti-inflammatories. But what he wouldn't know is that switchel has a fiery cousin called 'Super Tonic', which the Amish use to treat every ailment along the human digestive highway from sore throats to balky bowels. I've had plenty of both, and while I vastly prefer switchel, there's no denying the volcanic wallop that a shot of Super Tonic delivers when you're under the weather.

Switchel

INGREDIENTS

8 cups/2 litres water

1 cup/100 g grated ginger

2 tbsp honey

1 cup/250 ml apple cider vinegar

Optional modern addition: 1 hearty squeeze of lemon

INSTRUCTIONS

- Combine the water and ginger in a pan and bring to a gentle boil. Turn the heat down to a simmer and stir in the honey. Simmer for 2–3 minutes, then remove from the stove and let cool.
- Pour the ginger-honey water into a large jar and add the apple cider vinegar and lemon juice, if using.
- Top off the jar with water to fill. Chill and enjoy.

Amish Super Tonic

INGREDIENTS

4 cups/1 litre water

1 cup/100 g grated ginger

2–3 chopped garlic cloves

1 chopped yellow onion

1 tbsp ground red pepper, or fresh hot peppers

1 cup/240 g grated horseradish root

Apple cider vinegar

INSTRUCTIONS

- Combine the water and ginger in a pan. Bring to a gentle boil, then lower the heat and simmer for 2–3 minutes.
- Pour the ginger-water into a half-gallon/2-litre jar. Add the garlic, onion, horseradish and red pepper. Fill the jar to the top with apple cider vinegar.
- Give the contents a good stir and store in a cool, dark place. Stir the brew once a day while allowing to age.
- After 2 weeks, your tonic is ready. Strain into a clean jar and enjoy. Kind of.

6.4 AID STATION: CHECK YOUR BLOOD

Next time you run with two friends, check them out: one of you has no idea you're on the brink of a deadly disease that can be thwarted with a drop of blood.

That's the Russian roulette you're facing: one in three of us are pre-diabetic, but most of us (80 per cent!) won't find out until it's too late. The threat of full-blown diabetes is everywhere, so before starting your Two-Week Test, you should check your A1C blood sugar levels either with your doctor or a quick and easy at-home kit.

If you catch your diabetes in time, it's extremely manageable. Type 1 is a genetic disorder, often called Juvenile Diabetes because it typically shows up early in life. Type 2 is the one we're looking at: it's diet related and develops over time. For both types, your pancreas isn't creating the insulin you need to process blood sugars. That's why diabetics need to take insulin shots – and why pre-diabetics need to spot the danger they're in and do something about it.

The A1C only shows your average blood glucose level over the course of three months, which makes it *perfect* for the 90-Day Run Free programme. Two factors affect your blood glucose – high-glycaemic food, and exercise – which is exactly what the Run Free programme is designed to reboot. By taking the A1C test, you'll do two things: assess your risk for pre-diabetes, and establish a blood glucose marker as a baseline to monitor your progress. At the end of your 90 Days, you'll have spent three months eating better, clearing up nagging wobbles, and running more – and harder – than you have in years. Your next A1C test should be a victory lap.

But I'll be honest: I haven't checked my own A1C in

forever and I'm not looking forward to it. I picked up a kit from a pharmacy three days ago, and ever since, it's had me in a jam. I'm kind of dreading the results because I've been a slacker this year with my eating, but I also can't stand looking at that white box on my desk reminding me all the time why no one should ever bring Cinnamon Toast Crunch into the house.

So I'm with you. When I get to end of this chapter, I'm going to quit stalling and give myself the jab. There are four urgent reasons why:

1. If you're wondering which of your friends has the bullseye on their back, ask yourself this: *Are you a guy? Over forty-five? Who's a little heavy? And works out less than three times a week?* If so, you can probably quit wondering.
2. Have you had Covid? Due to the virus's effect on pancreatic cells, your diabetes risk just increased by 40 per cent. The reverse scenario is worse: if you first become diabetic and then get Covid, you're more likely to suffer severe complications.
3. Lots of us are high risk. If we're Black, Latino, Native American, Pacific Islander, or have diabetes anywhere in the family, the odds are stacked against us.
4. Don't kid yourself: if you think you can tell without a test, you're wrong. Pre-diabetes symptoms are mostly invisible, which is why eight in ten of us who are already in the hot zone don't have a clue.

That's why Thosh Collins began testing himself. To look at Thosh, you'd estimate his life expectancy to be about 250

As a Type 1 diabetic, Kaimana Ramos tracks his blood sugars on long runs with a glucose monitor patch.

years old. He works out hard. He eats so clean that the first time we were supposed to speak, he was out harvesting wild cactus buds for dinner. He's an expert in traditional Native American health and wellness. But he knows he's in danger.

'For most Native American men approaching forty and who come from a community with a high prevalence of T2D, I'd normally be considered high risk, which is a crazy notion to think about,' Thosh says. 'For people to not know any data on their biomarkers in this day and age is very risky when managing our health. If we can catch any blood sugar issues very early on, we can take action to help prevent the progression to Type 2 diabetes.'

So for the past five years, Thosh has taken an A1C test regularly. It was his Instagram post, publicly showing his own results, that spurred me to quit dillydallying.

The A1C kit has three parts: a mini blood collection unit; a test cartridge; and the cartridge reader. First, I prick my finger with the lancet, always easier than I think. Then, I tap a drop of blood into the collection unit and shake to mix.

Once the blood is ready, I pop the test cartridge into the reader. Final step: I insert the blood tube into the reader and sit tight, watching the five-minute timer click down until the results flash up. My results will fall somewhere on this scale:

Normal A1C: below 5.7 per cent
Pre-diabetes: 5.7 to 6.4 per cent
Diabetes: 6.5 per cent or more

My outcome: 5.2.

Just to be sure, I wait fifteen minutes for the reader to reboot and test again. This time: 5.4. I'll assume the higher score is accurate, since my fumbling with the first test might have thrown off the results. That leaves me .3 per cent above Thosh. Not bad, considering he's jacked beyond belief. But not great, since I'm now within .3 per cent of trouble. What bothers me most, though, is my nervousness before the test. We look forward to the races we've trained for, because even if we're jittery, we know we're ready. When we've cut corners, though – that's when we end up with a white box on our desk for three days.

So yesterday, my training goal was the Bird-in-Hand Half Marathon in five months. Today, it's an A1C test in three. Half-marathon PRs come and go, but tying Thosh's blood glucose level? That's a real victory.

> " WE LOOK FORWARD TO THE RACES WE'VE TRAINED FOR, BECAUSE EVEN IF WE'RE JITTERY, WE KNOW WE'RE READY. "

6.5 FOOD: **ACTION ITEMS**

1. Learn your 'Yes' and 'No' foods to prepare for the Two-Week Test.

2. Compile a recipe library of low-glycaemic meals. You'll find plenty on Phil Maffetone's website, but any online search of 'Low-GI meals' will turn up thousands.

3. Stock your pantry with low-glycaemic snacks. Start working them into your daily routine so they become your habitual go-to foods.

4. Take an A1C blood glucose test.

5. Continue practising Movement Snack exercises (see page 42).

Emmanuel Runes taps into natural elasticity to excel as a trail runner.

Fitness: Become the Master Mechanic

7

Back in 1878, a sickly teenager named Walter George had a revelation that remains, to this day, the gold standard of running wisdom. Walter didn't run very much at the time due to his asthma and fourteen-hour shifts as a chemist's apprentice, but he was still convinced he could break the world record in the mile.

And the reason he was so certain? The 100 Up.

Walter created the 100 Up from a combination of necessity and inspiration. Because he was stuck behind the pharmacy counter dealing with customers from dawn till after dark every day, he needed a quick and simple exercise he could do indoors. But the real creative force was his insight into running's raw mechanics. Like everyone else, Walter had always looked at running as an act of forward motion: you go from Point A to Point B, the faster the better.

But what if that's wrong? What if running wasn't about going from Point A to Point B – but Point A to Point A? Because think about it: what you're really doing is jumping off one foot and landing on the other. Before worrying about the forward part, Walter decided, maybe he should focus on the up and down.

So right there in the pharmacy, during those long hours at the counter, Walter George began experimenting with an exercise that took all the elements of running – knee drive, straight back, arm thrust, midfoot landing – and turned them *vertical*, instead of horizontal. It took a little trial and error, but before long, Walter had come up with an exercise that looked like nothing but delivered everything.

He called it the 100 Up, because that's exactly what it was: picking each foot up 100 times. The 100 Up has only three rules, but when it came to enforcing them, Walter wasn't messing around. 'Let me impress upon the student the necessity of maintaining *perfect form* in every practice,' he would stress. 'Directly the correct form is lost, the work should stop.'

For a perfect 100 Up, all you need to do is:

- Mark two lines on the ground, shoulder-width apart.
- Place one foot on each line.
- Keeping your back straight, raise one knee as high as your hip. Bring it back down. Repeat with the other leg.

You're marching in place, basically. Piece of cake, right?

But if you think you can kill it, the ghost of Walter George is ready to wipe that cocky smirk off your face. 'The exercise at first sight looks so easy of accomplishment that one might well think it possible to go a *thousand* up,' he warns. 'This is the result of not raising the knees to the prescribed height – the main point of the exercise – or of "galloping" through a short-timed movement in incorrect form.'

The true genius of the 100 Up is its built-in diagnostic tool – aka, those two marks on the ground. They're the unsung heroes of the exercise, because they're designed to capture any hidden wobble you might be harbouring. You'll be in the middle of performing the 100 Up, with all your focus on making sure each knee is driving up to your waist, and then suddenly, you glance down and discover some imbalance made you drift a half-foot off your hashmarks. If you've got a tight left hip, maybe, or a little forward lean from a lazy core, the 100 Up will sniff it out.

That's why Walter recommends starting with just twenty or thirty Ups, and recruiting a friend as a spotter to 'correct any shortcomings in your leg action or poise of the body'. When you can knock out a hundred perfect reps on each leg, you're ready to graduate from the 'Minor' to the 'Major': instead of marching, you now ramp up to running in place.

The Major begins Karate Kid style: you balance on the ball of one foot with your heel off the ground, while the other leg is cocked with the knee at waist height. Then, you spring into action: you leap off the balancing foot, land lightly and precisely on the other one, and swing your arms exactly as you would while running.

So does it work? Does all this hopping really pay off?

Holy smokes, it sure did for Walter George. For a year, he did almost nothing but the 100 Up, and when he finally got a chance to jump into some races, he found his asthma was under control and his leg speed was *insane*. By his twenty-first birthday, the chemist's apprentice was an international superstar, smashing records at every distance from 800 yards to 10 miles. His greatest flex was sauntering off on a twenty-four-hour drinking spree, then rocking up at the track in time to dazzle a jam-packed stadium by tearing off a 4:12 mile, setting a world record that wouldn't be touched for thirty years.

'By its constant practice and regular use alone,' Walter George said of the 100 Up, 'I have myself established many records on the running path, and won more amateur track championships than any other individual has won so far.'

You'd think that nowadays, with all the Nike money and nanotech devoted to building stronger, faster Superathletes, someone would have created a better training tool, but the 100 Up still ranks alongside the snap mousetrap as one of humankind's most enduring inventions: both were invented in the 1800s, both found the simplest mechanical solution to a biological problem, and both are easy enough for anyone to master.

The best part of the Walter George story is the irony: if the poor guy hadn't been stuck inside the drugstore all day, he wouldn't have gotten so fast. His accidental genius was discovering that the secret of running is strength, not speed. By building a solid foundation before he ever set foot on the track, Walter managed to bulletproof his body in a way that allowed him to train hard for years. More than a decade after his astonishing debut, he was still defeating all challengers and setting records as the most formidable racer on the planet.

But unfortunately, few of us ever learn the Lesson of the Pharmacist's Apprentice. We're so intent on going farther and faster, we never get good at going nowhere. We start running to get in shape, and never bother to get in shape to start running. And it doesn't help that in a lot of ways, we've actually got it worse than Walter. When it comes to fitness, we're dealing with disadvantages he never faced. Like cars. And Next Day Delivery. And squishy shoes, streaming channels, and jobs that plop us in chairs all day.

So to follow in Walter's footsteps, we can't just 100 Up. We have to catch up. We need to revive our legs by reawakening our joints and getting those mechanisms grooving again. Don't be daunted! These skills are as simple to learn as the 100 Up, and just as effective at fending off injuries. You're about to take control of your future and become your own body's master mechanic.

Pop up your knees and great form will follow.

7.1 LEG STRENGTH TOOL KIT

FOOT CORE

You're always told to train your abdominal core but never your foot core, which is probably even more important. This crucial muscle-craft is key to health and performance, because we can eliminate so much athletic dysfunction simply by training the feet. How we stabilise on the ground affects how we activate other muscles.

ONE-LEG BAREFOOT BALANCE

- Balance on one foot, on your forefoot, on a hard surface with the heel a little elevated so you feel nice and strong at the arch.
- Use a wall or chair or partner to help you stabilise when needed.

Note: This isn't a calf raise exercise, with up and down movement with the foot. There's no movement, just stabilising.

How many: 30–90 seconds per foot, or until you fatigue.

Pay special attention to: Where you feel it. Some may struggle with strength in their feet, others may be stronger in their feet and feel the most fatigue in their calves or glutes.

SIDE LIFT

- Balance barefoot on your right forefoot using a wall or chair or partner to help you stabilise.
- Keeping your right leg straight, raise your left leg sideways (think of half a pair of scissors opening).
- Raise your left leg only as high as you can while maintaining level hips, and then go back to the start position.

Note: This is a stabilising exercise for the stance leg, not a range-of-motion exercise for the moving leg.

How many: 15–25 reps, then repeat with the opposite leg.

KNEE LIFT

- Balance barefoot on your right forefoot using a wall or chair or partner to help you stabilise.
- Keeping your right leg straight, raise your right heel slightly.
- Now, lift your left knee in front of you as high as you can, and then go back to the start position. Keep your movements slow and controlled.
- The focus is on the stance leg, not the moving leg.

How many: 15–25 reps, then repeat with the opposite leg.

LEG STIFFENERS

Squishy shoes are energy thieves. Sure, they feel all plush and soft, but that's what every con man does: they make you comfy while they rob you blind. All that cushioning makes it *harder* to run, not easier. The more mush you have under foot, the less you're able to tap into your body's natural elasticity. Instead of springing you off the ground, all that free energy is absorbed into the foam. You now have to work harder to get back in the air.

What you really want is to bound along lightly. Leg stiffness is the key.

Leg stiffness doesn't mean muscle tightness or reduced range of motion. Instead, it's about creating a stiff base so our muscles and tendons can recoil as quickly as a bowstring. And the quicker you bound into the air, the less likely you are to get hurt. Mid-air is where you're safe; it's only when you're on the ground that you're at risk. As long as you're floating between strides, you're fine; it's landfall that causes trouble. Most injuries come from spending too much time on the ground, because all of your weight is supported on one leg at a time. The quicker you spring off that leg, the less your knee – or your calf, plantar fascia, or Achilles tendon – is forced to hold up your swaying body.

Remember Caballo's motto. You're about to learn the secret of 'light'.

POGO HOPS

Purpose: Engaging the arch and calves to activate natural elastic leg energy. We're learning to minimise ground contact and maximise elastic energy.

Pay special attention to: Getting off the ground quickly. Short, popping bounces are the goal, not height.

1) TWO FEET

How to:

- Barefoot is best.
- Hop quickly up and down, jumping from your ankles with as little knee flex as possible.
- Think mosh pit. Think Blondie, 1979.
- Once you get your pogo going, add variety: jump side to side, front and back, wherever your hops take you.

How many: Have fun with it and go for 30–45 seconds or until you can no longer pogo quickly, because slowing down increases ground contact time.

2) ONE FOOT

- Time for each foot to fly solo.
- Pogo like before – just one foot on the floor!

How many: 10–15. Stop before you fatigue, because slowing down increases ground contact time.

FOUNDATIONAL RUNNING MOVEMENT

100 UP

Purpose: Training active muscle pattern, especially for forefoot landing and knee drive. It's impossible to land on your heel while performing the 100 Up.

Pay special attention to: Standing tall with your back straight. You should feel your hips and lower back working. Push into the ground before pulling up your knee/leg, and notice how this keeps your feet stable and on point.

THE MINOR

How to:
- Barefoot is best.
- Mark two lines on the ground, shoulder-width apart.
- Place one foot on each line.
- Keeping your back straight, raise your right knee as high as your hip while driving your left arm forward.
- Drop your right foot back on its mark.
- Raise your left knee to waist height while driving your right arm forward – basically, marching in place.

How many: Form and precision are paramount. Stop as soon as you stray from your marks or struggle to lift your knee high enough.

THE MAJOR

How to:
- Same as above, but shifting from marching in place to running in place.

SINGLE-LEG WALL SQUAT

Purpose: Restore muscle equilibrium between quads and glutes. Many runners are quad dominant and lack glute activation, which leads to IT band issues, runner's knee and protesting hip flexors. Muscle tightness is caused by dominant muscle imbalances.

Pay special attention to: Initiating your squatting motion from your hips and glute, like sitting in a chair, rather than moving the knee first and forward past the toes.

How to:

- Barefoot is best.
- Stand next to a wall with the wall on your left side.
- Position your right leg about 2 feet away from the wall.
- Lift your left foot off the ground and slightly behind you.
- Using the wall for support, sink into a right-leg squat.
- Have the mindset of 'hingeing' at the hip.
- *Push* your support hand hard and continuously against the wall. That creates a stability challenge for your outside leg.
- Descend until your thigh is parallel to the ground, then rise.

How many: 15–30 reps on each leg.

RUN LUNGE

Purpose: If there is a single skill exercise that deserves mastery and craft work, this is the one. It highlights everything we need to be healthy, stable runners, including strength, stability, mobility and arm synchronisation.

Pay special attention to: As you lunge, switch your arms as you would while running. This is very challenging, so it can be helpful to use a mirror.

How to:

- Barefoot on a hard surface.
- Position yourself in a shallow lunge position.
- Make this a one-quarter squat, not deep, with your right foot under your hips and your left foot straight behind you.
- Raise and bring your left knee forward, raising it as high in front of you as possible.
- Swing your right arm forward in a running motion.
- Repeat on the other side.

How many: The goal is control and stability, so only do as many as you can comfortably, with a goal of 25+. Train your body to naturally find its balance points.

7.2
FITNESS: **ACTION ITEMS**

1. Acquaint your body with the Fitness exercises. Take your time, focusing on mastery and not quantity.

2. Assemble an experimental workout set, combining Movement Snacks with Fitness exercises. Take your pick of the exercises. The goal is to put them together in ways that feel fun and natural, so you'll feel at home when you meet them again in the 90-Day programme.

3. Power down with a low-glycaemic snack. Form the habit of reaching for a healthy food option when you're hungry after a workout.

After a lifetime of running injuries, Karma Park changed her life by changing her form.

Form: The Art of Easy

8

Eric promised he could teach running form in ten minutes. If I had to estimate, I'd guess he was miscalculating by a factor of at least 7,000 per cent, so I subjected his proposition to lab testing and gave it a try myself:

- I pulled up 'Rock Lobster' on my phone.
- I took about a half-step away from the wall, and hit Play.
- I began running in place to the beat.

I hit Pause and checked my watch. Then I tried it again. Each time, I found Eric's estimate to be wildly exaggerated. It wasn't even close to ten minutes. More like five.

One song. One wall. Three hundred seconds. If someone had only shared this secret with Karma Park, it could have saved her a world of misery.

Karma was such a disaster, the Navy honestly couldn't tell if she was a terrible runner or a terrific actor. How she even made it into boot camp was a mystery.

The strange thing was, running was her only weakness. Chuck her out of a boat at sea? No problem. Pull-ups, push-ups, crunches? Piece of cake. Karma was a competitive swimmer and varsity wrestler growing up, so two-hour workouts were in her blood. But ask her to run a mile and a half? In under thirteen minutes? Not a chance. Over and over she tried, and every time she ended up walking, grabbing her ribs from stitches and wincing from aches in her legs.

'I'm pretty sure the recruiter fudged the numbers on my Physical Readiness Test so she could get me in,' Karma believes. 'I finished the run and thought, *Oh crap, I'm a minute too slow*, and she's like, "No, no, you're good."'

When Karma got to basic training, she gritted her teeth and did her best. The Navy was her ticket to a dream life, so there was no way she was giving up. Karma was twenty-five at the time, with a wife in law school and hopes of becoming a surgeon. The surest path towards financing their future was a career in the military. Besides, she had a debt to pay back. Karma came to America from South Korea at age eleven, and while yeah, maybe Alabama wasn't the most welcoming place for a foreign kid with budding gender issues, Karma was still deeply grateful for the life her family was able to create there.

'I really wanted to serve this country,' she says. 'But in boot camp I was in and out of sick bay all the time.' Karma chanted the drill instructors' mottoes to herself – *Pain is only skin deep! Heel to toe! Heel to toe!* – but the harder she pushed, the more she broke down. 'At first maybe they were checking that I wasn't dogging it,' Karma recalls. 'I can see how I would be suspected because I feel that other recruits faked it to get out of running, but I was in so much pain, they knew something else was going on.'

Finally, Navy doctors diagnosed Karma with chronic hip displacement. She was ordered to report to the long-term sick bay, where she'd be stuck for as long as it took – a month, six months, a year – for her to either heal or quit. Those were her options: get better, get faster or get out.

Karma was crushed, but privately vindicated: ever since she was young and her mom would sign the whole family for local 5ks as a way of assimilating into their new home, Karma knew she couldn't run. 'My dad and I would walk at the back of the pack, and I thought, *This is the most ridiculous thing ever. We have cars and bikes, why are we running?* I was really fit in all the other aspects of PE, but with running, I tried and tried and never got any better.'

Back in civilian life, Karma struggled. She put her own education on hold and began managing a Subway so her wife could finish law school. She began putting on weight, but when she tried to exercise, her old leg injuries flared up and she finally discovered the real cause of her pain was rheumatoid arthritis. The medication made her lethargic and bloated, and her body ached so badly she needed a cane to walk.

Karma was in a bad spiral that nothing could stop.

Except her wife's lover.

'My wife had an affair with a guy who was really fit,' Karma says. 'When I confronted her, she told me I was fat. That hit me really hard.' So hard that after she and her wife separated, Karma decided to punish herself with the thing she detested most. 'I decided to drown my emotional pain by subjecting myself to physical pain,' she says. 'When I left the Navy I swore off running – *I hate it hate it hate it, never running again.* This time, I decided to run myself ragged into an early grave. I hated myself and hated running, so this is what I'll do.'

For once, Karma's injuries came to the rescue. Her legs seized up before her heart, and while she was searching for a new way to beat on herself, she had the enormous good luck to meet Sheridan. With that amazing woman by her side, parts of Karma that she hadn't even realised were hurting began to heal. For the first time, she had the confidence and support to face her gender identity and begin transitioning to the self that had always been buried.

She also resolved, once again, to get back into shape.

If you're keeping score at home, by now Karma has struck out three times as a runner. Over the years, I've heard a lot of stories like this from busted ex-runners – and lived one myself – but this is the first instance where I thought, okay, maybe it's time for the mercy rule to kick in and let it go for good. But against those odds, Karma stepped up again. When Sheridan gave birth to their first son, Karma set her jaw and decided their baby wasn't going to grow up with a parent hobbled with a cane or gone before their time.

'That's how I began my journey into learning how to run properly,' she says.

This go round, Karma attacked the problem from a different angle: What if her brain was the problem and not her body? Karma is a math whiz and comes from a medical family, so she was a little annoyed at herself for not realising sooner that if your equation keeps giving you the wrong result, adding the same numbers isn't going to help. Rather than running harder, she thought, maybe there was a way she could run smarter.

Her *eureka!* moment occurred soon after, when she noticed that her legs hurt more on downhills than ups. That's when it hit her: What if she treated the entire planet like a hill? Get up on her forefoot, in other words, instead of *heel-toe, heel-toe*ing it like she'd always been told.

'When I mentioned this to a friend, she immediately said, "Haven't you read *Born to Run*? That's what it's all about."'

Karma picked up a copy, and there, on page 181, she found the role model who would change her life. Not Ann Trason, the courageous science teacher who nearly outran a team of Rarámuri runners in the Leadville Trail 100. Not Scott Jurek, the gracious and unbreakable hero who rose from a rough Minnesota childhood to become the greatest ultrarunner of all time. Karma didn't even see herself in Jenn Shelton, that patron saint of human fireballs, or Caballo Blanco, the lovelorn loner who used running to heal a broken heart.

Nope. When Karma looked into the mirror, grinning back at her was Barefoot Ted.

I'm not happy about this now, but when Caballo Blanco and I first met Ted McDonald, we were ready to Rock-Paper-Scissors over who was going to clunk him on the head and chuck him into the canyon. Ted likes to say 'My life is a controlled explosion', which only confirmed my conviction that he has no idea what 'control' means.

I was slow to see what Jenn and Billy Bonehead and Manuel Luna liked about Ted. It took a few clashes before I finally got it, including a toe-to-toe shouting match in the middle of Death Valley, where I threatened to leave Ted by the side of the road to die while he was yelling in my face, 'I don't care how big you are! I'll fight you!' – at the very moment, by the way, when we were supposed to be crewing for Luis Escobar in the Badwater Ultramarathon.

But I couldn't miss the fact that lots of other people really enjoy him. Ted is a lot on a slow day, but he's also a huge-hearted friend and his own kind of genius. When I sent word to Ted that a group of my Amish ultrarunning buddies were travelling through Seattle en route to a Ragnar Relay, he immediately threw open the doors of his Luna Sandal shop and made them at home in an improvised bunkhouse. Nearly every year, Ted travels back down to the Copper Canyons and hands a wad of cash to Manuel Luna, the Rarámuri artisan who taught him how to make huaraches. Not because they're partners; because they're friends.

Still, it was gratifying to see that Luis had as much steam shooting out of his ears as I did after we invited Ted to join us in Colton for our photo shoot. For forty-eight hours we couldn't get a yes or no out of the guy, which would have been fine if he'd just stayed silent as well. Instead, Luis and I kept getting cryptic little teaser texts, like digital art smiley faces that dissolved from our phones a few seconds after appearing. It felt less like waiting for a friend to show up (or not) and more like being stalked by the Zodiac Killer.

Then lo and behold, an Amtrak train pulls into San Bernardino station and out pops Barefoot Ted, a big Santa Claus backpack full of sandal-making supplies over his shoulder. He'd spent six hours getting there, and immediately began hand-crafting a gorgeous pair of custom

Top: Barefoot Ted McDonald finishes the Leadville Trail 100 in homemade huaraches alongside pacer Christopher McDougall.

Bottom: In 2006, Barefoot Ted learned the art of sandal-making from Rarámuri craftsman Manuel Luna.

sandals for each of our volunteer models. While his hands were busy, so was his mouth: Ted cut loose with a thirty-minute spoken-word performance that left us all slack-jawed in astonishment as he prattled on, fluently and kind of brilliantly, about everything that had been rattling around inside his skull while he was captive on the train. ('Turning everything you see into food is a superpower. Do *you* have it?' is the only line I remember.) Soon after finishing a dozen sandals he was gone, grabbing a lift back to Santa Barbara that same night because, unbeknown to us, he'd had a pressing commitment there all along. What a guy.

As a runner, Ted was a true revolutionary. He was so far ahead of the pack when it came to minimalism, the rest of the country took years to catch up. Not that he didn't make a compelling argument from the start. It's just that in typical Ted fashion, the story took a direction only a man who calls himself The Monkey would follow.

If you recall, Ted only began running in the first place because he dreamed of becoming America's Anachronistic Ironman. Which meant, for reasons known only to Ted, he wanted to spend his fortieth birthday completing a full triathlon (2.4-mile ocean swim, 112-mile bike ride, and 26.2-mile run) but only using gear from the 1890s. If Ted has one quality greater than his raw athleticism it's his absolutely bulletproof self-confidence, so when he found he could handle the swimming and cycling but not the running, the problem couldn't be his body: it had to be the running.

Close: it was actually the running shoes. The first time Ted ran barefoot, his planetary axis shifted. 'I was totally amazed at how enjoyable it was,' Ted says. 'The shoes would cause so much pain, and as soon as I took them off, it was like my feet were fish jumping back into water after being held captive.'

On a barefooter's blog, he found the Three Great Truths:

- Shoes block pain, not impact.
- Pain teaches us to run comfortably.
- From the moment you start going barefoot, you will change the way you run.

Change the way you run …

That was the opposite of everything Ted had ever been told about running, but everything Ted had ever been told about running wasn't working. Besides, it immediately made sense. No decent basketball player just heaves the ball in the air and hopes for the best. No serious tennis player slashes their racket around like a club. Ted had spent a few years as a teacher in Japan, and he knew that sushi chefs and martial artists spend years perfecting the basic steps of their craft. In the world of movement, form and technique reign supreme.

Ted didn't know any barefoot runners in person, only online, so he set off on this quest for reinvention on his own. He found himself in the same predicament as a Czech soldier he'd heard about who, during the Second World War, spent his long nights on guard duty dreaming of Olympic glory. Rather than stand and shiver, the soldier began running in place, lifting his knees high to clear the snow and, to avoid being heard, landing as silently as possible in his heavy boots.

Back home after the war, the soldier replaced slippery snow with wet laundry: he washed his clothes by running on top of them in a bathtub full of soap and water. (Get a load of *that*, Mr 100 Up: one sloppy stride in a sudsy tub and you're not starting over, you're heading to the emergency room.)

Those weird home experiments paid off spectacularly. Coached only by his own ingenuity, Emil Zatopek pulled off the most stunning track performance in Olympic history: at the 1952 Games, he won gold in all three distance events, including *the first marathon he ever attempted*.

Despite how fast he ran, Emil took a ton of crap about how awful he looked. Upstairs, Zatopek was a horror. He'd get this grimace on his face, one sportswriter said, 'as if he'd just been stabbed through the heart'. Zatopek's head lolled around and his hands clawed his own chest like he was birthing an alien baby through his ribcage. But what sportswriters missed was that below the waist, Zatopek was a machine: rhythmic, precise, impeccable.

Ted never did get around to his Anachronistic Ironman – not yet, at least – but otherwise, he was unstoppable. Once he realised that running was a skill to be mastered and not a punishment to be endured, he became a Monkey on a mission.

More than a decade later, Ted is still handcrafting huaraches for runners.

Before long, he'd ripped out a marathon quick enough to qualify for Boston, and then ran Boston quick enough to qualify for the next one, and from there it was onwards and literally upwards, as he shifted from long roads to high-mountain ultramarathons.

But what Karma envied most wasn't Ted's remarkable twenty-five-hour finish at the Leadville Trail 100, or his out-of-left-field world record for skateboarding (242 miles in twenty-four hours). She didn't care if she ever ran as fast as Ted. She just wanted to be as healthy. She wanted to follow his footsteps from Hurt Ted to Happy Ted.

'I made a conscious decision to fully embrace forefoot running,' Karma says.

Maybe embrace isn't the right word. Since 3 May 2014, Karma hasn't missed a single day of running. Every evening, no matter what kind of storm is blowing through Birmingham, Alabama, no matter if she's fighting a cold or dealing with craziness at the medical office she manages, Karma pulls on her sandals and heads out the door.

Her eight-year-and-counting streak began in true Barefoot Ted fashion: bizarrely. Less than a year after changing her form, the woman who swore she'd never run again was bringing home her first marathon medal. Gone was the cane, forgotten was the spectre of crippling arthritis. By changing the way she moved, Karma discovered she could change the way she felt. She soon ramped up from a marathon to a 50k, and that's when things took off. The day after that first ultramarathon, Karma decided to test her

soreness by jogging an easy two miles. She was surprised to find her legs actually felt better after that run, so she went out again the next day … and the next … and thus a streak was born.

To maintain her daily running streak, Karma logs at least one mile a day, but that's just her baseline. During her first year of streaking she also tackled three ultramarathons, and then began creating streaks within her streak: she ran five miles a day for a full year, seven miles a day for ten months, and three miles a day for 1,300 days. Despite all these clicks on her odometer, Karma still felt she needed to borrow one more hack from Barefoot Ted: as a reminder to remain smooth and light, she always runs in a pair of his Lunas.

Karma had never actually met Ted in person until the day he hopped off the train in San Bernardino and blew into our photo shoot like a grinning bald tornado. Ted is usually quick on his feet, but when he came eye to eye with Karma, it took him a few beats to get his bearings.

The person who'd reached out to Ted years ago had never felt at home in her body and was facing two frightening transformations. The Karma in front of Ted today had made it through to the other end. In the past, Karma had looked to Ted for hope and guidance. Now, she deserved something very different. Ted understood, and delivered.

'If you have any questions, ask Karma,' Ted said, as he addressed the circle of very experienced and accomplished ultrarunners hanging on his every word about the art of minimalist running. 'She knows as much as I do.'

" SINCE 3 MAY 2014, KARMA HASN'T MISSED A SINGLE DAY OF RUNNING. "

8.1
THE ~~TEN-MINUTE~~ FIVE-MINUTE FIX

Running has a built-in catch-22: You've got to look down to see if your form is correct … but if you drop your head to look at your form, you mess it up.

Eric had to find some substitute for human eyes. He needed a biofeedback device that was as accurate as vision and provided an instant alert whenever an error was committed. Finally, he found the perfect tech.

A wall.

Next, he tackled tempo. Just like dancing, running is more than the moves; it also requires rhythm. Fixing one without the other is no fix at all, so Eric needed a foolproof system to marry movement to cadence. He knew exactly the beat he wanted, thanks to a happy collision between affordable consumer tech and a man who has nothing to do with Tennessee bourbon.

When cheap handheld video cameras first hit the market in the 1980s, it suddenly allowed anyone to become a guerrilla film-maker. One of those guerrillas was Jack Daniels, a two-time Olympic medallist turned college track coach. Daniels began filming elite athletes, and he noticed something fascinating: they all tended to run at about 180 steps per minute – ninety per leg – *whether going fast or slow*. To accelerate, they just lengthened their stride without changing that 180-beat rhythm. Daniels then turned his attention towards new runners, and found they typically had a much slower cadence, more like 160. The mistake these beginners were making, Daniels realised, was confusing *quick* with *hard*. It's actually easier to run at a quicker cadence, because you can bounce rather than *stop … go … stop … go …*

And the speedier you bounce, the more free momentum you generate.

But let's be real: Who wants to spend their runs counting steps and staring at a watch? For Eric's Ten-Minute Fix, he needed a painless way for runners to sink that rhythm into their muscle memory. And for that, we can thank the B-52s.

'Rock Lobster' clocks in at a crisp 92 beats per minute. If 80s alternative rock isn't your jam, then feel free to swap in 'Listen to My Heart' by the Ramones, 'ME!' by Taylor Swift, or our personal favourite, 'Verrazano' by Lady Southpaw, a punk rock marathoner who created an entire album deliberately timed to that 90-beat cadence. (You'll hear more from Lady Southpaw in Chapter 11 when we go toe-to-toe over running with music.)

So how do you put it all together?

1) Pogo up and down in place. You're not leaping for height; you're just popping up and down from your ankles. Don't futz around with your landing; just let your forefoot hit naturally with your heel kissing the ground.

2) Continue pogo-ing until it feels smooth and easy, as if you could do it all day. Think Muhammad Ali in the ring, Gwen Stefani at Riot Fest.

3) Got it? Now stand with your back nearly touching a wall. Run lightly in place. You're not hopping any more, you're running, but continue reaching for that quick, bouncing feel you had while pogo-ing.

4) If your heels hit the wall, you're kicking back. Pull your feet up instead. You want knee drive, not knee bend. That's the beauty of running in place: it's nearly impossible to do wrong. You can't heel-strike, you can't overstride. Your only risk is kicking back, which the wall has now corrected.

5) And now, the finale: keep your back to the wall, hit play on 'Rock Lobster', and run to the rhythm.

6) Feel it? You've now learned perfect running form.

MASTERING THE MOVEMENTS

RUNNING LOGS

PART 1

Purpose: The all-round kitchen-sink exercise. Helps to practise cadence, proper foot strike, stance leg, push off, and pulling leg over the log. Also helps to develop a feel for higher cadence, which is key.

Pay attention to: This isn't an agility drill where you're moving your feet as fast as possible. Your aim is to run over the logs smoothly and naturally.

How to:
- Create a ladder on the ground by spacing a dozen small logs in a row, each one about 3 feet apart. If you don't have firewood, use a dozen rolled up towels, or simply use chalk to mark lines on the ground. We used shoes here at the camp.
- Run the logs, gliding over and landing with one foot between each rung in the 'ladder'.
- Settle into an easy speed, making the run feel as natural as possible.
- Drive with your knee, stepping over the logs/shoes/chalk marks as if they were a half-foot high.

How many: As many as you like without tiring.

PART 2

Purpose: By gradually separating the logs at longer distances, we're feeling the push required to increase each stride. You'll need to push harder into the ground to clear the logs, which is also the way to generate speed.

Pay attention to: You want to *push* with your stance leg into the ground for extra distance, not reach with your lifted leg.

How to:

- Rearrange your ladder by making the distance between each log a little longer than the one before it, so the distance with each step over the log becomes longer. You can eyeball the distances, but you're basically adding 3–5 inches between each successive log.
  For example: log 1–log 2 = 3 inches …
  log 2–log 3 = 3.5 inches …
  log 3–log 4 = 4 inches …
- Adjust distances so you can still run but not leap.
- Run the logs, focusing on providing more force, and PUSH into the ground to navigate the extra distance.

How many: Have fun! Do as many as you like without tiring.

SKIPPING FOR HEIGHT

Purpose: Runners who have a hard time skipping are usually not sequencing their arms well with their legs during running, losing efficiency and stability. Poor arm swing throws off the legs, causing wobbles and wasted energy.

Pay attention to: Learning to feel relaxed *and* forceful. To get height, you need to relax and apply force while breathing and engaging core.

How to:

- In a normal skipping motion, drive the front knee *high*, focusing on gaining height not distance.
- Mimic running form, so your opposite arm and opposite knee are high in front.
- Skipping steps should be short, with lots of push off and strong, exaggerated arm swing to generate power.
- If you have a hard time coordinating your arms with your legs, practise skipping normally and then progress with height as you improve.

How many: 6–8 each leg. More is not better; more height and coordination is better. The more you do, the more you will fatigue and lose the purpose.

STICKY HOPS

Purpose: This specifically trains your ability to reduce ground contact time and engage the core.

Pay attention to: Land no deeper than a quarter squat, with the leg stiff and no up and down movement.

How to:

CONTROLLED

- Stand on one leg and hop forward, landing on the SAME leg in a shallow squat. Stick the landing and hold for a 3 count, then bound forward again onto the SAME leg. Continue this same-leg pattern.

QUICK

- Stand on one leg and hop forward, landing on the SAME leg in a shallow squat, and then quickly hop forward again landing on the same leg. Continue this quick hopping pattern, getting off the leg as quickly as possible.

How many: 8–10 each leg.

The Brain in Your Legs

Muscle memory is very real.

And a lot more powerful than most of us realise. Researchers discovered that when we exercise, a sort of recovery code is imprinted in our muscle cells. It's an archive of all the work we did to get stronger, so that even if we stop exercising for months – or even years – we can still switch on that recovery mode whenever we want. It's not a magic pill, but it is a shortcut. Strength and agility you developed in the past will return much faster than it took to build in the first place.

Gym rats figured this out for themselves long before scientists got involved. Weightlifters who'd stepped away from the steel and gotten soft realised that when they started lifting again, they rebounded in a fraction of the time they expected. They called it 'greasing the groove', the idea being that once you train your body to respond to a challenge, all you have to do is shock it back into action and it will soon glide along as it did before.

To test this, researchers at the University of Arkansas and the University of Kentucky put together a nifty experiment. They trained mice to scamper on a resistance running wheel, a kind of weight-and-cardio combo. After two months of workouts, the mice got three months off. That's roughly the equivalent of a seven-year layoff in human terms, because lab mice only have a three-year lifespan.

When the rested rodents were put back into action and pitted against mice that were new to the wheel, guess what? The retrained mice packed on muscle way faster than the newcomers. All the mice were out of shape when they started Round 2, but the mice who'd been down that road before were able to skip the intermediate stages and jump back into shape.

In cycling, old-school bike racers called this 'deep legs'. Their muscles didn't just get stronger from all those miles on the road; they got smarter. That's why a veteran rider coming back after an injury could quickly catch up with rookies, even though they were doing the same amount of training. Once you teach your legs the secret of easy movement, they'll never forget.

8.2 PERFECT RUNNING FORM PLAYLIST

You're not married to 'Rock Lobster'. The goal is to get any song at 90 beats per minute lodged in your hippocampus, so if the B-52s aren't your jam, take your pick from this Eric Orton-curated Run Free Playlist:

Lady Southpaw – 'Why I Run'/'Verrazano'
Hypnotic! Lady Southpaw created a perfect pair of 90-bpm Run Free anthems.

The Ramones – 'Listen to My Heart'
'Take it Dee Dee! 1, 2, 3, 4.' The original three-chord masters with a perfect 90-bpm short and fast track for those just starting.

Palace Winter – 'H.W. Running'
A free-spirit, lyrical journey at 90 bpm that will mesmerise and put you in the zone.

Led Zeppelin – 'Rock and Roll'
A legendary drummer and axe man warm up the legs with this 86-bpm classic that will keep you rocking and running.

Taylor Swift – 'ME!'
Grab a partner for this 91-bpm pop duet. You will be humming it all day and on your way to perfect pace.

The Rolling Stones – 'Everybody Needs Somebody to Love'
The Stones are rocking forever, and so too will your running to this simple 89-bpm blues rocker.

The Beatles – 'Help!'
The timing is there and gets better as the song plays. Ringo has your back – just when you're at risk of losing the beat, his drumming gets louder.

Olivia Rodrigo – 'deja vu'
Not the easiest beat to follow but worth it for this killer song.

Emmylou Harris – 'Born to Run'
Just a *scootch* below tempo, but we had to get one 'Born to Run' in here and Springsteen's is way too slow.

8.3 FORM: **ACTION ITEMS**

1. Experiment with the Running Logs drill and configure the most convenient system for you, whether shoes or chalk or towels.

2. Practise the 100 Up. It's fine to watch TV while you're 100 Up-ing, but be mindful of the rules: you need to bring your knees up to your waist with each stride and stay on your floor marks.

3. Cue up 'Rock Lobster', or any other 90-bpm tune, and practise running in place with your back against the wall.

4. See how lightly and easily you can run in time to the music. Can you relax enough to sing as you run?

5. Once you've mastered Basic Rock Lobstering, play around with your movements. Try lightly hopping back and forth, side to side, while staying in time to the beat.

6. Start practising all your Form exercises, acquainting your body with the movements so they'll feel natural when you begin the 90-Day programme.

Iman Wilkerson shifts into climbing gear in the California hills.

Focus: Faster, Farther and Forever

9

Beautiful! Thanks to Eric's strength exercises, your body is becoming an all-terrain vehicle, with a frame ready for both rugged climbs and highway miles. The 100 Up and other form skills are equipping you with puncture-proof tires, and your tank will always be filled with premium, now that you're pulling a Callie Vinson and cleaning up your meals.

Brains, body, belly: wheels, frame, fuel.

So what else do you need?

A motor.

Air is the all-important element that sparks this vehicle to life. How you breathe determines how fast you go, how long you can keep going, and how quickly you recover. That's the first thing every sports scientist looks at when they want to measure a runner's potential: How good is her breathing? Just like buying a car, what matters most is what's under the hood. No air, no go.

'Oxygen fires every cell in your body,' I was once told by Laird Hamilton, the big-wave surfing legend. 'Breath is what dictates failure. If you look at any fighter, any athlete, as soon as they start mouth-breathing, panting, they're done.

You can do without food for weeks, without water for days, but cut off oxygen, and you're gone in minutes. Breathing is your power.'

The reason I called a surf god rather than a track coach to talk about breathing is because, on one wild afternoon, two people came out the other end of a tragedy tunnel they really had no right to survive, and it was only because Laird had mastered the three main gears in any runner's motor.

Full Burn, Threshold and All Day.

Sports science textbooks call them anaerobic (gasping for air), threshold (decent air) and aerobic (plenty of air). You've experienced all three plenty of times. You know exactly how they feel. But do you know how to control

> **" HOW YOU BREATHE DETERMINES HOW FAST YOU GO, HOW LONG YOU CAN KEEP GOING, AND HOW QUICKLY YOU RECOVER. "**

them? Do you have any clue how long you can last at Full Burn? Or when you need to shift from Threshold to All Day to avoid flaming out in the middle of a run?

Because if you can't master those basic skills, then I'm sorry to say that you have no chance of becoming a centurion in Julius Caesar's Roman Legion. Caesar was one of the greatest military leaders in history, so when you consider that his troops covered thousands of miles on foot, the man has a few things to say about physical fitness. Caesar's forces were notorious for their unfreakingbelievable speed; enemy commanders would be rubbing their hands with glee, certain they had Caesar pinned down for good, only to hear arrows whizzing in from the rear and discover that overnight, the Romans had covered thirty miles at a run and penned them in from behind.

Caesar didn't have to hunt for great runners. He built them – and pace was his magic ingredient. During their first four months in the Roman army, new recruits were drilled relentlessly on timing. They embedded those three gears so deeply in their muscle memory that at a single command, even in the dead of night, 10,000 soldiers could instantly shift from a march to a trot without missing a step. They were put through the paces, you could say, on their paces.

As you can imagine, the supreme commander of the world's mightiest army wasn't a guy who liked to guesstimate. Caesar set his legion's All Day speed at exactly 'twenty Roman miles in five summer hours', or 15:00 minutes a mile. The next faster gear was double-time, a 13:30 clip that covered twenty-two Roman miles in five hours. When you factor in the gnarly terrain and 45-pound packs on their backs, that's a churn rate any ultrarunner would envy.

The Roman Legion's final gear … well, that's not one you ever wanted to see heading your way. Attack speed was a Full Burn charge, with every fighter closing fast on an enemy up to a quarter-mile away, yet not so fast that he out-sprinted his compatriots or had to drop his hands on his knees for a sec before swinging his sword. If you think that calculation is easy, try sprinting towards a power pole the next time you're on a run and see how ready you are to go into beast mode when you get there.

Tricky, right? Running hard is one thing. Running hard *with focus*, where you sync your pace to your goals and

> **TWO THOUSAND YEARS LATER, THE US MILITARY IS STILL CALLING SIGNALS FROM CAESAR'S PLAYBOOK.**

training, is a very different skill. Laird said, 'Breath dictates failure', but flip that sunny-side up and suddenly you're Caesar, where breath dictates success, and you can cruise along at speeds that seem dangerously fast yet perfectly match your oxygen limits.

So put yourself in Caesar's sandals for a moment. Heart-rate monitors and stopwatches haven't been invented yet. You've got crazy Gallic tribes coming at you from all sides, and the fate of the entire Roman Empire depends on one tricky math problem:

How the heck do you figure out the pace for each gear?

Why not, say, *eighteen Roman miles* in five summer hours? That's still pretty quick. Or twenty-five miles for quick-time instead of twenty-two? Seems manageable. Keeping in mind, of course, that if you miscalculate even a jot and your troops arrive a little too late, or a little too tired, your head is going home on a spear.

Caesar's solution to this problem was so ingenious, it's used to this day:

Singalongs.

If you want to determine the top speed a runner can move and still have plenty of air, make them sing. To calibrate the next faster gear, increase the pace until they can barely talk. Ramp it up again, so they can only bark out a few words at a time.

And there you have it: by using soldier chants, Roman commanders got both a test and a teaching tool. Most of those Roman Legion classic hits have been lost over time, but the fragments that remain indicate they were perfectly synced to troop speeds and bawdy enough to keep the boys engaged, usually about Caesar having sex with a lot of Roman wives who weren't Mrs Caesar.

Two thousand years later, the US military is still calling signals from Caesar's playbook. Today, combat boots tromp along at nearly the exact speed as those hobnailed sandals of the past. Even the singalong system is identical, apart from references to raunchy Romans.

In boot camps across America, fresh recruits are learning All Day speed by chanting in unison as they go:

We *are Alpha*
Mighty mighty Alpha
Rough and tumble Alpha
Straight-shooting Alpha
Better than Bravo
Better than Charlie
Chicken chicken Charlie …

For double-time, drill sergeants cut back on the words, replacing a steady refrain with call-and-respond:

Sarge: *Motion in the ocean—*
Grunts: *His air hose broke!*

Sarge: *Lots of trouble*
Grunts: *Lots of bubble!*

Sarge: *Rock, rock—*
Grunts: *Rock lobster!*

Granted, that call-and-respond isn't standard military issue, but it could be.* Because according to US Army Training Circular 3-21.5, section II, 4–14, official double-time cadence for all troops is a precise, time-tested, very Jack Daniels approved …

180 steps per minute.

In All Day gear you're pushing, not straining.

* *Real double-time marches are more like:*
Sarge: Charlie, Charlie, where you been?
Grunts: Round the world and back again!

Sarge: Charlie, Charlie, how'd you go?
Grunts: In a big ugly RATT rig moving real slow!

9.1 DO GEARS REALLY MATTER? WELL …

About two miles off the coast of Maui, Laird Hamilton found himself relying on those same three gears in his own kind of ultramarathon. It was December 2007, and early that morning, Laird got word that a series of rogue waves was coming in hot.

Laird and his buddies quickly loaded their boards on the backs of jet skis and boomed out to sea. They were heading for a break that was so far offshore, Laird himself had only found out about it recently and he'd lived in Hawaii his entire life. As the surfers approached the swells, they craned their necks back in awe. Laird had ridden some of the biggest waves any human had ever surfed.

These … these were not those.

'My personal Poseidon Adventure,' one of Laird's friends would say. 'Times *ten*.'

These waves were like a genetic experiment gone wrong, creating monsters so massive they were beyond the capability of any human control. In other words, you probably couldn't ride them; these freaks were sucking so much water towards their peaks that a surfer trying to slide down their face would get pulled *backwards* instead, rising higher and higher until the wave broke and crushed him towards the ocean floor.

Laird slid onto his board anyway.

What happened next is described in spellbinding detail by Susan Casey in her terrific book *The Wave*. For all its surfing suspense, I kept thinking that I'd never come across a better teaching parable for *See, THIS Is Why You Need to Learn Your Gears and Learn Them Now!* Laird suddenly

found his life depending on those three major speeds, and it started the moment he realised the giant he was on was about to crash.

Laird dove back into its face a moment before the world exploded. He was tossed, pummelled, spun around, but fought back to the surface, where he saw good and horrible news roaring towards him at the same time. His friend Brett was racing to the rescue on a jet ski, but hot on Brett's heels was another massive wave. Laird had just enough time for a big gulp of air before he, Brett and the jet ski were crushed under an avalanche of water. The two surfers came up gasping, only to be hit by another monster … and another … pushing them 500 yards down to 'the pitch-black depths'.

Laird went into All Day gear. With no idea when the onslaught would relent, his only move was to activate the surfer's equivalent of an overnight march and roll with the ordeal as long as it lasted. Finally, it calmed enough for him to surface and look around, and that's when he spotted Brett floating seventy yards away in a pool of blood.

Laird launched towards Brett at Full Burn. One of the metal fins on the surfboards had ripped Brett's leg open to the bone, shredding the flesh so badly that to Laird it looked 'like a smashed orange'. Laird quickly stripped off his wetsuit and knotted it around Brett's leg in a makeshift tourniquet. They needed to get to shore, and fast, but when Laird scanned the horizon for the jet ski, it was a half-mile away, surging out to sea with the current.

Laird strapped Brett into his flotation vest, then thrashed off in pursuit of the runaway ski. His only hope was nailing his Threshold pace. All Day, and he'd never catch up. Full Burn, and he'd never make it. Or even *see* it, because when your oxygen flags, so does your eyesight. That's another price you pay for oxygen debt. To you it's just a sprint, but to your Stone Age nervous system, a jacked-up heart rate and shortness of breath is a red alert that a fight for survival is in progress. All non-essential functions are temporarily suspended. Your eyesight constricts to tunnel vision, so you can see only what's directly ahead. You literally cannot focus.

If Laird pushed too hard, he'd not only gasp out too soon, but also lose the ability to spot either the jet ski in the distance or Brett behind him. He and his dying friend would both be lost at sea. Luckily, Laird clocked it perfectly. After fifteen minutes of hard swimming, he got a hand on the ski. And that's where the story shifts from 'Wow!' to *What the actual hell?*

Because the ignition key for the ski was still strapped to Brett's wrist.

Laird rummaged in the glovebox, found a pair of iPod headphones, and – while fighting an ocean churning with man-eating mega-waves and the pressure of knowing his friend was bleeding to death behind him – he somehow managed to hotwire the jet ski and roar back to the rescue. Laird radioed for help, hauled his dying friend onto the ski, and blasted the mile or so back to shore.

An ambulance was waiting by the time Laird skidded up on the sand. Paramedics surrounded Brett and began working feverishly to stop the bleeding. Laird, still naked, finally stood up and took a calming breath, looking back on

the mayhem he'd barely survived. Those insane skyscraper waves were still rising and crashing, booming a warning to stay away.

So Laird borrowed a pair of board shorts, recruited a fresh jet ski driver, checked on Brett, and headed back out to sea.

Because, you know. Poseidon Adventure times ten and all.

9.2
FOCUS TRAINING: ATHLETICISM = AWARENESS

My version of Laird's Impossible Adventure began the day I first met Eric Orton at the park in Denver to interview him for *Men's Journal.* **My assignment was to chronicle Eric's multi-faceted approach to endurance training, but after one workout with me, Eric ripped up all the facets except one.**

Eric could tell at a glance that my running form was rubbish, and a few simple exercises (the same ones he'd later use to assess Jenna, Iman and Emmanuel at our photo shoot) quickly revealed my strength issues. Wheels and frame both needed work, that much was clear. But the big mystery was my motor.

If there was going to be any chance of me stepping up to the starting line with Caballo and the Rarámuri, Eric had to see what kind of transmission I was working with so he could lay out a training plan. Runners, he explained, have eight gears:

1st Gear = Super-slow, running drill pace
2nd Gear = All Day speed (endurance)
3rd Gear = Marathon training pace
4th Gear = Half-marathon training pace
5th Gear = Threshold (10k pace)
6th Gear = 5k training pace
7th Gear = Full Burn (sustainable speed)
8th Gear = Finish-line burst

Think of those three main gears – All Day, Threshold and Full Burn – as the 'Drive' on your automatic transmission:

they handle just about every job you have, and you can click right in without giving them much thought.

The other five? They're the *S* and *L* options on the shifter: you know they exist, kinda, but you don't use them enough to remember the exact feel of sprightly *Sport* or tractor-pull *Low*, or when you really need them.

You can really dial in the exact differences between these gears by using a heart-rate monitor and chest strap, but do you want to spend your runs pushing buttons and peering at numbers on your wrist? Or would you rather develop a natural feel for each speed so you can tell, instantly, when you're in the right gear?

So when Eric was explaining his coaching method to me in the park, he showed me a technique that does the same thing for pace that the Two-Week Test does for food. Once you learn it, he said, you'll know right away if you're on target.

Eric told me to kick off my shoes. Together we began jogging barefoot around the park. He pointed ahead.

'When we reach that tree, sprint to the next one,' he said.

'You mean, like—' I fumbled, oddly confused by those simple instructions. The last time anyone told me to sprint, I was playing high-school basketball. For the next forty years, I'd probably cartwheeled more than I'd sprinted, and I can't cartwheel. Anyone who's ever ripped a hamstring racing a nine-year-old knows there's only one sensible way to run, and that's to find your groove and stick to it. Sometimes we go a little faster, often a little slower, but mostly we trot at whatever pace lets us finish a few miles with an acceptable degree of discomfort. Nobody *sprints*. Talk about a recipe for disaster.

'Fast as you can,' Eric insisted. 'Let 'er rip for about thirty seconds. Then settle back to a jog.'

Twenty seconds into a thirty-second sprint, I flamed out and had to walk. I hadn't sprinted in so long, I'd forgotten how. It was equal parts embarrassing and annoying. What was the point anyway? Did I have to remind this guy I was training for fifty miles, not fifty yards?

Eric didn't give me time to mope. As soon as I recovered, we went at it again. And again. And by the fourth or fifth rep, I noticed a weird sensation, like your hand tingling back to life after you've banged your elbow: instead of getting tired, my legs felt looser, stronger, fresher, than when we'd started. The faster I ran, the better I felt. I was straightening my back, deep breathing from the gut, driving with my knees.

'Good, right?' Eric asked. 'Feeling bouncy?'

Running fast can help autocorrect your biomechanics, he explained, while slow leads to sloppy. That's a big reason I was always hurt; my plodding pace had me balancing too long on each leg, leaving all those tissues and tendons exposed to serious torque as my body weight swayed around. For years, I'd been a human version of Barefoot Ted's big-wheel Victorian bike, trundling along with just one gear.

'It doesn't mean you've got to sprint all the time,' Eric said. 'But the technique is the same. Believe it or not, running fast is the best way to learn how to run slow.'

Because no matter the speed, my cadence shouldn't change. I should still be Rock Lobster-ing along, *pop-pop-popping* my feet at a steady 180 steps per minute. To go faster, Eric explained, I just had to lengthen my stride a little. That change alone would go a long way towards curing my injuries and building my strength and stamina.

As he was talking, I was suddenly struck by a revelation. So *that's* why Caballo was so hung up on that stuff about 'First focus on Easy …' At the time, I thought he was mostly sharing a little smokin'-herb-by-the-river hippie philosophy, but listening to Eric, I started to get it. Caballo was actually revealing the most important bit of running wisdom he'd picked up from the Rarámuri:

Easy is everything, he was telling me, *except easy*.

> " RUNNING FAST CAN HELP AUTOCORRECT YOUR BIOMECHANICS, WHILE SLOW LEADS TO SLOPPY. "

Luckily, Eric had a system for teaching Easy that didn't require a fifteen-year sabbatical at the bottom of a canyon.

Soon after I got home, he told me to run a single mile as fast as I could and then send him my time. We didn't live near a high-school track, so I used the odometer on the pickup truck to measure a mile on the flattest road I could find.

I parked the truck back home, then jogged two easy miles back to the starting line I'd created by dragging my foot across the dirt road. I set my watch, sucked in a few deep breaths, and was off. I loved the quick feel of my Rock Lobster cadence, plus all the new power I was getting from my freshly straightened back and knee drive.

I came off the dirt road at roughly the half-mile mark and turned onto pavement, accelerating exactly as I'd planned. I made the move I'd been waiting for, using the smooth asphalt to speed along and slingshot myself into the last—

Goddammit. A quarter-mile from the finish, I ran out of air and slowed to a walk. I dug my phone out of my back pocket, too annoyed with myself to wait before calling Eric.

'Good!' replied Mr Half Full. 'Better to go hard and fall short than finish strong and wonder how much you had left.' Eric told me to take a day off, then hit it fresh. This time, I jogged the course backwards before I started. I focused on the distance, my pace, how my breathing should feel.

Six minutes and change later, I was already smiling before I reached for my watch and hit STOP.

ONE-MILE TEST

Why one mile: This middle distance is a good benchmark for calculating the maximum speed that can be sustained for a relatively long period before going into oxygen debt. Your one-mile time will provide the ranges for your running gears and become the foundation for your 90-Day programme.

Note: Wait until this test is assigned in the 90-Day programme.

Course: The One-Mile Test is best done on a running track for accuracy and repeatability. If you don't have access to a running track, find the flattest course you can that's as free of cars and intersections as possible.

Warm-up:
- Run easy for 15 minutes.
- Perform 1–2 sets of Skills (Skipping for Height/Pogos/Sticky Hops)
- 5 x 30-second accelerations where you gradually pick up your speed throughout the 30 seconds, finishing each at a comfortably fast speed. If you dread these, you're going too hard. Take a 1–2 minute rest interval between each.

Test: Run as fast *and* as steadily as you can for one mile. Avoid going out too fast (*cough*McDougall*cough*).

Cooldown: Relax into an easy 5–10 minute run/walk.

FOCUS TRAINING

How Focus Training works: Too many runners try to increase endurance by piling on long, slow miles, rather than building their strength and speed. It's an understandable mistake, but fortunately, it's one that Emil Zatopek managed to avoid. When Emil was training for his marathon debut at the 1952 Olympic Games, he was ridiculed for doing one-hundred-yard dashes instead of long miles.

'I already know how to run slow,' he shrugged. 'I thought the point was to run fast.'

Zatopek's marathon gold medal is pretty good proof he was right. But instead of following his example, most runners continually train at goal pace, rather than working their other gears. Ask yourself this: if your dream is a four-hour marathon, are your daily runs mostly clocking in around 9:00 minutes a mile? If so, you're not building speed and stamina. You're getting good at staying slow.

The remedy: Don't train for twenty-six miles. Learn how to run one mile fast and repeat it twenty-five more times.

GEAR 2: ALL DAY

This steady endurance gear not only conserves oxygen, but also allows you to access your richest source of energy. By keeping your heart rate in All Day range, your body learns to tap into fat as fuel rather than relying on fast-burn sugars and high-glycaemic carbohydrates.

What it should feel like: Chatting pace, when you can sustain conversation but still remain aware of steady effort.

Focus on: Quick cadence, relaxed swinging arms, keeping things easy and rhythmic. Remember foot strike by visualising Running Logs as you go. Stop occasionally and run in place to re-engineer the feeling, then continue.

GEAR 5: THRESHOLD

This is your 10k speed, a pace you can maintain for 45–60 minutes of all-out effort. Too many runners do the bulk of their training too far below this pace, resulting in meagre gains and long plateaus. Threshold is where the magic happens, providing the most dramatic bumps in speed and distance.

What it should feel like: You'll notice a shift in breathing from steady to more laboured but rhythmic. Not huffing and puffing, but where you can speak in separate words rather than sentences – an effort you can maintain during 45–60 minutes of steady effort. Training intervals of 4–20 minutes are used at this effort.

Focus on: Pushing into the ground to get your speed. Resist the temptation to stretch out your leg and overstride. As you settle in after a few minutes, your breathing becomes rhythmic and sustainable. Relax and feel the arm swing.

GEAR 7: FULL BURN

VO_2 max is the gold standard for endurance diagnostics, because it measures the maximum amount of oxygen you can suck in and utilise during intense effort. When Laird Hamilton says, 'Breath is what dictates failure', VO_2 max is what he's talking about: How hard can you go before you run out of air?

Just like Threshold, Full Burn is trainable. As you improve your oxygen intake at Full Burn, those gains transfer to the other gears as well. Full Burn is the first building block for improving performance at longer distances and faster speeds. It's why Emil Zatopek learned to run fast before he ran far.

What it should feel like: Run-like-you-stole-it effort. If you can still run after 2–4 minutes, you're going too slow.

Focus on: Try taking TWO breaths in and one breath out, rather than the normal one in, one out. Notice how this helps you focus and get into the flow. Each breath in should be timed to each foot strike. Stay consistent with your foot strike, remembering to drive into the ground rather than reaching for speed.

YOUR HANDY PACE-TO-GEAR CONVERSION CHART

Check this chart to see how your one-mile personal best translates into a minutes-per-mile pace for longer runs. Remember, your ultimate goal is to get used to how each gear feels, but comparing them to times on your watch isn't a bad way to learn. Each gear has a 30-second pace range (like, 16:43 and 16:12 for Gear 2 if you're a 12-minute miler). Your sweet spot is anywhere in between.

One-Mile Time	Gear 1	Gear 2		Gear 3		Gear 4		Gear 5		Gear 6		Gear 7		Gear 8	
12:00	> 16:43	16:43	16:12	14:55	14:24	14:24	13:48	13:32	13:12	12:51	12:36	12:15	12:00	11:34	11:24
11:55	> 16:36	16:36	16:05	14:49	14:18	14:18	13:42	13:26	13:06	12:46	12:30	12:10	11:55	11:29	11:19
11:50	> 16:30	16:30	15:58	14:43	14:12	14:12	13:36	13:21	13:01	12:41	12:25	12:05	11:50	11:24	11:14
11:45	> 16:23	16:23	15:51	14:37	14:06	14:06	13:30	13:15	12:55	12:36	12:20	12:00	11:45	11:19	11:09
11:40	> 16:16	16:16	15:45	14:31	14:00	14:00	13:25	13:10	12:50	12:30	12:15	11:55	11:40	11:15	11:05
11:35	> 16:09	16:09	15:38	14:25	13:54	13:54	13:19	13:04	12:44	12:25	12:09	11:50	11:35	11:10	11:00
11:30	> 16:03	16:03	15:31	14:19	13:48	13:48	13:13	12:59	12:39	12:20	12:04	11:45	11:30	11:05	10:55
11:25	> 15:56	15:56	15:24	14:13	13:42	13:42	13:07	12:53	12:33	12:15	11:59	11:40	11:25	11:00	10:50
11:20	> 15:49	15:49	15:18	14:07	13:36	13:36	13:02	12:48	12:28	12:09	11:54	11:35	11:20	10:56	10:46
11:15	> 15:42	15:42	15:11	14:01	13:30	13:30	12:56	12:42	12:22	12:04	11:48	11:30	11:15	10:51	10:41
11:10	> 15:36	15:36	15:04	13:55	13:24	13:24	12:50	12:37	12:17	11:59	11:43	11:25	11:10	10:46	10:36
11:05	> 15:29	15:29	14:57	13:49	13:18	13:18	12:44	12:31	12:11	11:54	11:38	11:20	11:05	10:41	10:31
11:00	> 15:22	15:22	14:51	13:43	13:12	13:12	12:39	12:26	12:06	11:48	11:33	11:15	11:00	10:37	10:27
10:55	> 15:15	15:15	14:44	13:37	13:06	13:06	12:33	12:20	12:00	11:43	11:27	11:10	10:55	10:32	10:22
10:50	> 15:09	15:09	14:37	13:31	13:00	13:00	12:27	12:15	11:55	11:38	11:22	11:05	10:50	10:27	10:17
10:45	> 15:02	15:02	14:30	13:25	12:54	12:54	12:21	12:09	11:49	11:33	11:17	11:00	10:45	10:22	10:12
10:40	> 14:55	14:55	14:24	13:19	12:48	12:48	12:16	12:04	11:44	11:27	11:12	10:55	10:40	10:18	10:08
10:35	> 14:48	14:48	14:17	13:13	12:42	12:42	12:10	11:58	11:38	11:22	11:06	10:50	10:35	10:13	10:03
10:30	> 14:42	14:42	14:10	13:07	12:36	12:36	12:04	11:53	11:33	11:17	11:01	10:45	10:30	10:08	9:58
10:25	> 14:35	14:35	14:03	13:01	12:30	12:30	11:58	11:47	11:27	11:12	10:56	10:40	10:25	10:03	9:53
10:20	> 14:28	14:28	13:57	12:55	12:24	12:24	11:53	11:42	11:22	11:06	10:51	10:35	10:20	9:59	9:49
10:15	> 14:21	14:21	13:50	12:49	12:18	12:18	11:47	11:36	11:16	11:01	10:45	10:30	10:15	9:54	9:44
10:10	> 14:15	14:15	13:43	12:43	12:12	12:12	11:41	11:31	11:11	10:56	10:40	10:25	10:10	9:49	9:39
10:05	> 14:08	14:08	13:36	12:37	12:06	12:06	11:35	11:25	11:05	10:51	10:35	10:20	10:05	9:44	9:34
10:00	> 14:01	14:01	13:30	12:31	12:00	12:00	11:30	11:20	11:00	10:45	10:30	10:15	10:00	9:40	9:30
9:55	> 13:54	13:54	13:23	12:25	11:54	11:54	11:24	11:14	10:54	10:40	10:24	10:10	9:55	9:35	9:25
9:50	> 13:48	13:48	13:16	12:19	11:48	11:48	11:18	11:09	10:49	10:35	10:19	10:05	9:50	9:30	9:20
9:45	> 13:41	13:41	13:09	12:13	11:42	11:42	11:12	11:03	10:43	10:30	10:14	10:00	9:45	9:25	9:15
9:40	> 13:34	13:34	13:03	12:07	11:36	11:36	11:07	10:58	10:38	10:24	10:09	9:55	9:40	9:21	9:11
9:35	> 13:27	13:27	12:56	12:01	11:30	11:30	11:01	10:52	10:32	10:19	10:03	9:50	9:35	9:16	9:06
9:30	> 13:21	13:21	12:49	11:55	11:24	11:24	10:55	10:47	10:27	10:14	9:58	9:45	9:30	9:11	9:01
9:25	> 13:14	13:14	12:42	11:49	11:18	11:18	10:49	10:41	10:21	10:09	9:53	9:40	9:25	9:06	8:56
9:20	> 13:07	13:07	12:36	11:43	11:12	11:12	10:44	10:36	10:16	10:03	9:48	9:35	9:20	9:02	8:52
9:15	> 13:00	13:00	12:29	11:37	11:06	11:06	10:38	10:30	10:10	9:58	9:42	9:30	9:15	8:57	8:47
9:10	> 12:54	12:54	12:22	11:31	11:00	11:00	10:32	10:25	10:05	9:53	9:37	9:25	9:10	8:52	8:42
9:05	> 12:47	12:47	12:15	11:25	10:54	10:54	10:26	10:19	9:59	9:48	9:32	9:20	9:05	8:47	8:37
9:00	> 12:40	12:40	12:09	11:19	10:48	10:48	10:21	10:14	9:54	9:42	9:27	9:15	9:00	8:43	8:33

One-Mile Time	Gear 1	Gear 2		Gear 3		Gear 4		Gear 5		Gear 6		Gear 7		Gear 8	
8:55	> 12:33	12:33	12:02	11:13	10:42	10:42	10:15	10:08	9:48	9:37	9:21	9:10	8:55	8:38	8:28
8:50	> 12:27	12:27	11:55	11:07	10:36	10:36	10:09	10:03	9:43	9:32	9:16	9:05	8:50	8:33	8:23
8:45	> 12:20	12:20	11:48	11:01	10:30	10:30	10:03	9:57	9:37	9:27	9:11	9:00	8:45	8:28	8:18
8:40	> 12:13	12:13	11:42	10:55	10:24	10:24	9:58	9:52	9:32	9:21	9:06	8:55	8:40	8:24	8:14
8:35	> 12:06	12:06	11:35	10:49	10:18	10:18	9:52	9:46	9:26	9:16	9:00	8:50	8:35	8:19	8:09
8:30	> 12:00	12:00	11:28	10:43	10:12	10:12	9:46	9:41	9:21	9:11	8:55	8:45	8:30	8:14	8:04
8:25	> 11:53	11:53	11:21	10:37	10:06	10:06	9:40	9:35	9:15	9:06	8:50	8:40	8:25	8:09	7:59
8:20	> 11:46	11:46	11:15	10:31	10:00	10:00	9:35	9:30	9:10	9:00	8:45	8:35	8:20	8:05	7:55
8:15	> 11:39	11:39	11:08	10:25	9:54	9:54	9:29	9:24	9:04	8:55	8:39	8:30	8:15	8:00	7:50
8:10	> 11:33	11:33	11:01	10:19	9:48	9:48	9:23	9:19	8:59	8:50	8:34	8:25	8:10	7:55	7:45
8:05	> 11:26	11:26	10:54	10:13	9:42	9:42	9:17	9:13	8:53	8:45	8:29	8:20	8:05	7:50	7:40
8:00	> 11:19	11:19	10:48	10:07	9:36	9:36	9:12	9:08	8:48	8:39	8:24	8:15	8:00	7:46	7:36
7:55	> 11:12	11:12	10:41	10:01	9:30	9:30	9:06	9:02	8:42	8:34	8:18	8:10	7:55	7:41	7:31
7:50	> 11:06	11:06	10:34	9:55	9:24	9:24	9:00	8:57	8:37	8:29	8:13	8:05	7:50	7:36	7:26
7:45	> 10:59	10:59	10:27	9:49	9:18	9:18	8:54	8:51	8:31	8:24	8:08	8:00	7:45	7:31	7:21
7:40	> 10:52	10:52	10:21	9:43	9:12	9:12	8:49	8:46	8:26	8:18	8:03	7:55	7:40	7:27	7:17
7:35	> 10:45	10:45	10:14	9:37	9:06	9:06	8:43	8:40	8:20	8:13	7:57	7:50	7:35	7:22	7:12
7:30	> 10:39	10:39	10:07	9:31	9:00	9:00	8:37	8:35	8:15	8:08	7:52	7:45	7:30	7:17	7:07
7:25	> 10:32	10:32	10:00	9:25	8:54	8:54	8:31	8:29	8:09	8:03	7:47	7:40	7:25	7:12	7:02
7:20	> 10:25	10:25	9:54	9:19	8:48	8:48	8:26	8:24	8:04	7:57	7:42	7:35	7:20	7:08	6:58
7:15	> 10:18	10:18	9:47	9:13	8:42	8:42	8:20	8:18	7:58	7:52	7:36	7:30	7:15	7:03	6:53
7:10	> 10:12	10:12	9:40	9:07	8:36	8:36	8:14	8:13	7:53	7:47	7:31	7:25	7:10	6:58	6:48
7:05	> 10:05	10:05	9:33	9:01	8:30	8:30	8:08	8:07	7:47	7:42	7:26	7:20	7:05	6:53	6:43
7:00	> 09:58	9:58	9:27	8:55	8:24	8:24	8:03	8:02	7:42	7:36	7:21	7:15	7:00	6:49	6:39
6:58	> 09:55	9:55	9:24	8:53	8:21	8:21	8:00	7:59	7:39	7:34	7:18	7:13	6:58	6:47	6:37
6:55	> 09:51	9:51	9:20	8:49	8:18	8:18	7:57	7:56	7:36	7:31	7:15	7:10	6:55	6:44	6:34
6:53	> 09:49	9:49	9:17	8:47	8:15	8:15	7:54	7:54	7:34	7:29	7:13	7:08	6:53	6:42	6:32
6:50	> 09:45	9:45	9:13	8:43	8:12	8:12	7:51	7:51	7:31	7:26	7:10	7:05	6:50	6:39	6:29
6:48	> 09:42	9:42	9:10	8:41	8:09	8:09	7:49	7:48	7:28	7:24	7:08	7:03	6:48	6:37	6:27
6:45	> 09:38	9:38	9:06	8:37	8:06	8:06	7:45	7:45	7:25	7:21	7:05	7:00	6:45	6:34	6:24
6:43	> 09:35	9:35	9:04	8:35	8:03	8:03	7:43	7:43	7:23	7:18	7:03	6:58	6:43	6:32	6:22
6:40	> 09:31	9:31	9:00	8:31	8:00	8:00	7:40	7:40	7:20	7:15	7:00	6:55	6:40	6:30	6:20
6:38	> 09:28	9:28	8:57	8:29	7:57	7:57	7:37	7:37	7:17	7:13	6:57	6:53	6:38	6:28	6:18
6:35	> 09:24	9:24	8:53	8:25	7:54	7:54	7:34	7:34	7:14	7:10	6:54	6:50	6:35	6:25	6:15
6:33	> 09:22	9:22	8:50	8:23	7:51	7:51	7:31	7:32	7:12	7:08	6:52	6:48	6:33	6:23	6:13
6:30	> 09:18	9:18	8:46	8:19	7:48	7:48	7:28	7:29	7:09	7:05	6:49	6:45	6:30	6:20	6:10
6:28	> 09:15	9:15	8:43	8:17	7:45	7:45	7:26	7:26	7:06	7:03	6:47	6:43	6:28	6:18	6:08
6:25	> 09:11	9:11	8:39	8:13	7:42	7:42	7:22	7:23	7:03	7:00	6:44	6:40	6:25	6:15	6:05

One-Mile Time	Gear 1		Gear 2		Gear 3		Gear 4		Gear 5		Gear 6		Gear 7		Gear 8	
6:23	>	09:08	9:08	8:37	8:11	7:39	7:39	7:20	7:21	7:01	6:57	6:42	6:38	6:23	6:13	6:03
6:20	>	09:04	9:04	8:33	8:07	7:36	7:36	7:17	7:18	6:58	6:54	6:39	6:35	6:20	6:11	6:01
6:18	>	09:01	9:01	8:30	8:05	7:33	7:33	7:14	7:15	6:55	6:52	6:36	6:33	6:18	6:09	5:59
6:15	>	08:57	8:57	8:26	8:01	7:30	7:30	7:11	7:12	6:52	6:49	6:33	6:30	6:15	6:06	5:56
6:13	>	08:55	8:55	8:23	7:59	7:27	7:27	7:08	7:10	6:50	6:47	6:31	6:28	6:13	6:04	5:54
6:10	>	08:51	8:51	8:19	7:55	7:24	7:24	7:05	7:07	6:47	6:44	6:28	6:25	6:10	6:01	5:51
6:08	>	08:48	8:48	8:16	7:53	7:21	7:21	7:03	7:04	6:44	6:42	6:26	6:23	6:08	5:59	5:49
6:05	>	08:44	8:44	8:12	7:49	7:18	7:18	6:59	7:01	6:41	6:39	6:23	6:20	6:05	5:56	5:46
6:03	>	08:41	8:41	8:10	7:47	7:15	7:15	6:57	6:59	6:39	6:36	6:21	6:18	6:03	5:54	5:44
6:00	>	08:37	8:37	8:06	7:43	7:12	7:12	6:54	6:56	6:36	6:33	6:18	6:15	6:00	5:52	5:42
5:58	>	08:34	8:34	8:03	7:41	7:09	7:09	6:51	6:53	6:33	6:31	6:15	6:13	5:58	5:50	5:40
5:55	>	08:30	8:30	7:59	7:37	7:06	7:06	6:48	6:50	6:30	6:28	6:12	6:10	5:55	5:47	5:37
5:53	>	08:28	8:28	7:56	7:35	7:03	7:03	6:45	6:48	6:28	6:26	6:10	6:08	5:53	5:45	5:35
5:50	>	08:24	8:24	7:52	7:31	7:00	7:00	6:42	6:45	6:25	6:23	6:07	6:05	5:50	5:42	5:32
5:48	>	08:21	8:21	7:49	7:29	6:57	6:57	6:40	6:42	6:22	6:21	6:05	6:03	5:48	5:40	5:30
5:45	>	08:17	8:17	7:45	7:25	6:54	6:54	6:36	6:39	6:19	6:18	6:02	6:00	5:45	5:37	5:27
5:43	>	08:14	8:14	7:43	7:23	6:51	6:51	6:34	6:37	6:17	6:15	6:00	5:58	5:43	5:35	5:25
5:40	>	08:10	8:10	7:39	7:19	6:48	6:48	6:31	6:34	6:14	6:12	5:57	5:55	5:40	5:33	5:23
5:38	>	08:07	8:07	7:36	7:17	6:45	6:45	6:28	6:31	6:11	6:10	5:54	5:53	5:38	5:31	5:21
5:35	>	08:03	8:03	7:32	7:13	6:42	6:42	6:25	6:28	6:08	6:07	5:51	5:50	5:35	5:28	5:18
5:33	>	08:01	8:01	7:29	7:11	6:39	6:39	6:22	6:26	6:06	6:05	5:49	5:48	5:33	5:26	5:16
5:30	>	07:57	7:57	7:25	7:07	6:36	6:36	6:19	6:23	6:03	6:02	5:46	5:45	5:30	5:23	5:13
5:28	>	07:54	7:54	7:22	7:05	6:33	6:33	6:17	6:20	6:00	6:00	5:44	5:43	5:28	5:21	5:11
5:25	>	07:50	7:50	7:18	7:01	6:30	6:30	6:13	6:17	5:57	5:57	5:41	5:40	5:25	5:18	5:08
5:23	>	07:47	7:47	7:16	6:59	6:27	6:27	6:11	6:15	5:55	5:54	5:39	5:38	5:23	5:16	5:06
5:20	>	07:43	7:43	7:12	6:55	6:24	6:24	6:08	6:12	5:52	5:51	5:36	5:35	5:20	5:14	5:04
5:18	>	07:40	7:40	7:09	6:53	6:21	6:21	6:05	6:09	5:49	5:49	5:33	5:33	5:18	5:12	5:02
5:15	>	07:36	7:36	7:05	6:49	6:18	6:18	6:02	6:06	5:46	5:46	5:30	5:30	5:15	5:09	4:59
5:13	>	07:34	7:34	7:02	6:47	6:15	6:15	5:59	6:04	5:44	5:44	5:28	5:28	5:13	5:07	4:57
5:10	>	07:30	7:30	6:58	6:43	6:12	6:12	5:56	6:01	5:41	5:41	5:25	5:25	5:10	5:04	4:54
5:08	>	07:27	7:27	6:55	6:41	6:09	6:09	5:54	5:58	5:38	5:39	5:23	5:23	5:08	5:02	4:52
5:05	>	07:23	7:23	6:51	6:37	6:06	6:06	5:50	5:55	5:35	5:36	5:20	5:20	5:05	4:59	4:49
5:03	>	07:20	7:20	6:49	6:35	6:03	6:03	5:48	5:53	5:33	5:33	5:18	5:18	5:03	4:57	4:47
5:00	>	07:16	7:16	6:45	6:31	6:00	6:00	5:45	5:50	5:30	5:30	5:15	5:15	5:00	4:55	4:45

* Reminder: Speed Zones are in minute-per-mile pace.

9.3 FOCUS: **ACTION ITEMS**

1. If you haven't started running already, this is a good time to begin. Remember: for Beginners, you're running gently three or four times a week for 10–20 minutes. Dabblers, likewise, or a little longer. Veterans, if you've taken a week off already, you can begin getting back out there.

2. Be mindful of Form and Focus as you go. Think of these runs as dance rehearsals rather than exercise: your goal is to master moves and rhythm, not just bash out distance. It's tricky to combine mindfulness and relaxation, but that's the aim.

3. Experiment with your gears. Run slowly enough to sing as you go, then gradually pick up the pace until you can only puff out a few words at a time.

4. Work your way up and down the gear range, mixing in a few short bursts so you remember what it feels like to go Full Burn.

5. Before you start your run, plan your snack. Get in the habit of deciding what you're going to eat when you get home, so you're not tempted by the half a jam doughnut your son left in the fridge.

Footwear: First, Do No Harm

10

When *Born to Run* came out, it ignited a firestorm with a single sentence:

Running shoes may be the most destructive force to ever hit the human foot.

Podiatrists and running-store owners called me 'dangerous'. Sports scientists accused me of somehow oversimplifying *and* overstating the facts. My personal favourite was the famous Olympian-turned-marathon-guru who began spreading a rumour he'd invented that I'd secretly suffered a stress fracture while running barefoot and had snuck off into hiding to conceal it.

World War Shoe had begun. And I was just warming up.

'If running shoes never existed,' I went on, 'more people would be running. If more people ran, fewer would be dying of degenerative heart disease, sudden cardiac arrest, hypertension, blocked arteries, diabetes, and most other deadly ailments of the Western world.'

The entire running-shoe industry, I contended, was built on nothing but guesswork and bullshit.

Rather than firing back for themselves, Nike and Brooks and the rest of Big Sneaks did their best to stay out of it. They knew there was no science on their side. For decades, study after study had shown that running shoes did *nothing* to prevent injuries or improve running performance. One withering report found that the more you paid for your shoes, the more likely you were to get injured. Nike's own top scientist discovered that all the extra cushioning they were sticking in their shoes actually *increased* impact shock instead of reducing it. An Australian biomechanist was so bewildered by his inability to find *any* studies that justified the use of Stability and Motion Control shoes that he challenged the companies to share their research.

> ❝ THE ENTIRE RUNNING-SHOE INDUSTRY, I CONTENDED, WAS BUILT ON NOTHING BUT GUESSWORK AND BULLSHIT. ❞

Their response?

Silence.

So I wasn't surprised that the shoe companies decided to basically plead the Fifth. But I was completely blindsided by some other voices that entered the fight. Like Dr Irene Davis, one of the country's top biomechanical researchers and head of Harvard Medical School's Spaulding National Running Center. Irene has studied human movement for decades, and was a firm believer in the need for structured shoes.

Was being the operative word.

'I didn't run myself for thirty years because of injuries,' Irene was now saying. 'I used to prescribe orthotics. Now, honest to God, I run twenty miles a week, and I haven't had an injury since I started going barefoot.'

Pause for a sec and let that sink in. The top authority on running injuries at Harvard Medical School just suggested that running shoes may have been the most destructive force to hit her own feet.

And she was just warming up as well.

Modern running shoes are 'stupid', Irene told super-scientist Neil deGrasse Tyson during a podcast to discuss *Born to Run*. 'The earliest shoes', Irene explained, 'were just to protect our foot, very much like most of the other clothing we wear. What is stupid is that we then started to add all this technology. We're adding cushioning when our muscles can do that cushioning. We're adding motion control when we can control our feet with the muscles that we have. By doing that, we're actually setting our feet back.'

Neil got it immediately. 'If you look at human beings as a species, we spent much more time *not* wearing shoes than wearing shoes,' he agreed. Neil's own father was a nationally ranked runner who continued competing long after college, and Neil was struck by the simplicity of his shoes. 'There wasn't all this extra rubber, and tech, and heel,' Neil pointed out. 'It was like hardly anything covering his foot.'

For a scientist with Irene's background, her conversion to minimalism was astonishing. But for decades, she explained, she'd seen every possible innovation rolled out and none of it worked. Not the springy shocks. Not the stability wedges. And definitely *not* Asics's 'menstrual shoe', which a podiatrist shilling for the company gamely attempted to claim was necessary because, you know, the

ladies need special cushioning 'in harmony with a woman's hormones'. Granted, maybe you could cut the menstrual-shoe podiatrist a little slack for this silliness, because back in the old days, even doctors believed a bunch of dumb stuff about women's bodies.

Except this was 2010.

Irene was genuinely interested in finding a scientific explanation for how running shoes reached that level of stupid, so she went to Nike's top designer and asked. The response was a classic tale of a committee trying to design a horse. Back in the 80s, new runners began having Achilles issues because their tendons had shortened after so much time without exercise.

'Hey, easy fix,' sports podiatrists told Nike. 'Just build up the heel and you'll take pressure off the Achilles.'

Cool! Except when you lift the heel, your foot slides forward and your arch collapses.

Back to the drawing board. This time, they not only lifted the heel, but also narrowed the toe box and jacked up the arch to lock the foot in place.

Dang it. Now there was no room for the foot to spread on landing. It tried to roll instead, and rolling ain't good. Maybe inserting hard wedges in the midsole would help? You'd have to add more foam to cover them, of course.

By this point, there had to be a nagging voice in the back of the designers' minds saying, *Hang on, why don't we just tell runners to warm up a little instead?* But on they forged, lifting the heel, narrowing the toe box, jacking up the arch, inserting hard wedges, pumping in extra foam, and—

And that's how a magnificent horse that worked beautifully for 2 million years becomes a $200 camel you're supposed to replace every three months.

Irene put it this way: 'My view is that the running-shoe companies, rather than have the runners adapt to the sport, which is what everyone did in the past, they took the shoe and adapted it to the runner and ended up, I think, doing more harm than good.'

So now that the top minds in the field have proven the junk doesn't work, why is it still being sold?

'We've got shoe companies who are very much invested in the cushioning, the support, and all of the technology that they put into shoes,' Irene said bluntly.

> **AND THAT'S HOW A MAGNIFICENT HORSE THAT WORKED BEAUTIFULLY FOR 2 MILLION YEARS BECOMES A $200 CAMEL YOU'RE SUPPOSED TO REPLACE EVERY THREE MONTHS.**

Basics don't bring in the bucks, in other words.

But junk is a goldmine.

Irene reached her conclusions through controlled studies in her lab with runners covered in electrodes. Curt Munson had to figure it out in his socks.

Curt was the first shoe-store owner to call me after *Born to Run* was published. He wanted a face-to-face with me at his store, Playmakers Performance Footwear in Okemos, Michigan. Why he thought I was dumb enough to walk into an ambush by a pissed-off sneaker salesman in the backwoods of Michigan, I have no idea, but it's testament to Curt's salesmanship that after a few calls, he actually talked me into it.

I didn't feel much better when I pulled into the parking lot and Curt insisted on taking me, alone, into a back room. I figured he wanted to rip me a new one in language not suitable for customer ears, so I braced for a good old-fashioned Okemos face-melter. Instead, Curt flicked on the lights and showed me his mini-museum of old running shoes. The footwear told their own story: for years, they slowly got higher and softer, until suddenly the Brooks Beast arrived in 1992 and launched an arms race for bigger and ever-Beastier.

'I've been a runner my entire life,' Curt said. 'I've seen every kind of shoe for fifty years. And look what I'm wearing.'

He pointed to his feet. To my amazement, I hadn't noticed he had on a pair of Vibram FiveFingers.

Curt told me that as he'd gotten older, he'd struggled so much with injuries that he began running less and biking more. One weekend, he was in a triathlon and realised just before the final leg that his running shoes were missing. He charged off without them, unfazed by the optics of Michigan's best-known sports-shoe magnate trotting through the streets of Lansing in his socks.

When he hit the finish line, Curt was floating. Something about that run had set the clock back thirty years for him. His back, his knees, his feet, *everything* felt better. He got on the phone with New Balance, which often relied on Curt's expertise, and made them a pitch: *If you design a barefoot-style shoe*, he offered, *I'll teach people how to use it.*

Two beautiful babies were born from this union: the fabulous New Balance Minimus line, and Playmakers' 'Good Form Running' programme. Curt not only offered free Good Form lessons to anyone, customer or not, who stepped into his shops, but he also trained dozens of salespeople *who worked at competing stores*.

'Everyone wins,' he shrugged, when I asked why he was:

a) not only empowering shoe buyers to run barefoot, but
b) persuading the rest of the shoe industry they should too.

'Healthy runners are happy,' the Running Shoe King of Okemos declared. 'Happy customers trust you and keep coming back. They'll always need shoes. But they have to learn there's a right way to use them – and a right way to choose them.'

Hawk Harper wasn't waiting for anyone else to make him a happy customer.

Hawk grabbed me at the Outdoor Retailer Convention a few months after *Born to Run* came out and told me he'd been hacking shoes on his own for years. As a 240-pound defensive end in college, Hawk had blown out all the cartilage in his knees. Doctors warned him his running days were over, which by the laws of Harper Hardheadedness meant his running days had just begun.

Hawk went on to finish seventy-plus marathons and win St. George with a sizzlin' 2:22. He opened Runner's

Corner in Orem, Utah, in the 1980s, and it was there that Harper Hardheadedness went pro. Hawk's shop became the Church of Last Resort for runners from across the state whose physicians had told them to give up. Hawk loved it when they came limping in with their chronic pain and dire diagnoses. He'd show them his own scars, then let them in on his secret formula for defying the doctors:

It's easy, he'd confide. *Just think like a Kenyan*.

That's how Hawk bounced back after his football injuries. He studied what the world's best marathoners were doing, and simply copied their form and footwear. Elites *never* wore thick shoes, he noticed, not even in training, and they always pattered along lightly with their legs bending beneath them, not locked out in front.

But even as a shoe salesman, Hawk was finding it harder and harder to find any model that wasn't overloaded with fat heels and motion-controlling inserts. If he couldn't buy them, he decided, he'd bake them. Hawk stuck a shoe in the toaster oven and set it at 275 degrees Fahrenheit. He waited for the glue to melt, then pulled off the outsole, ripped out all the extra foam and junk he didn't want, and glued the outsole back on.

Ta-da! When Hawk tried on his Frankenshoe, he was ecstatic. His feet were finally free enough to pop along as lightly as the Kenyans'. From then on, whenever a customer complained of sore knees or aching Achilles that no shoe could relieve, Hawk fired up the toaster oven and set to work.

But it was Hawk's mad scientist son I really wanted to meet. Golden Harper is Hawk with a head start. Hawk was in his thirties before he figured out how to rip and rebuild his shoes and stride, but Golden was already showing exquisite form and a sceptical mind by the time he was out of diapers.

By age nine, Golden was fitting customers in the family store. By ten, he was running marathons. At twelve, he set an age group world record with a 2:45 marathon that stands to this day. But the more Golden learned about running, the more he struggled with his faith. By the time he reached college, Golden no longer believed in the Church of Last Resort.

'I've been lying to people my whole life,' he realised. 'All the things I've been telling people about shoes that have been told to me by the shoe companies are scientific *lies*.'

> " HAWK STUCK A SHOE IN THE TOASTER OVEN AND SET IT AT 275 DEGREES FAHRENHEIT. "

Golden was majoring in biomechanics and exercise science at Brigham Young University–Hawaii, and that gave him the opportunity to dig into the medical and engineering principles behind Stability running shoes. What he found was appalling: *None of it was real*. It wasn't science: it was marketing masquerading as science.

'We like to think the engineers and biomechanists are designing new products down in the Nike lab. Bull crap!' Golden says. 'The reality is that you don't have any actual biomechanics people designing shoes. It's all coming from the marketing people.'

Until he discovered who was really driving the design changes, Golden was always mystified by why they never worked. Every six months, the shoe companies unveiled their latest amazing gimmick – *High-efficiency foam! Carbon-fibre plates! Heel-to-toe rocker soles!* – but injury rates remained the same.

'Nike put elevated heels on its shoes and no one did a thread of research on it,' Golden fumed. 'And since then, everyone has just copied it. It made a ton of money, so everyone just copied the same thing.'

Back in Utah, Papa Hawk was struggling with his own dark night of the soul. 'If my dad doesn't run with good technique, he can't run at all,' Golden says. 'His knee blows up to epic proportions. So he taught himself how to run like the Kenyans, and we became really good at showing that to customers, usually in a quick five-minute lesson.'

But what was the point? 'We teach everyone how to protect their body,' Hawk lamented, 'and then we sell them a pair of shoes that undoes it all.'

It was *insane*! Even the guy who created the market for Stability shoes was now admitting he'd made a huge mistake. Dr Benno Nigg is co-director of the University of

Quick feet and a forefoot strike are the secret to all-terrain running.

> **" EVEN THE GUY WHO CREATED THE MARKET FOR STABILITY SHOES WAS NOW ADMITTING HE'D MADE A HUGE MISTAKE. "**

Calgary's prestigious Human Performance Lab. Back in 1985, he floated the notion that maybe it was harmful for the foot to roll inward on landing, or pronate. Big Sneaks seized on the idea and flooded stores with Stability shoes. But in 2005, Benno recanted, calling the anti-pronation theory 'completely wrong thinking' that led to 'blunders in sport-shoe construction'.

Blunders?

If the Food and Drug Administration were in charge of squishy running shoes, they'd be announcing a recall and yanking them off the shelves. Millions of people trusted their health to these devices because they were recommended by specialists and cloaked in medicalese. Yet even though the top Stability guy was now saying, *Oops, my bad!* – and the *British Journal of Sports Medicine* was following that up with a blistering report which showed that every woman who wore motion-control shoes for a thirteen-week study ended up injured, *a 100 per cent fail rate* which indicated the shoes were useless at best, and dangerous at worst—

None of it made any difference. Stability shoes were – and remain – a booming business.

'There's this huge focus on pronation,' Golden points out, 'but there's no connection between that and injuries. *So why are we focusing on it?*' He paused for a dramatic beat, then let fly with his verdict. 'Because it's a way to create more types of shoes to sell.'

The godfather of Stability, however, wants nothing to do with the trouble he unleashed. Ask him today what he recommends for runners, and Benno Nigg sounds a lot like Barefoot Ted.

'You don't need any protection at all,' the world's most respected sports-shoe scientist admits. 'Except for cold. And, like, gravel.'

Golden now had everything he needed to go into the Frankenshoe business for himself: real science, a toaster oven and a parade of human guinea pigs.

His goal was simple: instead of stripping the junk out of overbuilt shoes, why not build one without any junk in the first place? But first he had to figure out what that shoe would look like, and that's where the guinea pigs came in.

Golden began with the easiest hack: widen the stinkin' toe box. No human foot looks anything like the shape of a running shoe. Our feet are boxy; running shoes are pointy. Long ago, Hawk figured out he could solve 75 per cent of his customers' plantar fascia and other foot problems just by sticking them in a bigger shoe and loosening the laces.

Next, Golden broke out the power tools. He grabbed some Saucony 'Jazz Originals' from the discount rack and hired a cobbler to grind the heels and thin the midsoles so the shoes would be totally flat. He called these misfits 'Jazzy Zeroes', because now there was zero drop in height from heel to toe. Plus, 'Jazzy' sounded better than 'Fugly'.

'We started by testing them on our hopeless customers,' Golden says. 'Those who had tried the most cushioned shoe, the most supportive shoe, orthotics, but still had the same injury problems.' Golden also gave the Running Hopeless a survey and promised them ten bucks if they returned it in six weeks with feedback.

'The crazy thing is that before the surveys came back, their friends started coming in, saying things like "You gave Joe a pair of these hacked-up shoes and now his knee doesn't hurt as bad. Can I try a pair?"'

Within a year, Golden had data from more than a thousand customers who'd bought his glued-together, stretched-out Franken-Zeroes. 'You don't sell a thousand shoes you hacked from a cobbler unless they're really good,' Golden says. 'And the results were unreal. We had a 97 per cent success rate on injury or pain reduction in the five major running injury areas: plantar fascia, shin splints, runner's knee, IT band and lower back.'

This was already bigger than Golden could handle. His cobbler could only grind down so many Jazzies a day, and besides, the Harpers were just one family store in the mountains of Utah. Think how many injured runners across the country – around the world! – would be overjoyed to

For Caballo, a good day began with tortillas, a tin mug of coffee, and big miles in battered sandals.

stick their feet into a shoe that would finally let their toes spread and foot aches melt away.

Hawk had scores of contacts in the shoe industry and every one of them patted Golden on the head and told him to take his proven model and 97 per cent success rate and piss off. Which, of course, is exactly the wrong thing to say to a Harper if you really want them to go away.

Golden had begun the experiment out of curiosity; now he was on fire. 'These people don't give a crap about whether people are getting injured in their shoes or not,' he fumed. 'So I felt like we were both trying to fix injured humans and a broken industry as well.'

Golden and his MacGyver-like cousin Jeremy went hunting for allies, and soon discovered an underground army of crack engineers who were sick of getting pushed around by marketing honchos. 'I'm reading stuff to them out of *Born to Run*, and they're saying, "Yeah, yeah, we know that stuff is right. But they would never let us make a shoe like that."'

❝ I FELT LIKE WE WERE BOTH TRYING TO FIX INJURED HUMANS AND A BROKEN INDUSTRY AS WELL. ❞

A Shoe Like That became Golden's obsession. 'We were trying to mimic the Tarahumara experience,' Golden says. 'Reading about them in *Born to Run* really influenced our first shoe. We decided to make a Tarahumara sandal, the same thickness and ride, but with modern materials.'

They had a team. They had a dream. Now they needed a name. This rebel alliance was on a mission, not an ego trip, so they didn't flounce around with Greek goddesses or Roman acronyms or personal vanity. Instead, they seized on a single word that captured their disgust for what the running industry had become and their hope for what it could be.

They called themselves *Altra* – 'To repair what's ruined.'

10.1
BUILDING YOUR QUIVER

Not surprisingly, Altras are the shoes we recommend to start your 90-Day Run Free reboot. After debating a variety of models and brainstorming with seasoned runners who share our natural-movement mindset, we settled on two top picks:

For trails:
Altra Superior (zero drop, 21mm stack)
For roads:
Altra Escalante (zero drop, 24mm stack)
Altra Escalante Racer (zero drop, 22mm stack)
(Side note: The Escalante Racer would have been our undisputed pick for roads, but Golden Harper pointed out that the regular Escalante is basically the same as the Racer if you pull out the insole, giving you two shoes for the price of one at $10 less. I also lobbied valiantly for two Xero Shoes models – Zelen and Mesa – but I was overruled because minimalist shoes can be an extreme transition for many runners.)

Why Altras? Three reasons.
1) *Natural feel*: With these two creations, Golden Harper succeeded in his quest to build shoes with modern materials that still give the feel of a Rarámuri huarache. Some Altra models have more cushioning than we prefer, because they're designed for ultramarathons on the roughest trails.
2) *Flexibility*: We opted for the Superior and the Escalante because they're the lightest and most flexible in the Altra line-up, hitting the bullseye between just enough protection and not too much.
3) *Shelf life*: We didn't want to recommend a shoe that undergoes a major structural facelift every six months, Nike

Pegasus style. The template for both the Superior and the Escalante is locked in, so the version you get in years to come will match the one you have today.

But if you'd rather choose your own gear, go for it. We applaud your rebel spirit! Pick whatever you like it, as long as it retains the four key features of natural footwear:

1) Wide toe box: no pinch on either side of your foot
2) Ample length: 1.5 inches of space past your longest toe
3) Low heel (or 'Drop', or 'Heel-to-toe offset')
4) Minimal cushioning (or 'Stack Height')

If the first two seem obvious, think again. House odds say you've been blowing those decisions your entire life.

'Every time a new customer comes in, I guarantee they're picking shoes a full size too small, minimum,' says Nathan Leehman, owner of the Ultra Running Company in Charlotte, North Carolina. 'That's the easiest fix for so many problems – *just size up!* – but wow, you wouldn't believe the resistance we get. You tell some people that they're an 8.5 when they think they're a 7, they'll walk out the door.'

> **❝** IF NATHAN COULDN'T FIND A RUNNING STORE HE COULD TRUST, HE'D OPEN ONE HIMSELF. **❞**

For a long time, Nathan was his own worst customer. He was a Michelin exec who only got into running because he was spending too much time with a phone in one hand and Oreos in the other. He started with one mile every other day, huffing along at barely faster than a walking pace, but as his endurance increased, so did his excitement.

'I used to hike Moab and Colorado, never realising you could *run* those trails,' Nathan says. 'That's when running became all about getting someplace on my feet that no one else gets to visit.'

Because he's got that kind of mind, Nathan became a scientist of the sport and kept experimenting with ways to increase his range and speed. Before long, the four-miles-a-week guy was ripping his way up the ultramarathon ladder, knocking off hundred-milers in fifteen hours (yes, that's four consecutive trail marathons in less than four hours each), and finishing Top 50 at the legendary Tor des Géants, a brutal 205-mile race through the Alps which requires three times as much climbing as an assault on Everest.

At first, Nathan just bought whatever *Runner's World* and his local shoe guy recommended. But you can't spend years on the retail side of the tire business without developing a bloodhound's nose for bullshit, so it wasn't long before Nathan began pushing back and asking hard questions.

'I did a treadmill test once and the shoe guy tells me I have great form. Then he hands me a Stability shoe,' Nathan recalls. 'Wait, why do I need an anti-pronation shoe if I'm not overpronating? I can't get him to explain why in plain English, so I keep pushing. Finally, he goes, "Well, that's the best we have in your size."'

Got it. 'Best' meaning 'most expensive'. Nathan had one of those *Sixth Sense* flashbacks where he suddenly realised this was nothing new, just the latest in a long series of rip-offs he'd never caught before. If he was angry at anyone, it was at himself for not spotting it sooner. *Of course* the stores didn't believe any of this stuff actually worked. How could they, when every six months they told you that whatever you bought last time was obsolete and ought to be replaced? Even iPhones don't expire that fast.

Well, to hell with that. If Nathan couldn't find a running store he could trust, he'd open one himself.

'We came up with the tag line *Learn to Love to Run*,' Nathan says. 'Because the learning portion is so much more important than what you put on your feet. If I could sell the education and give away the shoes for free, I'd do it.'

That was the inspiration. The execution depended on six golden rules he's followed since the doors opened in 2013:

#1. Protection, Not Correction

'I tell my vendors if they can show me one study that says a Stability shoe will make my customers healthier, I'll carry their whole line. No one can do it. At one point we were Hoka's biggest retailer on the East Coast, but we didn't carry a single one of their Stability shoes. We told them, "We support you, but not when you make stuff up."'

#2. No Fancy Insoles

'All they do is make a lot of money for the store. They don't do anything for runners. Nothing. If you sell insoles, that's a sign to me that you've lost your North Star.'

#3. No Heel Higher Than 8mm

This may sound like Shoe Geek territory, but it's the gold standard for running footwear. 'Drop' is a term invented by Golden Harper, and it describes the difference in height from heel to toe. Flat shoes, like the Altras and Rarámuri sandals, have zero drop. The Brooks Beast is colossal, at 17mm. Hokas actually have a relatively slight drop, about 4–6mm, although their cushioning is substantial. 'I drew an arbitrary line at 8mm,' Nathan says. 'Any more than that, it forces you to run poorly and straighten your leg so the heel can clear the ground. Running is hard enough already, why put the brakes on?'

#4. No Born-Broken Tests

Nathan doesn't believe there's anything wrong with your body that a shoe can fix. That's why he won't measure your pronation, or assess your 'Habitual Motion Path' – the latest gimmick in the trade – to determine your 'unique joint movements'. As a rule of thumb, any time a conversation about running shoes includes the words 'unique', 'special' or 'individual', your pocket is about to get picked.

#5. Rock Lobster Rules

Like Eric, Nathan discovered he can teach ideal running form in about five minutes. He'll strap a Zwift RunPod on your foot and have you hop on the treadmill. As you run, the pod flashes your steps-per-minute cadence on the treadmill display. 'Typically, new customers will sound like a herd of elephants, with gigantic strides and lots of vertical oscillation.' Then Nathan feeds them two simple cues: shorten your stride, raise your cadence to 180. 'The difference is night and day. Suddenly, they're bending their knee, landing lightly. It's always an electrifying moment.'

But sometimes, the Rock Lobster romance dies as soon as the treadmill powers down. Some people are stoked beyond belief to discover a magic formula for stronger, healthier running; others aren't in the mood just yet for a running-form reboot. That's when Nathan unveils his Rule to End All Rules:

#6. Running Is Just Grown-up Recess

'My goal is to make everyone happy and healthy and eager. If someone is running a trail 10k in two months, darn right I'm putting cushion under them. But long term, we always encourage people to run minimal. I have a fundamental belief that everyone is built to run long distances barefoot, but very few of us put in the time and effort to develop the skills to do that. If you get that concept and pursue that goal, then my whole wall is yours to choose from.'

Jenna Crawford combines trail stamina with the road speed of a 2:51 marathoner.

Nathan's Footwear Wall is a bizarre experience, at least if you're used to other running stores. As you take it all in, you'll have the strangest sensation of being … not confused. There are no gimmicks or confusing jargon, none of the make-believe stuff about Motion Control and Stability.

You only have to consider the two factors that matter: How much cushion do you want? And how much heel?

'Most people are right in the middle: medium drop, medium cushion,' Nathan says. And that's where you'll find them on the wall: dead centre. Nathan arranges his shoes left to right according to heel height, and top to bottom by cushioning. That puts Luna Sandals at top left (zero drop, zero cushion), and the Hoka Bondi on the bottom right (4mm drop, 33mm cushion), with everything else in between.

One fun perk of Nathan's wall is it also functions as a motivational ladder. Whenever you return, you can gauge how much progress you've made on your running form by whether your eye is now drawn higher and more leftward towards the Luna side. That's another refreshing feature of the Ultra Running Company system: even when shoe models are updated and everything has new names and colours, you can still tell at a glance exactly what each shoe offers and how it compares to what you're wearing now.

For himself, Nathan likes to keep a quiver of three or so different shoes and work his way up the cushioning scale as the week goes on. He'll start super-minimal on Tuesday when his legs are fresh, switch to mid-cushion by Thursday when fatigue is setting in, then treat himself to something a little more plush for his Saturday long run, like the Saucony Endorphin Speed, which Nathan calls 'the best Hoka that Hoka never made'.

'I can run in anything under 10mm and it won't affect me, but I do this for a living,' Nathan says. 'The lower you go with your drop, the more likely you'll land under your centre of gravity. It's just easier.'

When new customers ask Nathan what to do, he tells them, 'I'll put you in minimal shoe and you'll run a mile, and it will be your best mile ever. So freeing! But then you'll sit on the couch for a week with sore calves because you overstressed. Or I can put you in a cushioned shoe and you'll have fun and build up at the same time.

> **'I FEEL … WOW.'**
> **FOR A SECOND, I COULDN'T**
> **REMEMBER WHICH FOOT**
> **HAD THE PROBLEM.**
> **'LIKE, PERFECT.'**

'But—' Nathan adds, reaching for his favourite hand-on-heart metaphor to make sure his point sticks. 'We tell people what we've shown them about form is more important than any shoe on this wall. Stay focused. Keep your North Star.'

Personally, Eric and I aren't 100 per cent on board with Nathan's cushioned shoe cheat day. We're also not 100 per cent against it.

We know a lot of extremely capable trail runners, like Karl 'Speedgoat' Meltzer and triathlon legend Bree Wee, who follow the same approach as Nathan. The Dirt Diva herself, Catra Corbett, runs almost exclusively in a hearty pair of Hokas and it hasn't slowed her any: Catra has finished more than a hundred 100-mile races, and runs every day with a sense of joy and, often, a dachshund.

But for us, cushion is a slippery slope to sloppiness. You can get away with it for a while – for a very *long* while, if you're as form-savvy and disciplined as Nathan – but our feeling is the more you cut off ground contact, the easier it is to degenerate back to bad habits. Your North Star will disappear into darkness.

I learned that lesson first-hand. Back in 2007, I was in the middle of work on *Born to Run* when something peculiar happened: my foot started to hurt again.

I was in London at the time attending a workshop on natural movement. The whole point of the conference was the elasticity of human tissue. The whole point of my book was about how elasticity can lead to injury-free running.

So why the heck was my heel sore?

By that point, I'd been training with Eric for more than a year and had transformed my running so dramatically that within eight months, I'd clicked off three ultramarathons. My running form was *dialled*. My conditioning was peak. I was even back to the same pants size I wore as a college rower.

I was also limping.

It was mystifying. I hadn't checked in with Eric in months, because there wasn't any need. My goal all along had been to run wherever I wanted, as far as I wanted, without worrying about races or personal bests, and in that mission, Eric had more than succeeded. One night, I jumped in to run twenty miles with Jenn Shelton when she was struggling to finish the Vermont 100. Not long after, I signed up for a local 50k right before the starting gun because I heard they served hot french fries at the halfway point.

Yet suddenly, that old familiar ache was biting at my right heel. I'd ignored it for a few weeks, hoping it would fade on its own, but the walk through London every morning to the conference was becoming more painful every day. A friend suggested I go see Lee Saxby, a boxer-turned-fitness-coach who had an underground reputation as a miracle worker.

The underground part turned out to be literally true: Lee held court in a tiny gym in the basement of a nondescript hotel. 'What's with those shoes, mate?' Lee said, as soon as I arrived and told him my problem.

'I've been learning to run barefoot style,' I explained. After the Copper Canyon race, I'd come home fully convinced that Caballo and Barefoot Ted were right *in theory* about the evils of cushioned shoes. But in practice, I wasn't yet ready to commit. So I struck what I considered to be a nice compromise with a Nike shoe that seemed halfway between flat and fluffy.

'That's why I prefer minimal shoes like these,' I said.

'Those?' Lee snorted. 'They're sofa cushions.'

Lee had me kick them off. He then handed me a weightlifting bar and showed me how to ease down into a full squat, with my back straight and my feet flat on the floor.

'Ten of those,' Lee said.

'Ten more,' he commanded once I'd finished. 'You're staggering all over the place. Give us a proper ten.'

It took about forty reps before I managed a clean ten squats in a row. 'All right,' Lee said. 'Now outside.'

We went out to the sidewalk. Lee pointed down the street and told me to run to the corner and back, barefoot, while chanting, '*1-2-3-4, 1-2-3-4 …*'

After my fourth lap, Lee said, 'Okay, you're good.'

'"Good" meaning …?'

'Good. All sorted. How do you feel?'

'I feel … wow.' For a second, I couldn't remember which foot had the problem. 'Like, perfect.'

'Just run back to your hotel barefoot. Lock in the feeling.'

'Really? Through central London?'

'You'll be fine. You need to wake up those feet. And if I were you I'd stuff those things—' he pointed towards my Nikes. 'Straight into the rubbish.'

It took me a bit to process what happened, and once I did, I never wore a cushioned shoe again. Lee's squats cured my symptoms (a tight plantar fascia tendon beneath my heel) but his barefoot cadence drill fixed the cause: my running form had degenerated. Running-shoe companies are constantly trying to one-up each other with the latest, techiest, cushiest super shoe, but the reality is, all they're doing is reverse engineering what you can already find on the end of your leg.

Eric had taught me to run with a quick, light, forefoot stride, but bit by bit, I'd been backsliding into old habits. In my mind's eye, I was as easy-light-and-smooth as Caballo – but in reality, I'd regressed to a heavy plod. Because of the cushioning in my shoes, I never noticed the difference.

I thought I was playing it safe by slowing my transition to minimalist shoes. But when it comes to running form, I'm convinced it's the riskiest move you can make. Cushioning is a narcotic. It's a numbing agent. The more you have, the less you feel. So Eric and I strongly recommend you train in the Altras, or a similar low-drop shoe.

But if you're in Nathan's camp and want an occasional cushion-shoe cheat day, consider meeting us in the middle with my genius wife's technique. Mika will set off barefoot, holding a shoe in each hand. As soon as she feels any discomfort – tired calves, pebbly ground, whatever – she pulls her shoes on and continues her run. That barefoot period at the beginning of her run is just enough to spark her good-form muscle memory so afterwards, it doesn't matter what she's got on.

For the rocky and muddy Ohana trail, Chris likes his three-year-old pair of Altra Vanish XC.

10.2
A HUNTER'S GUIDE TO ELUSIVE AWESOMENESS

Like all true treasure, minimalist shoes are tough to find but a blast to discover.

Most big companies don't even make a minimalist line any more, but in some ways, that's actually a plus. It's opened a space for homegrown innovators, like Barefoot Ted and Xero Shoes' Stave Sashen, and scrappy purists, like Vivobarefoot and Inov-8, to create small-batch beauties they truly believe in. Still, a good number of our recommendations may vanish by the time you finish this sentence, so don't think of this as a buyer's guide. It's more a lesson in what to look for. Fantastic running shoes are all over the place. You may have to research a bit or scour eBay to find them, but when you're flying through the woods and feel like you're wearing handmade moccasins, you'll be glad you did.

AMY STONE, ULTRA RUNNING COMPANY SHOE EXPERT

'I have a titanium plate in one leg from a car wreck, so I'm *very* mindful of good form and a soft landing,' Amy says. She's also an expert on mistakes that women runners can make when choosing shoes, and No. 1 is going too small.

'A lot of people have the misconception that shoe size is a universal unit of measure, but a size 8 in one shoe isn't always an 8 in another,' she says. 'Plus if you're 8 in a pump or stiletto, you're a 9 or 9.5 in a running shoe. And getting too small a shoe is really detrimental to foot health.'

Amy has a great hack for women runners: when you decide what you want, buy the men's model instead. 'It's a crazy thing that the entire industry has decided that women have narrow feet,' she says. 'Why would a woman with a similar stature to a man be given a shoe that's more narrow?' And please, she begs, don't buy a shoe based on appearance. 'Believe me, no one cares,' she says. 'You're the only one paying attention to whether your sneakers are cute.'

AMY'S TOP 5

1. Long trail runs: **Altra Superior**

2. Shorter trail runs: **Xero Shoes sandal**

3. Roads: 'The first-generation **Altra Solstice** is my all-time favourite, then they turned it into a gym shoe and ruined it. So now I prefer:

4. The **Altra Escalante**, and—

5. Several of the **Xero Shoes** are also great on roads.'

NATHAN'S TOP PICKS

1. Road shoes: **Altra Escalante Racer** for early in the week, **Saucony Freedom** for later. 'I like significant cushion when my legs start to feel sore, or for long runs.'

2. For exceptional long road runs, twenty-plus miles: **Saucony Endorphin Speed**, 'the best Hoka that Hoka never made. It's the first 8mm shoe I've run in for a decade.'

3. Trails, thirteen miles or less: **Altra Superior**.

4. Trails, thirteen miles or more: **Hoka Speedboat Evo**, 'my favourite all-round high cushion shoe'.

MARGOT WATTERS, ALPINE ULTRARUNNER

Margot is often on extremely rocky technical trails, or training for long miles on roads. She likes a little more forgiveness in her cushioning, while retaining a low ride which won't interfere with her form.

1. Saucony Peregrine trail: Margot relied on her Peregrines for a 200-mile race in the Alps. The Peregrines are low to the ground with a modest 4mm drop, but have solid rock protection and a confident grip.

2. Saucony Kinvara road: Margot's favourite long-distance road shoe, a road version of the Peregrine with a 4mm drop.

3. Dynafit Feline Up trail: A lightweight mountain shoe with 4mm drop and a precision fit, this is Margot's footwear of choice for shorter, faster races and fast technical training.

4. Inov-8 Roclite 290: The go-to for mountains with dry, hard rock, like Wyoming's Grand Tetons, and a great all-rounder on mixed terrain.

5. Altra Escalante Road: With slightly more cushion than the Escalante Racer, this is Margot's top choice for strength and speed training on roads.

ERIC ORTON'S TOP 5

Eric Orton lives in the Grand Tetons and tackles a lot of snow and rock, so his Top 5 have more bite and muscle.

1. Inov-8 TerraUltra 270: 'For me, this is one of the best all-rounder trail shoes. It has a perfect combo of stack height and protection, with natural flexibility in a lightweight, zero-drop package. This shoe is very responsive with great energy return.'

2. VJ Spark: 'It has a more precision fit through the midfoot than the Inov-8, which I like because of my narrow feet, but still has a wide toe box. It's nimble, with a low-to-the-ground platform and great grip and protection. On technical trails, it's a Ferrari.'

3. Altra Escalante Racer: 'My go-to road shoe. The Escalante is a great option for both longer and faster runs, and the perfect choice for runners looking to transition to a low-drop shoe.'

4. Xero Shoes Speed Force: 'Super lightweight and minimal, with a well-thought-out design that allows your foot to articulate naturally. A true minimal shoe that feels like a Rarámuri huarache, yet still has enough protection for both roads and trail.'

5. Inov-8 Xtalon 210: 'Lightweight and minimal, with an aggressive lugged sole that's perfect when precise footing is vital. In snow they're sublime; in summer, they're great on soft and muddy trails. When the lugs wear down, they become my track shoes.'

CHRISTOPHER MCDOUGALL'S TOP 6-ISH

Pro tip: 'My first move for any shoe is to rip out the insoles. You'll be amazed at how much better they feel without that useless layer of mush.'

1. Luna Sandals Leadville: 'The original and, for me, the most versatile of Barefoot Ted's creations. The first time I tried a pair, Ted strapped them on my feet just before I paced him over the last thirteen miles of the Leadville Trail 100. An off-road half-marathon isn't the best place to experiment with huaraches, but they worked beautifully.'

2. Xero Shoes Zelen: 'I stayed away from Xero Shoes for a long time out of loyalty to Barefoot Ted, as they were direct competitors in the huarache space, but once Xero rolled out a road shoe I was free to give it a try. And wow, am I glad I did. The Zelen is a dream on roads and trails, and Xeros are the only shoes with an insole so well-proportioned that I don't have to take them out. Excellent designing across the board.'

3. Xero Shoes Mesa Trail: 'My desert island pick if I can only have a single footwear choice. The Mesa is like a bouldering shoe up top but an all-terrain vehicle down below, with a sole so grippy it feels like an ATV tire. The mesh upper drains water so fast, you can blast through creeks without feeling soggy.'

4. Bedrock Sandals Cairn Pro II Adventure: 'Water is low-key Kryptonite for nearly all huaraches because it causes your feet to slide around on the footbed, except somehow, the wizards at Bedrock solved that problem without sacrificing any of its flexible feel. I love everything about these all-terrain beauties.'

5. New Balance Minimus (MT00, M10v1, M10v4, MT20): 'Pour one out for a true masterpiece, gone before its time. New Balance delivered natural feel with just a breath of cushioning, but this line of true barefoot shoes was tragically discontinued and can only be hunted down on eBay. I recently found a pair of the MT00, that beautifully crazy one-off that looked like a translucent ballet slipper with a bubble sole. You'll have to wrestle them off my cold, dead feet.'

6. Altra Vanish XC: 'Every time I wear these tissue-thin beauties, I wonder what kind of wizardry keeps them from falling apart. The upper is open mesh, making it a dream in the heat and maybe the best swim-run shoe ever.'

10.3 AID STATION: YOUR BRAIN ON BARE FEET

During a hike in the Scottish Highlands back in 2016, two visiting scholars from Florida were so enchanted by the soft heather that they pulled off their shoes and began running barefoot. They had a blast, but were surprised afterwards that their legs felt great but their minds were just … drained.

Why, they wondered, was running barefoot so mentally exhausting?

Being psychologists, they decided to put it to the test. Drs Ross and Tracy Alloway teamed up with Dr Peter Magyari, a University of North Florida exercise physiologist, and created an experiment. They gathered seventy-two volunteers, a diverse mix ranging from ages 18–44, and had them run for sixteen minutes both barefoot and in shoes. Before and after the runs, the test subjects' working memory was tested and compared.

A 5 per cent improvement would be terrific, because the more you remember, the better you feel. Your working memory affects not only your academic and professional performance, but your mental health: a little cognitive slip is a big contributor to anxiety and social friction. You don't just lose your keys; you forget names, have trouble following directions, make poor decisions, get stressed and anxious.

So a 5 per cent boost would be significant. But running barefoot, the Florida researchers found, *tripled* that score. Working memory performance improved by 16 per cent. 'There was no significant increase in working memory when running with shoes,' they noted.

Why? Ross Alloway has a theory: 'It's possible that the barefoot condition required a more intensive use of working memory because of the extra tactile and proprioceptive

demands associated with barefoot running, which may account for the working memory gains.'

You're putting together a puzzle, in other words. Whenever you run barefoot, you're not numbing your legs with two slabs of foam and blindly thumping along. You're scanning the terrain, quickly assessing each landing spot and mentally comparing it to scenarios you've encountered before: Smooth or stony? Prickly or soft? Muddy or firm? Your memory is engaged and activated, serving as the working link in your brain–body connection. All that information is zipping around the brain's decision-making frontal lobes, forming faster-than-thought choices about exactly where, and how, you should touch down for each stride.

Your bare feet don't increase your risk of injury, in other words; they *lower* it. 'If a barefoot runner has better proprioception through a more direct coupling to the ground, it stands to reason that the barefoot runner would be far less likely to suffer injuries related to balance and terrain irregularities,' Dr David Jenkins, a podiatric professor and board member of the American Academy of Podiatric Sports Medicine, has noted. 'Indeed, several investigators have demonstrated that unshod athletes had significantly better lateral stability and ability to discriminate ankle inversion movement.'

No wonder the Alloways were so wiped after trotting across that Scottish sheep meadow. Beautiful as it was to the eye, to their feet it presented a minefield of 'sheep poo' they had to avoid. But for barefoot runners, one person's poo is another's Lumosity: 'If we take off our shoes and go for a run,' Ross Alloway concluded, 'we can finish smarter than when we started.'

10.4
FOOTWEAR: **ACTION ITEMS**

1. Take your current favourite running shoes and pull out the insoles. That thin layer of padding may look inconsequential, but when you put your shoes back on, you'll feel significantly more stable and lower to the ground. Run without insoles for a few days to transition to the feel of minimal shoes.

2. Visit your local running store and check out their selection of neutral and minimalist shoes. Ideally, you'll find one of our recommended models. Don't let them upsell you into some cushioned monstrosity.

3. When you've made your choice, be careful about sizing. Take Golden Harper's advice and make sure you have plenty of length and width. Too big isn't a problem. Too small is a disaster.

4. Break in your new shoes by working your way through the skills you've accumulated: wear them for Movement Snacks, Rock Lobstering against the wall, and your Form and Fitness exercises. Get used to the feel of landing lightly without artificial cushioning.

5. Try your new minimalist shoes on your shortest run of the week. Remember to relax and keep your cadence high. Don't *try* to make your foot land a certain way. If you've been Rock Lobstering and practising the 100 Up, you just need to keep popping along with a high cadence and you'll be fine. But if your legs rebel in any way – tight calves, twingey feet – call it a day and walk it in. Think of this as a post-operative period: you're reawakening muscles that have been asleep for a long time.

6. Experiment with running barefoot. Try it Mika style: set off with your shoes in your hands. As soon as you feel any discomfort, pull them on to finish your run.

Karma Park's best runs combine sandals, her dog, and at least one son.

Fun: If It Feels Like Work, You're Working Too Hard

11

'Great tattoo,' a friend said, after I pulled the bandage off my arm to see if it was still bleeding.

'I love it. Thanks.'

'Um – you know it's missing a toe, right?'

I checked again. One, two, three— Yup, he was right. The wicked-cool *Born to Run* logo with the bare foot I just inked on my body for life was actually a wicked-cool, four-toed *Born to Run* logo.

Which made it perfect. If you're going to get a tattoo from a motorcycle biker on parole in a battered RV parked between a tequila-shots aid station, a dirt wrestling ring, and the finish line of a 200-mile footrace directed by a guy who's wearing a mariachi suit and searching for the shotgun he's lost (again), then c'mon – what's the point if it doesn't miss a digit? Or spell *Born* with a P?

I could have gone back for another toe, but the line outside Honest Bob's RV was getting long and I'd risk missing the Beer Mile, or the Rarámuri ball games, or an explanation for why everyone was spanking the guy running through the crowd in a Mexican *lucha libre* mask. It was only 8:40 in the morning, but at Luis Escobar's 'Born to Run Ultramarathon Extravaganza', that's already the white-hot centre of the circus.

Back in 2010, Luis had called me to ask, very kindly and unnecessarily, if I was cool with him using the name for a special kind of event. Luis wanted to bring Caballo's vision to life in a way that a cantankerous canyon loner never could. Caballo always felt that marathons had become way too commercial and solitary, with a bunch of strangers being herded through a merchandising mall before plodding off through the streets, identified only by numbers on their shirts like a bunch of prisoners.

Caballo wanted Dancing! And Storytelling! And then a No-Mercy, Lung-Scorcher of a Trail Race! Before getting right back to Partying and Dancing and Storytelling again!

That was the true magic that Caballo had discovered in the Copper Canyons. That's why the Rarámuri were such sensational distance runners. Chia seeds, natural running form, minimalist footwear – sure, they're all important, but they're only the means to an end. They're the tools you use to reach the real goal: making running feel wonderful.

And that's where the Rarámuri reign supreme. If you want to become a great runner, as coaching legend Dr Joe Vigil realised when he first saw the Rarámuri at Leadville, you've got to make it fun. The same lightbulb flashed for Caballo when he was invited to his first *rarájipari*, the Rarámuri ball race. Caballo was delighted to discover that the Rarámuri never forgot that running is supposed to be a party, not a punishment. They don't race the way we do, with thousands of strangers at a starting line staring silently into the distance, waiting for a gun to blast so they can charge off into their own solitary cave of pain and self-doubt.

Instead, two villages gather to spend the night drinking homemade corn beer and placing bets. The next morning, each village fields a team of eight or so runners. For the next twelve hours, or twenty-four, or sometimes forty-eight, the two teams will race back and forth along a one-mile stretch of trail, each one chasing down their own crazily ricocheting wooden ball and flicking it, fast break style, from teammate to teammate.

When the race is over, it's party time again. Bets are settled, corn beer is shared, bad decisions are encouraged. The runners all meld back into the celebration as if they'd been on the same team from the start – and that, of course, is exactly the reason the Rarámuri created this game in the first place.

Caballo had never witnessed anything like it. While the two teams were charging up and down the racecourse, their families and neighbours and besties were whooping it up on the sidelines, cheering and singing, offering *iskiate* and encouragement, lighting torches at night, making the entire experience feel as much like a party as possible. No one is

going to feel jolly after forty-eight hours on their feet, of course. But you can try, right?

Because anything else would be crazy. Suffering isn't the point of running; at worst, it's collateral damage you hope to avoid. Getting hurt is the opposite of getting better. If you told Arnulfo or Manuel Luna they ought to Goggins themselves into the hospital to become 'the hardest man ever created', or they ought to 'suffer in order to grow', they'd either hand you the moonshine jug or gently remove it from your hands.

Why would you ruin the only body you'll ever have? How is making yourself so sore you can't walk a *good* thing? No rational mammal would ever damage themselves by choice. Unless, maybe, they'd been duped into believing that alpha-male Rambo cosplay makes you a 'hard MFer' – or that acting tough is more important than getting better.

I still don't understand how Caballo Blanco, the least sociable man on earth, pulled together the wackiest and weirdest week-long bout of running and partying I'd ever seen.

But the Copper Canyon Ultramarathon would always be a miracle that only the lucky few could experience. The journey is tough, and the danger from local narco lords is so unpredictable that in 2015, the race had to be cancelled after two local police officers were dragged out of the station in the centre of town and murdered.

So Luis came up with a plan of his own. What if he staged the Burning Man of running races, a long weekend on a wild California ranch where everyone camped out, partied hard, and ran even harder? Luis debuted the Extravaganza in 2010, and it quickly became clear that 'Extravaganza' was an understatement.

To give you a sense of what Luis created, these are the events that I, personally, witnessed during one half of only *one* of the Extravaganza's four days:

Saturday, 5:45 am Mariachi trumpets blare in the dark. 'Runner up!' someone shouts. Four-Day Runners who began on Wednesday are coming through camp on another loop, or maybe it's the 100-Milers who started last night. Other early risers join the cry: 'RUNNER UP!' If you're trying to sneak in a little more sleep, forget it.

6:00 Barefoot Ted and I join Luis on top of a hay wagon to lead a thousand or so runners and friends in Caballo's pre-race oath. Right hand on heart, left hand up: 'If I get hurt, lost or die, *it's my own damn fault!*'

6:45 Luis finds the shotgun he lost the day before either killing a rattlesnake or blasting the start for the Beer Mile, he can't remember which.

7:00 *BLAM!!* Luis fires both barrels and all of us in the 'shorter' distances – 100k, 50k and 10 miles – charge off together, cresting the first hill as the sun hits the Pacific.

7:00:01 Friends who'd emerged from tents wrapped in blankets to see us off immediately pivot and head for the food truck, where Luis's sister and bro-in-law are serving breakfast tacos that smell so delicious, I'm tempted to DNF.

7:20 Hey, it's Pat Sweeney coming towards me, and as he crests the hill in the midst of the Four-Day Race, I'm happy to see he's wearing shorts. Pat is a nudist and former pro Frisbee player who once finished the Chicago Marathon only to run all the way to New York in sandals to do another one. Pat is the unchallenged champion of both the Naked Beer Mile and Beer Half Marathon (thirteen miles, thirteen beers), because who else wants to try? Pat also leads the Extravaganza's most popular seminars, like:

*History of the California Missions. Bring four beers.

*Trail runner's guide to California flora and fauna. Bring four beers.

*Quiet Reflections with Patrick Sweeney. Bring four beers.

8:40 Approaching the 10-mile finish, I'm having such a good time I'm tempted to switch to the 50k and keep going. But I want to see what else is happening, so I accept my handmade finisher's necklace that's placed around my neck by Pat Sweeney, who somehow beat me to the finish even though he's still facing another thirty hours of running.

8:50 Honest Bob's Tattoo RV is open for business, so I slide in and pull off my shirt. Honest Bob keeps the door open as he works, which means every time a friend pops in to say 'Hi!' the whole RV rocks and he's got to quickly lift the needle from my arm. His ability to anticipate wobbles is uncanny.

9:30 Freshly inked, I get a whomping bowl of homemade *menudo* from Luis's sister's food truck, and also discover my wicked-cool tattoo is missing a wicked-cool toe.

10:00 'ON YOUR MARKS!'

Just in time, I make it to the starting line of the 0.0 Race.

'GET SET …'

Luis fires the shotgun.

'*DO NOTHING!*'

Racers congratulate each other on completing zero miles in zero minutes.

'It's an ultrarunning gateway drug,' Luis explains.

10:01 Kris Brown and Brian Gillis, two strangers from Oakland and Seattle, are fighting furiously for first as they sprint towards the finish of the 50k when they spontaneously grab hands and cross the line together.

Taking the Caballo Oath at the Born to Run Extravaganza. Pictured: Luis Escobar, McDougall and Barefoot Ted.

Spectators applaud the sportsmanship. Luis is outraged.

'Hell no!' he shouts. 'You're not on a date. You're in a race.' The Extravaganza is fun, and it's a run, but it ain't no fun run.

Luis gives them a choice: to determine first place, they can either wrestle or shotgun a beer. They elect to shotgun. Kris and Brian chug the beers and hold the empties over their heads. Invalid: Luis detects dribbling. In the second attempt, Kris finishes two gulps ahead and is declared the 50k champion. He dons the *lucha libre* mask and cape and, in keeping with Extravaganza custom, runs through a paddywhack gauntlet of spectators who swat him on the ass to keep him humble.

10:30 I head over to Barefoot Ted's Luna Sandal tent, where he's hanging out with the Rarámuri legend Arnulfo Quimare. Ted set Arnulfo up with a batch of huarache materials, so I grab a seat as the master craftsman makes me a pair of sandals.

Arnulfo has become an Extravaganza regular, as has his *Born to Run* rival, Scott Jurek. One year, Luis passed around a hat until it was stuffed with cash, then goaded Arnulfo and Scott into a one-hundred-yard rematch for all the money.

'Arnulfo was on fire,' Luis recalls. 'It wasn't even close.'

11:00 'This guy is dying to fight you,' Luis says. 'You up for it?'

Professor John Vanderpot teaches a class on *Born to Run* at San Diego State University. Every year, the Extravaganza has an all-comers wrestling tournament to raise money for combat veterans. This year, Dr Vanderpot wants to tangle with me.

'He's in the middle of the 100k,' Luis says. 'He'll pull off the course long enough to wrestle.' Last year, one runner ended up in hospital because he forgot that tapping out was an option. Plus, Luis admitted that the literature professor I was up against had wrestled in college. Still, I figured I had a fair shot against a 52-year-old academic who'd just run thirty miles and had another thirty to go. Man, did I figure wrong.

12 noon Musicians are tuning banjos and guitars on the hay wagon in preparation for the evening's Dirt Bag Prom, scheduled to begin just after the 100-Milers finish and between laps for the Four-Day Racers so they can pop in for a few dances.

Lots of runners bring wild gowns and outfits for the Prom. Quite a few finish without them. Skinny-dipping is common, despite the ranch having no standing water.

'Many relationships have started and ended at Born to Run,' Luis says. 'There's been one wedding. Too many proposals to count. A couple divorces. At least one confirmed conception. That baby is now six years old.'

Zach Friedley was just there to make coffee.

He wasn't interested in Proms or Wheelchair Jousting or prisoner-on-parole tattoos, and he sure as hell wasn't at the Extravaganza to run. Guys with one leg don't run trails.

Zach was born missing a right leg above the knee and three fingers from his right hand. He got into wrestling as a kid, because it was the one sport for which bear-crawling around the house was terrific training, but by high school, opponents worked out that they could neutralise his advantage by keeping their distance. He began losing against wrestlers he'd once dominated, and by senior year, his hopes for a college scholarship had faded.

That's also when Zach discovered the one thing they don't tell you about prosthetics as a youngster: when you grow up, you're on your own.

The free care he'd gotten from Shriners Children's Hospital was over, which meant it was now up to Zach to source – and pay for – his own artificial legs. Keep that in mind the next time you see a Paralympian in action: before even getting to the starting line, they've already faced the extraordinary challenge of finding, fitting and financing their own custom prosthetics.

'They break, too,' Zach says. 'And they can hurt like hell.'

Zach spent his early twenties limping around awkwardly because his specialist assured him that pain was the reality of adult devices. Finally, Zach set off on a last-chance power drive to the manufacturer's headquarters in Indianapolis. He walked the halls, looking for someone who could help, until his athletic build caught the attention of a sports-prosthetic designer who let him try on a sprinter's blade.

Sprinting is what adaptive athletes did: they ran very short races on very smooth tracks. Zach tried it, and was so good they let him keep the specialty blade, but sprinting was kind of a dead end: if you weren't world-class, there wasn't much else for an adaptive runner to do. But at least he got the leg, which is exactly what he needed when cannabis came a'calling.

A high-school friend, Teresa Shiflett, needed strong backs at her cannabis operation in the mountains of Northern California. She warned Zach that the terrain was way too rugged, but he convinced her that with some duct tape and an old running shoe, he'd be able to adapt his skinny sprinter's blade for backcountry climbing.

'People didn't think I'd be worth a shit, but I could work harder and faster than anyone,' Zach says. The pot business is no stoner's paradise. Zach was up each day by 4:30 am, pulling tarps off the plants by 5:00, and hauling five-gallon buckets of water 1,200 feet up from the creek until the sun went down. The steep climbs were as brutal as Teresa promised, but Zach was discovering he could move in ways he'd never attempted before.

Friends said he was nuts for clambering around those rocky cliffs on his wacky taped-on sneaker, but as far as Zach was concerned, the real Queen of Crazytown was Teresa. Despite the grinding work, she was training at the same time for a hundred-mile race. Zach couldn't wrap his head around the idea that any human could move that far under their own steam, no matter what locomotion they had below the waist. So when Teresa invited him to come check out Born to Run with her, he couldn't resist.

Zach rolled up to the Extravaganza with a trunk full of coffee beans and a pro-grade grinder. A coffee company which contributes to social causes had agreed to help Zach raise money for disabled children. 'My plan was to spend all day handing out really good coffee to these amazing runners, but when I got there, I was surprised to find they weren't all that amazing,' Zach says. 'Honestly, I see all these people and they aren't super freak athletes. They're just totally normal, but doing this thing that seems unfathomable.'

'So how come you're not running?' Luis asked.

'Is it even possible?' asked Zach. The most he'd ever run was a 5k, on smooth roads, and it sucked. 'Can a prosthetic handle these trails?'

Luis shrugged. Behind them, a bunch of Extravaganza runners were holding a demolition derby by smashing into each other in plastic kids' cars while racing down a giant hill. Half the racers had bounced out and were sprawled on their faces.

'A lot of crazy shit goes on here,' Luis said. 'I never thought *that* was in the cards. But here we are.'

Inspired either by Luis or the devil-may-care carnage on Car Crash Mountain, at dawn the next day Zach raised his right hand, swore that his death would be his own damn fault, and launched himself into the hills as a human engineering experiment. He finished the day in tears – with a 10-mile finisher's medallion around his neck.

'I showed up as a coffee vendor,' he says. 'I left a trail runner.'

When he got home to Mendocino, Zach was in the grocery store when he bumped into pro ultrarunner Kris Brown, the same guy I'd watched shotgun two beers at the Extravaganza to decide the 50k winner. Zach went full fanboy. ('He's an animal!' Zach gushes.) Zach couldn't resist peppering the pro with newbie questions, until Kris cut him off. 'Let's just run sometime,' he offered.

Kris began guiding Zach through the mountains, and encouraged him to extend his range from ten miles to a hundred. 'You just gotta jump,' Kris kept saying, but c'mon: Zach didn't want to punk in front of his new hero, but if things went south, he and his one leg would be *waaay* out in the woods on their own in the middle of the night, with no Kris Brown around to get him out of there.

But then Zach heard what two other adaptive pioneers were up to, and it made him think he'd had the wrong idea about running all along. Dave Mackey was a two-time Ultrarunner of the Year before having his left leg amputated below the knee in 2016 after a near-fatal fall off a trail. Since then, he's run the Leadville Trail 100 twice and conquered the 'R2R2R' – the Grand Canyon rim-to-rim-to-rim challenge, forty-seven miles with more than 10,000 feet of climbing.

Jacky Hunt-Broersma wasn't even a runner when she lost her leg to cancer in 2001. She mostly became interested because it was high on the list of things she was told she wouldn't be able to do. 'Of course everyone was saying, no, amputees don't run trails!' Jacky told *Canadian Running*

Zach Friedley made it his mission to lead more adaptive athletes onto the trails.

Zach's prosthetic taught him a key lesson for all runners: form and balance are everything.

magazine. She soon found out why: prosthetics snap, rubber treads tear off the bottom, blood blisters and chafing are the price of admission, and if it's muddy and steep, expect to see Jacky come sliding downhill on her butt.

'Your brain doesn't recognise the prosthetic as part of your body, so you have to teach your brain to trust this foreign object on your leg,' Jacky has said. Imagine walking with your eyes closed, never knowing exactly what your foot is about to land on, whether it will grip or slide or jar, and you begin to have a sense of what it's like to run on an artificial limb.

Which, of course, is why she likes it. As every trail runner and six-year-old can tell you, play time is no fun without some blood and mud. In five furious years, Jacky ramped up from three miles, to forty, to all 120 miles of the TransRockies Six-Day Stage Race. In May 2022, she set a world record by running 104 marathons in 104 days, the longest consecutive streak by *any* runner, male or female, with or without prosthetics. (The men's record for daily marathons, by the way? Fifty-nine, according to Guinness.)

But what put a gleam in Zach's eye wasn't the Mackey and Jacky parade of triumphs. It was their flameouts. Like in 2019, when Dave Mackey stepped onto the biggest stage in ultrarunning, the Western States 100, and came away with a Did Not Finish. And the time Jacky attempted to take on the Moab 240, only to find that wet rocks wouldn't allow her to make the aid station cut-off. Another DNF.

Those three letters put a chill in Zach's heart. If there's one thing he hates more than being That Guy – the adaptive athlete everyone wanted a selfie with because they'd never seen one before – it's being That Guy Who DNF'ed. A DNF cut right to Zach's greatest fear: that he wasn't as good as everyone else, and shouldn't be out there in the first place.

So when he DNF'ed in a thirty-mile race with only five miles to go, Zach was mortified. He was determined to put that memory behind him, so he trained like crazy for an even longer race – a fifty-miler – and crashed even faster, breaking down from heat and prosthetic problems before he even made it halfway. Humiliated, he phoned his coach from the middle of the woods for, basically, permission to quit.

'I'm so proud of you!' Chris Palmquist said.

'You're not disappointed?'

'No!' she replied. 'Pull that plug. Don't do damage.'

Starting a race is brave, she explained. Finishing it when you're hurt is ego. 'If it's going to knock you out of training for three days,' she told Zach, 'then call it a day.' The Three-Day Rule was Chris's yardstick: continuing to run when you know you won't be able to walk for seventy-two hours means it's time to question why you're running in the first place. If it's because you've got something to prove, then it's only a matter of time before you get injured for real or quit for good. The extraordinarily successful Illinois high-school track coach Tony Holler calls this philosophy *Don't burn the steak*. 'Kids are good at what they like, obsessed with what they love,' he explains. Push too hard today, and they won't be back for many tomorrows.

'I'll always take a Did Not Finish over a Did Not Start,' is how Zach's coach put it.

But that kind of Mackey–Jacky wisdom can be hard to come by, as Zach can tell you, so he and Luis Escobar began scheming. How could they get more people – adaptive or otherwise – to give trail running a try? How could they be encouraged to take Kris Brown's advice and just jump?

Easy! Make it impossible for them to fall.

> **"AT THIS YEAR'S EXTRAVAGANZA, ZACH AND LUIS ARE CUTTING THE RIBBON ON 'BORN TO ADAPT', THE FIRST EVER ADAPTIVE ATHLETE TRAIL RACE."**

At this year's Extravaganza, Zach and Luis are cutting the ribbon on 'Born to Adapt', the first ever adaptive athlete trail race. 'Running of all forms is welcome, including blades, crutches, ninja-sticks (forearm crutches), wheelchairs or crawling,' Zach says. 'My goal is to get someone who has never run a mile, or maybe only done a couple laps around the track, and give them an invitation into trail racing.'

Together, Zach and Luis came up with a brilliant twist: Born to Adapt is a race-the-clock contest to see who can complete the most 5k loops in three hours. Runners will be constantly lapping and encouraging each other, with the option of resting or racing as much as they want.

You can win, you can run your guts out for every second of the three hours, you can cover a mile and call it a day, but the one thing you can't do is DNF: whenever you're done running, you've already reached the finish line. Your day is done when you've had enough fun.

And somewhere, of course, Caballo Blanco is taking a bow.

No race ever meant more to him in his life than his first, against-all-odds, rub-my-eyes-is-it-really-happening Copper Canyon Ultramarathon. Caballo had dreamed forever of getting the Rarámuri to show their stuff against the best athletes from the outside world – but then, just when he reached the middle of an event that shouldn't have happened in the first place and might never happen again, right in front of the townspeople of Urique who'd all turned out to watch, Caballo suddenly dropped out of his own race.

It wasn't even a hard decision. Watching the joy on everyone else's face, he decided, was a lot more fun than finishing.

11.1 TIME TO SCOOT

In 2005, at age forty-one, Matt Carpenter raced a hundred miles across the sky faster than any human ever has, setting a course record at the Leadville Trail 100 that still stands today. When I asked him how, he led me into the garage.

First we checked out his treadmill, which he used to calculate exactly how many sips of water he needed to stay hydrated (eighteen an hour). We moved to his shoe rack by the door, where he'd tinkered with his laces until he'd dialled in the precise degree of tautness that kept his running shoes from flying off while remaining loose enough to switch out quick.

And then he moved to the secret weapon.

The worst thing you can do with running, he said, is force it. Sometimes your body is beat, other days your

head's not there, but you're afraid you'll pay a price if you ditch a workout. 'You can only run so much,' says the guy who *twice* won a mountain marathon and half-marathon on consecutive days. 'Then you've got to vary it up or you'll do more harm than good.'

The solution? Same as with any other love affair: Keep it fun. Keep it fresh. But most of all, keep it honest.

And that's the beauty of a scooter. Or in Matt Carpenter's case, a Kickbike – the high-end, higher-performance, Scandinavian version. Don't feel guilty about running around behind your marathon schedule's back, because as fun as they are, scooters are also fantastic running-form teachers. You glide around like Tony Hawk, but deep inside your muscle memory, all kind of reconditioning is going on.

'Often I run into stubborn "heel bangers" who just can't

> **IN ABOUT THREE SECONDS, I DISCOVERED THAT SCOOTERS ARE AN INSTANT REWARD SYSTEM FOR GOOD BALANCE AND BIOMECHANICS.**

seem to break the habit of landing heel first. Here is where the scooter comes in,' notes Tom Miller, the PhD physiologist in Utah who specialises in coaching elite Masters athletes. For decades, Tom has come up against runners who resist change despite years of chronic setbacks. Finally, Tom learned to save his breath, stick them on the scooter, and bid them peace out. Within a minute, the hardheads are doing everything they told Tom they couldn't.

'Scootering allows heel bangers to experience what it feels like to push off from well beneath the centre of gravity,' Tom points out.* 'Those who land heel first while on the scooter immediately feel the impact slamming up through their extended legs as they jerk awkwardly along. Within a few minutes, their foot contact adjusts and begins to feel natural.

'As soon as I see this happening, I immediately have them run while imitating the scootering leg movements,' Tom continues. 'The transformation is often spectacular.'

I started scooting back when I only thought it was fun. My Amish neighbours in Peach Bottom, Pennsylvania, prefer vehicles that keep you connected to the earth and close to home, hence buggies over cars and scooters instead of bikes. The Amish-built scooters look so simple, I didn't realise how brilliantly they're engineered until my daughter wanted one for her eighth birthday and I took it for a spin.†

---

* *For a pioneering look at the connection between scooters and running biomechanics, check out* Programmed to Run *by Thomas S. Miller.*
† *Read* Running with Sherman *to find out what she wanted for her tenth.*

In about three seconds, I discovered that scooters are an instant reward system for good balance and biomechanics. Nail your kick and you're sailing; shank it, and you're making twice the effort to go half the distance. 'No different with running,' Eric says. 'The scooter demands consistency. After you push off, the leg cycles back into position for the next foot strike with no reaching or overstriding. This teaches good bent-knee drive, like running in place. The scooter really helps you feel this.'

What I feel is absolute joy. In the ten years since I filched a scooter from an eight-year-old, I've used it nearly every day. Our post office and local country store are at the top of a two-mile climb, and bombing back home down that long, winding hill is such a blast that instead of driving to the supermarket, I got in the habit of throwing on a backpack and wrapping the day's dinner shopping around that four-mile scoot.

What's weird is that even when my legs are feeling busted, a half-hour's scoot revives them so much that I come home feeling fresher than when I left. I can't fully explain the magic, but my best guess is that the scooter's two main motions – pumping the stance leg up and down in quarter-squats, while extending the drive leg way out on the follow-through – have the same effect as a sports massage, recharging your run-weary legs by flushing blood and lactic acid out of your muscles.

I've now got two: my ten-year-old Amish-built with the 24" front tire, and a new 26" Schwinn Shuffle. They cost the same (about $200), but I was surprised to find I prefer the old-school Amish whip. The Amish want to go hard, not look pretty, so their floorboard is comfortably low for easy kicking and the handlebars are purpose-built, not Beach Cruiser carryovers. Plus, you can swap out the Amish tires for wheelchair tubes with solid rubber cores, so you'll never have a blowout. I've been tempted to try the Kickbikes, especially that boss-looking Sport G4 with rad adjustable bars and 28" front slick, but at 500 bucks, I could never justify buying one for the same price as two Amish originals.

This past November, I was scooting down a long hill on a freezing morning when I had the urge to dig my phone out of my pocket with one hand while balancing with the other so I could call Eric. 'I feel like I've broken through to something new,' I shouted over the wind. 'It's like, euphoria. I think I'm in the best shape of my life.'

'*Maaay*be,' Eric began, in the kind of tone you'd use with a buddy who thinks he can make it from the top of his chimney to his neighbour's backyard pool. 'Or maybe you're just having fun. Could be both. Probably the fun.'

11.2
RUNNING WITH MUSIC

The elephant in the room is those buds in your ears.

Here's the dilemma: Eric and I are a big, head-shaking *Nope* whenever we're asked if it's okay to run with noise in your ears. If you're not Rock Lobstering in your living room, you're better off without the earblasters. But personal preference may be colouring our opinion, as witnessed by the fact that I couldn't resist calling it 'noise' instead of 'emotionally uplifting melodies that have been clinically proven to release mood-enhancing hormones and create lasting sensations of happiness and well-being'.

We're not anti-happiness and well-being, and it's impossible to escape that fact that no one has ever run worse while listening to Gloria Gaynor. But if you have to Gaynor, we're convinced, you've already lost.

For us, music is audio ibuprofen, a numbing agent that's probably masking a bigger problem you ought to be addressing head-on. We'll ride or die to the bitter end that once you learn to focus on the rhythm of your breathing, the Rock Lobstering of your cadence, and the elegance of your footfalls, music will become an annoyance and distraction.

Unless we're dead wrong. Lady Southpaw thinks so, and she created an entire album to prove it.

> **LUCKILY, THE LEGEND HIMSELF AGREED TO ENTER THE ARENA: RICK RUBIN, THE LAST WORD ON ALL THINGS LYRICAL *AND* A DEDICATED BIOHACKER AND FITNESS STUDENT.**

Lady Southpaw is a New York punk musician who decided to follow in the marathoning footsteps of Alanis Morissette (4:28, NYC), Flea of the Red Hot Chili Peppers (3:42, LA), the Clash's Joe Strummer (4:13, London, plus a rumoured 3:20 as an anonymous bandit in the Paris Marathon after a ten-pint night) and Eminem, who never actually entered a race but earns honorary status for the sheer persistence of his daily seventeen miles.*

Lady Southpaw thought a good backbeat could steady her cadence, so she sang one. Eighteen of them, actually: her album, *Marathoners Rocking New York*, is a full forty-five-minute soundtrack of eighteen original cuts, all of them 180 beats per minute with a sound straight from Ramones-era punk – because that's when the NYC marathon was born.

To Lady Southpaw, running with music is the same as sneaking food into the movies and smoking weed in Texas without a prescription: no matter what you say, everyone's doing it anyway. 'Maybe it's worth having the conversation in the open about how to do it safely and responsibly,' she messaged me. 'Like sex education ;)'

Fair point. It's time we sat down and had The Talk.

Flea represented one side, Lady Southpaw more than held her own on the other, but when the dust settled, we were left with a great debate but no clear victor. We needed a tiebreaker, someone trusted by all who truly understands the human experience of movement and music. Luckily, the legend himself agreed to enter the arena: Rick Rubin, the last word on all things lyrical *and* a dedicated biohacker and fitness student.

Here's how it played out:

* *'I became a f—ing hamster,' Eminem told* Men's Journal *magazine. 'Seventeen miles a day on a treadmill. I would get up in the morning, and before I went to the studio, I would run eight and a half miles in about an hour. Then I'd come home and run another eight and a half.'*

Runner's World magazine: How did you get into running?

Flea: Well, I was never much of a runner before – maybe a little jog here and there, probably never more than a mile in my whole life. Last year, I read *Born to Run* and it affected me profoundly – the concept of our bodies being used for their real purpose when they're running. I thought, *F—k it. I'm gonna run a marathon and raise money for the Silverlake Conservatory of Music*. As a musician I'm about expressing what's inside, and I think everyone has a song in them that they need to get out, whatever their gig is. And with running, my body has another way to express itself.

RW: Do you listen to music when you run?

Flea: Never. Never have done it, don't want to. When I'm running, my senses are so alive and full. I'm listening to my body, I'm listening to my breath, I'm listening to nature around me, I'm listening to my footsteps and paying attention to what's going on. I'm trying to nurture this energy and get into the run. When I listen to music, I focus solely on what I'm hearing, and I just don't want to do that when I'm running. I want to focus on the running itself and all that entails, and I feel like that's plenty.

But why settle for 'plenty', Lady Southpaw wonders, when you can have *extraordinary*? As she writes:

Going back and rereading some of my favourite sections of *Born to Run* is reminding me of my initial inspiration to make music for running. They both have the power to unlock this higher plane of experience. You can call it flow, the 'zone', or the 'runner's high'. You can get it from either one individually but the combination is pure magic.

I think any runner knows when the forces all align during an amazing run, you have that feeling like you understand the universe and your place in it and it's this hard-won euphoria. There's a similar flow experience in playing and even listening to a great song, especially if you can dance around to it in a big crowd of people who all love the same song.

Basically, I believe music can play the role of a guide to getting you to that runner's high (especially if you are someone relatively new to and not already

in love with running). It helps organise your mind and body so you're not wasting too much energy extraneously. Running already takes a lot of energy so there are big gains in being as efficient as possible, and properly timed music is a really good tool. Music can also tap into positive emotions and help your mental game, getting you psyched up to run.

I'm really cautious about blasting my music at the expense of everything else and everyone else in my environment. I know that it can be annoying to my fellow pedestrians to downright dangerous (even fatal) if I'm sharing the road with vehicles and bikes. I would always advise extreme caution in a situation involving any kind of traffic (which in NYC is practically every situation). It's totally possible to find a level that allows for you to also hear your surroundings, check in with your body, and save the occasional blasting for the treadmill, track or other safe, secluded path.

When I got more serious about running and started training for a marathon for charity, I got the idea to write a song for running and use it as part of my fundraising promotion. That's what motivated me to really dig deeper and investigate what made a song good for running. That's when I had the 180-bpm breakthrough, and it was transcendent! The basic premise was that after studying Olympians, running coach Jack Daniels discovered that the vast majority tended to run at or around 180 steps per minute. Conversely, the most common mistake beginners would make was having long, bouncy strides that often led to injury. When people learned to shorten their stride and increase their turnover, their gait would naturally become a lot more efficient. As a universal training tool, 180 steps per minute is amazing! I figured it out by running in place to a 180-bpm song in my living room and then moving forward really gradually. Once you can do that, you can use the cadence at any pace.

So, I started finding songs that were already 180 bpm and putting them together into playlists for myself. The first place I took it was to that gym treadmill and I was so blown away. After getting the feel of that cadence at my usual pace, that thirty minutes just flew by and I didn't feel tired, I felt energised! I felt like I had discovered the secret of life!

I began to feel there was a visceral connection between music and running. As you point out in *Born to Run*, 'recreation has its reasons'. The heartbeat, the breathing, the repetitive rhythmic physical movement: I wouldn't be surprised to learn that there was some basic form of music occurring in ancient people's minds while they were running to help pass the time and keep them going on those long expeditions. I'm really inspired by the idea that the first music we each hear is in the tones of our mother's voice, her heartbeat, and rocking motions; initially in the womb and then as babies.

This all led me to feel passionately that there was this huge unlocked potential for a genre of music made for running. Imagine a whole narrative that could lead you through an emotional story that was written with the experience of running in mind. Where the beat was always consistent and easy to hear and at a perfect 180 bpm or thereabouts. There's something beautiful in the idea that there's a tempo that most people can use and it may even help them to be a better runner. This was the inspiration behind *Marathoners Rocking New York*. What other sport allows a normal person like me to participate in the same event as the top professional competitors? What sport is more inclusive than that?

Music isn't necessary for every single run, especially when you are outside connecting to nature. Keep your volumes low enough to hear what's going on around you. And in racing situations, I'm always unplugged. But when you're racking up easy miles on a safe path, or just trying to get some treadmill time before work, why make running harder than it has to be? As long as humans have run the earth, the beat has been there. Use it.

—Erin, AKA Lady Southpaw

Coach Eric examined Lady Southpaw's argument from all sides, and beyond our fundamental belief that music is the enemy of body awareness, he didn't find much daylight to squeeze in any fresh objections.

'On the trail, my ears are my eyes,' he stressed, which sounds like a knockout punch until you realise he's mostly talking about listening for mountain lions and grizzlies in the Grand Tetons, a bit of a niche concern. Besides, the Lady did recommend keeping volumes down so you can still hear and deferring to the voice of Mother Nature when available.

Rick Rubin considered both sides, then weighed in with the key point we were all missing. Because that's what Rick Rubin does.

If you're not familiar with Rick's work, you've either been Captain America-ed in ice since 1984 or tipped off that Rick would never define what he does as 'work'. His preferred title is 'music enthusiast', which is about as low-key as you can get for a guy who launched LL Cool J and the Beastie Boys to fame *from his college dorm room* and went on to guide a staggering galaxy of superstars, everyone from Jay-Z and Kanye West to Adele, Metallica, the Red Hot Chili Peppers and Eminem (that's Rick headbobbing by Em's side in 'Berzerk').

Nobody was paying any attention to washed-up Johnny Cash until Rick led him out of obscurity and on to a string of Grammys. Johnny Cash, for his part, missed what was so great about Nine Inch Nails's 'Hurt' until Rick finally talked him into it – and another Grammy. Barbra Streisand didn't get why Rick wanted her to do a bossa nova version of The Cure's 'Lovesong' – until Adele turned it into a smash hit. It was Rick's idea for Run-DMC to 'Walk This Way' with Aerosmith, but it took a ton of Rick-suasion.

Over the past decade Rick has also devoted himself to learning as much about his body as he does about music. He's smart about managing food and stress, and regularly subjects himself to oxygen-starving underwater workouts and freezing plunges with sub-Arctic ice-bather Laird Hamilton. He was already a devoted barefooter before reading *Born to Run*, so when it comes to minimalism, he's right there with us.

But when Rick and I spoke about running with music, he

put it in terms I'd never considered. 'The question is this,' he said. 'When do you want to be at the mercy of the music?'

On a treadmill, you're at the mercy of the machine. The only sights you see are the ones the machine is facing, the only sounds you hear are the ones the machine is making. Instead of stimulated, your senses are numbed by the motor – unless you fight back with music of your own.

'When I'm on the elliptical, I would play 60s psychedelic music and go in the rhythm,' Rick says. 'And if the music had me going slower than the energy output, I had the control to make the activity make sense with the music.'

But as soon you step outside, you shift from predictable to chaotic. The outside world is where music is born. It's the source of our all our rhythms and melodies and emotion, everything from the floating lilt of laughter to that goddamn car alarm in the Safeway parking lot. The 70s street-gang punk that Lady Southpaw loves? It came straight from the clash and bang of New York City streets. Tune out the garbage trucks, and say goodbye to Blitzkrieg Bop.

You have to absorb the unpredictability of the outside world, Rick believes, because otherwise, you lose the source of inspiration. It's not always bluebirds and whispering pines, but if you clear your mind and free your ears, you'll come home with ideas you didn't have when you left. Don't drown out the music of the world with the music in your pocket.

Just when I think Rick has settled the subject – indoors, good; outdoors, bad – he buttonhooks. 'Sometimes,' he muses, 'I do listen to music for a particular reason. Last summer in Kauai, I was listening to a DJ set in the car and it was so great, I wanted to continue.' Even though he was about to walk the shores of the Pacific, Rick let the DJ drown out the waves. 'I remember it was a great experience.'

We were right back at our starting point, a big old *You do you* shrug – but Rick had one more thing to say. 'That's what it is,' he went on. '*A particular purpose.*' When he works out, Rick likes to repeat the Metta Sutta, a Buddhist prayer of health and compassion. The prayer is only four short sentences, and the more you repeat them, the more love and compassion you create: first, for yourself, and gradually for your family, your community, and finally, the world.

> **IN HIS OWN INSTINCTIVE WAY, RICK STUMBLED ACROSS THE SAME ANCESTRAL CONNECTION BETWEEN MOVEMENT AND MEDITATION.**

'I found the phrases difficult to remember because they're not naturally musical,' Rick explains. 'Then I realised I could assign a metre to them and link them to any activity. I always look for opportunities to link things so I can do them more. Without linking things, you may not schedule them.'

Rick might forget to do his chants, he might not be in the mood to do his squats, but lash them together and instantly, his mind has a new focus. He's doubled his motivation and slashed the monotony.

'When you're swimming a mile, it's one repetitive movement over and over, no variety. So attaching something bigger to it gives the exercise a higher purpose,' he says. 'And it feels completely natural. I'll go:

May I be filled – *stroke!*
With love and kindness – *stroke!*
May I be well – *stroke!*
May I be peaceful – *stroke!*
And at ease – *stroke!*
May I be happy – *stroke!*

'And over time,' Rick concludes, 'you have the pleasure of extending the circle outwards, taking in more people.'

May my *spouse* be filled
With love and kindness …

May my *family* be filled
With love and kindness …

Climbing the Ohana Trail high above Oahu.

May the *world* be filled
With love and kindness …

Having never seen a wheel, in other words, Rick accidentally chiselled a stone into a perfect circle. Unlike Callie Vinson, he didn't know about prayer runs, that beautiful Native American tradition of dedicating the effort of each run to a loved one in need. But in his own instinctive way, Rick stumbled across the same ancestral connection between movement and meditation – and the perfect answer to our question.

So if you're wondering if it's okay to run with music, consider it the same way you would your food choices, your footwear and your running form:

- Is it making you stronger, or hiding a weakness?
- Is it helping you get better, or get it over with?

Because maybe you're a Rick Rubin, and you know when to pop the buds in and when to keep them out. Maybe you're a Lady Southpaw, and you've figured out that cranking up the beat (*safely!*) will keep your spirits high and your cadence on point.

Or maybe it's a blah Wednesday and you need some Kesha straight to the brain.

Just for today.

11.3 AID STATION: FUN RUNS AMISH STYLE

'Good morning friends!' read the email from my Amish friend Amos King.

'I would love to hear what is the top thing you put in place this year that will change the trajectory of your life??' he continued. 'Here's the plan: 5–7 miles of fellowship. Time: 6:30 am tomorrow.'

Within seconds, a reply pinged from the message chain:

Oh boy that's a bit deep for this early in the morning.

But before the sun was up that Saturday, eight runners were already deep in conversation in the freezing dark near a trailhead in Lancaster, Pennsylvania. Most were members of *Vella Shpringa* ('Let's All Run' in Pennsylvania Dutch), which has to be the world's only Amish ultrarunning club.

Amos started the group after catching the running bug about ten years ago, when some of his co-workers on a roofing crew invited him to join them in a 5k. Since then, Ame has run multiple fifty-milers and trimmed his Boston Marathon personal best to a smokin' 2:54.

Now, on every other weekend in any kind of weather, a rotating gang of Ame's friends sets off into the woods in the dark. Keeping a running club together isn't easy, especially when most of the members work on their feet all week and have farm chores waiting back home, but Ame came up with a strategy that's both innovative and ancient as time:

He created his own hunting pack.

For starters, Ame always pre-games with a group message before the run about whatever bug has burrowed into his mind that week. (My personal favourite: *Would you rather lose everything you've earned but keep all you've learned, or lose all you've learned and keep what you've earned?*)

Second, he's serious about the 'all' part of 'Let's All Run'. Everyone is welcome – Amish or not, fast or not-so-much – which means on any given Saturday, you might find Ame's wife, Liz, in her traditional long dress and apron, or Zach Miller, the elite pro runner who grew up nearby and took such a liking to Vella Shpringa that he joins these pre-dawn chat fests whenever he's not competing overseas.

Building the runs around banter was a stroke of genius. Whether by accident or inspiration, Ame hit on a foolproof system for locking in the perfect pace for a long run without a watch or heart-rate monitor. You can't talk if you're out of breath. You can't be heard if you're rocketing off ahead. So if you want to cruise along in the sweet spot just below your red zone, all you have to do is suggest to Ame that Sigmund Freud didn't know crap about human nature compared to Viktor Frankl, and you'll have a debate on your hands that won't end until you're back in the parking lot.*

---

* *Vella Shpringa member Jake Beiler set that morning's topic, because he was pretty miffed by Freud's contention that humans are captive to their biological urges with little capacity for free will.*

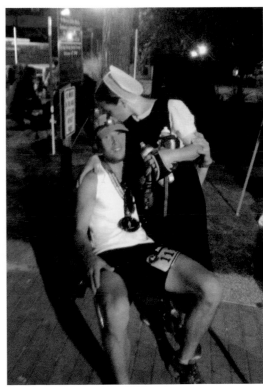

Amos King ran his first 100-miler in 23 hours, crewed by his wife, Liz. Liz King routinely wins 5ks and qualified for Boston in her first marathon.

11.4
FUN: **ACTION ITEMS**

- **Mika's Little Free Library Loop** – Nothing makes a long run easier than breaking it into a bunch of mini destinations. My wife and her friends realised there were at least four Little Free Library book boxes within a few miles of their neighbourhood. So every week or so, they load a backpack with books they've finished and run the loop, dropping off discards and picking up fresh titles. In one run, you get the self-satisfaction of donating with the joy of free shopping and the thrill of the hunt. My friend Dennis Poolheco used to train for ultramarathons by running a big loop across Hopi tribal land in Arizona to visit all his relatives. His young cousins would race out to meet him as soon as he came into view, turning each stop into a joyful little reunion.

- **Movement Snacks!** – Besides the selection we've included, Julie and Jared have plenty more movement snacks on their website. If you're ever feeling a little *blah* and not in the mood for a run, grab a few friends and work through a Movement Snack selection (see page 42). Julie calls them 'sneaky hard', but mostly they're sneaky fun: when you finish, you'll stand up and discover your mood is soaring and your entire body feels lighter, looser and more relaxed.

- **Adrenaline is a Superfood** – Rory Bosio skyrocketed from paediatric nurse to two-time champion of the Ultra-Trail du Mont Blanc, a ferocious Alpine ultramarathon, and she gives much of the credit to Alejandro, her creaky beach cruiser bike that she rides up a mountain pass about once a week before hurtling back down. In winter, Rory performs hill repeats by charging up snowy peaks and sledding down. Amelia Boone, the Spartan obstacle-course superstar, is a fan of long, hilly climbs and white-knuckle descents on her ElliptiGO (basically a stairmaster on wheels). Both of these champions realised that some of the best workouts are the ones you invented at age eight.

- **Get Weird** – My old hometown of Philadelphia has always been an oddball incubator, starting with Benjamin Franklin and his naked 'air baths' and developing, today, into a hotbed of underground urban adventuring. Take Rebecca Barbour: after she found out that if you connected all the landmarks that Rocky Balboa supposedly passed on his morning run it would cover thirty miles, she created the 'Rocky 50k', an annual ultramarathon attracting hundreds of runners in grey sweats and black Converse All Stars. Another Philadelphian persuaded a bunch of people (including me) to raise money for charity by racing up and down Rocky's iconic Art Museum steps for twenty-four hours. A local parole supervisor called Gags saw a photo of Philly taken from outer space and was inspired to run the city's entire seventy-six-mile perimeter, fuelling himself at convenience stores along the way. 'The best races,' a wise old trail runner once told me, 'start where you scratch a line in the dirt with your foot.'

The Black Men Run Boston crew on their regular Saturday-morning route through the streets of Dorchester.
Front: Jeff Davis. Row 2: Carlos Nobles, Serghino René, Chernet Sisay, Amannuel Abate.
Row 3: Khalil Saddiq, Ray Antoine, Kyle Ofori.
Row 4: Jeff Joseph, Abiodun Otu.

Family:
Those Who
Sweat Together
Soar Together

12

In March 2010, a wild-looking stranger showed up at the starting line of the Big Island International Marathon in Hawaii the way most people appear at a hotel breakfast bar: barely dressed, on a whim, and at the last minute. His long hair was flopping around his face, and even though it was wet and windy, all he had on was shorts and running shoes.

Two hours later, race volunteers were frantically hopping in and out of a van just in front of him, hurrying to stop oncoming cars and put down traffic cones as he sped towards the finish line. Race policy is to leave the road open until frontrunners are in the final stretch, but no one paid any attention to Tarzan until they suddenly realised that instead of flaming out, he was actually getting faster.

Despite the battering headwind, he finished first in 2 hours 50 minutes. The sports reporter for the *Hawaii Tribune-Herald* was curious to find out more about this unknown kid who'd erupted from nowhere and caught race

officials napping, but by the time the reporter got to the awards area, he'd disappeared.

'Who was that?' the reporter asked.

Race officials shrugged. His name and age were on the race entry, but otherwise, he was a mystery. 'No idea,' they said. 'The guy's a ghost.'

The name stuck. For the rest of that year, the Ghost kept winning races all over Hawaii. He broke the course record in one 50k, beating everyone including the relay teams, and was gone before most of the runners-up trickled in. Not that he wasn't a friendly ghost. Everyone who had a chance to chat with the guy said he was a total Casper, sweet as could be. It's just that he was always in a hurry to grab breakfast or go surfing, and cared so little about results that he had no idea he'd won seven races in a row until a competitor told him.

By late 2010, though, more and more Hawaii runners were getting this nagging feeling they'd seen the Ghost before. They went home and searched their bookshelves.

There he was, right on the cover of *Born to Run*: Billy 'Bonehead' Barnett.

Billy had come to Hawaii to visit his brother in the Navy and liked it so much that, somehow, he persuaded the owner of a luxury bed-and-breakfast who was looking for an experienced innkeeper to hire the Bonehead instead. Setting Billy loose in Hawaii was like releasing a pet dragon back into the wild. He turned heads wherever he went, and he went everywhere. Billy surfed when he wasn't running, and ran when he wasn't surfing, logging 120 miles a week on trails he'd never seen before and jumping into every rando race from road 5ks to backcountry ultras.

That same year, I was visiting Oahu when Billy flew over from the Big Island to meet me for a run. I was waiting at the trailhead when a car pulled up and Billy tumbled out, bare-chested and trailed by a cloud of smoke. He waved goodbye to the new stoner friends who'd picked him up hitchhiking from the airport, then chased after the car to retrieve his luggage: a T-shirt he'd left on the back seat.

We had a blast together, running an ancient trail leading down the mountain to a waterfall. The route was about ten miles for humans and twenty for pet dragons, because Billy spent as much time charging off to explore stray paths and climb tropical fruit trees as he did on trail. We were starving by the time we popped out of the woods, so my wife and kids picked us up and took us straight out to eat. Even though Billy's legs were caked with mud and he was wearing the same sweaty tee that had been tucked into the

back of his shorts all afternoon, he sent an electric charge through the restaurant that I had only seen once before: when Jake Gyllenhaal suddenly popped into a coffee shop in Leadville, Colorado, at five in the morning. Waitresses who had nothing to do with our table kept filling Billy's water and triple-checking his food was okay. Even my daughters noticed the unusual amount of attention our table was receiving, and they were in elementary school, but the Ghost himself was oblivious to the raw hot-guy magnetism he was projecting. When I dropped him at the airport the next morning for his flight home, his legs and tee were still streaked with mud; he'd declined the offer of a shower and fresh shirt as not worth the trouble.

For the next ten years, Billy lived the Ghost life: running huge miles, surfing monster waves, so content to go his own way that even soap was too much of a social burden. His romance with Jenn Shelton was over but they remained each other's spirit animals. Jenn seemed determined to one-up Billy by taking the Ghost life international: she guided river expeditions in Oregon before heading to Texas to become Lance Armstrong's running buddy, then moved to Italy to try ski-mountaineering but shattered her leg, recovering her strength on a fishing boat in the Bering Sea until she had a baby in Utah and moved to Alaska to homestead. Because, of course.

Billy, meanwhile, remained on the Big Island and got a master's in special education so he could teach emotionally challenged youngsters. It turned out to be the perfect

Alyx Barnett and baby Cosmo cheer Billy to a third-place finish in the 2021 Honolulu Marathon.

occupation for a guy who wakes up each morning with his nose in the air for the next adventure. Every day in the classroom is a new test of his stamina; every student outburst is a fresh reminder that the secret of strength is staying cool; and every afternoon by 3:01, he's free to blast out the door and into the mountains.

Until suddenly, the Ghost's solo life came to an end: in 2019, Billy met Alyx Luck, the only woman on the planet who could out-Jenn Jenn Shelton.

Alyx began her coaching career while serving three years in a maximum security women's prison after road-tripping across Wyoming with a friend who'd stolen a bunch of credit cards. Alyx didn't think it was fair that the men's penitentiary had a better gym than the women's, so after she persuaded the warden to beef up their equipment, she began teaching some of her fellow inmates how to train. Her dad was a track coach and Alyx herself had been a rugby player and national champion endurance equestrian as a youngster, so she knew her way around a weight room. When Alyx was released, she still owed a fortune in restitution. The best financial option for an ex-con, she found, was prison muscle.

'I was waitressing and bartending and working at two gyms, and when someone offered me a thousand bucks for an MMA fight, I jumped,' Alyx says. 'I loved it! Really fun. The

second I got off parole, I left Wyoming and began fighting all over the country.' Alyx battled her way into King of the Cage matches, but after a while, she noticed an unsettling trend among her fellow fighters: a lot of them were going back to prison. 'They were dealing drugs, living the drama life. I could see where this would end. So I got out.'

With her savings, Alyx moved to California and opened her own gym. She became a triathlete … then a professional bodybuilder … then a magazine-cover fitness model, absorbing a wealth of training knowledge along the way. The one goal she didn't achieve was dodging drama: as an Instagram influencer with 400,000 followers, she became embroiled in a messy fight when she was accused of cutting the course at Decaman USA, a race to complete ten consecutive Ironman triathlons in ten days. Around the same time, she decided the best way to end her marriage to a Marine-turned-fitness-model was to disappear: she secretly packed a bag, told her husband she was off to a race, and snuck off to Oman to figure out her next move.

Which brought her face to face, and lip to lip, with the Ghost. While hiding out from her soon-to-be-ex, Alyx reached out online to Billy for advice about a Big Island trail race she was considering. Emails grew into phone calls, and those phone calls ended with a dare: 'If you like what you see,' Alyx told Billy when he offered to pick her up at the airport, 'kiss me.'

And thus, two solitary satellites collided with a bang.

Billy, who'd made the Ghost life his calling, fell in love with Alyx, who'd made it her business. Few sports are more isolating than ultrarunning and surfing, which demand self-reliance and endless hours alone, and Alyx had found them. Triathlon may seem like the ultimate time hog, but bodybuilding is literally a trophy system for selfishness; you only triumph if you are thinking about yourself all the time. The second you stop inspecting your body in the mirror and obsessing over your hourly calorie intake, you're settling for second place. 'It requires you to focus on your eating and diet to flawless perfection,' Alyx says. 'You can't make a mistake.'

But by the time she met Billy, Alyx sensed her life needed another course-correction. She'd gotten into the fitness industry as a necessity after her release from prison, but after a decade as both coach and competitor, she'd grown to despise it. 'I was getting a lot of magazine traction as a fitness model, and it was all so destructive,' she says. 'People are being told they should look like us, and meanwhile I'm watching these models snort coke and inject steroids so they can sell a 10-Minute Booty Builder.'

Her career was on the rise, but she suspected it led off a cliff. 'I was the best I ever looked, but I had to take the escalator because walking a flight of stairs was too painful,' Alyx recalls. 'My joints hurt so much I was crying. And that's the body image that's on magazine covers.'

Already, she'd begun studying healthy eating and natural fitness as a way to guide her coaching clients away from extremes and into an approach that valued plenty of rest and daily well-being assessments ('Forget how you look. How do you feel?'). Even though the timing was ridiculous, Alyx decided the moment had come to commit to her own advice: she received her online doctorate in naturopathy and nutrition in the same week she was appearing onstage in Las Vegas at the Arnold Fitness Expo, a showcase honouring the Emperor of Anabolic Excess.

Living with Billy in Hawaii, Alyx threw herself into the ultrarunning life. She completed the notorious HURT 100, a five-loop ass-whupping on Oahu's rainforesty Mount Tantalus, and created her own Hawaii Mountain Running race series on the Big Island. Together, Alyx and Billy were training smart, eating clean, and running their best.

Or so they thought – until, in 2021, they made the greatest performance discovery of their lives: they had a baby.

Billy's 120-mile weeks came to a screeching halt. Alyx's strength and stamina days were replaced by, first, a substantial pre-birth slowdown, and then a gradual postnatal recovery for both her and her newborn. Even when Cosmo was old enough for a stroller, their walks were only as long as his naps. 'I'd do one-mile loops around the house to see how Cosmo was coping,' Billy says. 'You learn pretty fast to let go of that desired outcome. If I head out and he's crying, we turn around.'

Because Alyx had Cosmo all day while Billy was teaching, his afternoon runs became her first free time of the day. 'My life-hack for running with a jog stroller,' Alyx says, 'is to get my spouse used to it.' Consequently, all of Billy's training was tailored to his baby's moods: if Cosmo was content, Billy went long. If Cosmo wasn't feeling it, they played on the floor instead. One day a week, Billy did a blazing hard run on his own. The other six were all gentle baby jogs.

Billy's mileage plummeted from twenty miles a day to twenty-five miles a week, and remained there for seven months until, a few days before the Honolulu Marathon, he decided to hop in just for kicks. At age thirty-seven, with no build-up, no prep and no taper, Billy ripped out the fastest marathon of his life, chopping a full three minutes off his personal best to finish third overall in 2:36:48.

'I had no idea I could run a PR, especially in a healthy way,' Billy told me afterwards, still slightly dazed by the experience. 'You only associate personal records with the razor's edge of injury, but I was totally relaxed. My only goal all year was to spend as much time as possible with Cosmo and Alyx.'

One month later, Alyx suddenly discovered she'd been granted a waiting-list entry for the HURT 100, giving her all of two weeks to prepare for a hundred-mile trail race. She shrugged, kissed Billy and Cosmo goodbye, and *clobbered* it. Alyx beat not only her own personal best but also Billy's, taking two hours off her previous record and forty-five minutes off the mark that Billy had set seven years earlier at the peak of his Ghost-racing prime.

'I didn't know where my body was at so I decided, *Hey, just be in the moment*. It was a beautiful day and I got to spend solo time with my friend Anna,' Alyx recalls. 'From now till the end of time, I can also say I beat Billy Barnett. It just takes a hundred miles to get there.'

So what's the secret? How did two extremely experienced athletes turn their worst year of training into the best races of their lives?

They found a performance-enhancing substance, of course. And it was lying in the crib.

Eric grasped it right away. 'Getting better looks different than most people think,' he said. We've been sold on this mindset that running is a solitary pursuit, but that's a very modern – and unnatural – concept. And as usual, we pay a price every time we think we can outfox Mother Nature.

Humans are the world's greatest team players. That's how we've rolled since the dawn of time, and it's worked out beautifully. For millions of years, we tackled every job as a team. We hunted together, hauled nets and worked fields and built homes together. Think of an Amish barn raising, and you're not just looking at your past: you're seeing your DNA in its natural habitat. For millions of years, no one would bend their head to a job without a partner to watch their back, and no parent would leave their children behind with predators afoot. Humans alone were prey; humans united were an unstoppable force.

We broke through as a species the day we became running buddies. That was our superpower: our ability to head off across the savannah with no natural weapons except our ability to run any creature alive into heat exhaustion. You couldn't do it alone, of course. You needed savvy old-timers who could read tracks at a glance, followed by a band of men and women in their physical prime who could surge ahead and seal the deal, trailed by youngsters at their heels who were learning the craft. Only a diverse and well-coordinated team had any chance of wearing down a healthy antelope.

Solidarity was survival. We ran like crazy and stuck together, because that's all we had going for us. Which means, topsy-turvy as it sounds, sharing your run may be the best selfish move you'll ever make.

> **" ALL GREAT RUNNING CULTURES, FROM NATIVE AMERICAN TRIBES TO FINNISH TRACK STARS, BUILT THEIR MIGHT BY MIMICKING HUNTING PACKS. "**

Sports scientists have been waving this flag for so long, they're getting a little pissy about it. 'Academics in interdisciplinary fields have known about these findings for decades,' complained a 2019 study about group exercise by the American College of Sports Medicine, 'but this work and its implications have only recently begun to trickle into the discussions of major health organizations.'

Personally, my favourite in the literature is a 2015 study which took a bunch of hard-drinking, overweight bar-stool soccer fans in the UK and somehow persuaded them to temporarily trade their pints for weights. *Football Fans in Training* 'explicitly targeted middle-aged men who were overweight or obese and at high risk of ill health'. The Fans were asked to work out together only one day a week for three months, after which they could either stick together as a team or ditch it and go off on their own. At the end of a year, researchers found that the Fans not only largely maintained their team workouts, but 'demonstrated significantly greater weight loss' than a control group. By making them a team, it took just twelve days to transform guys who'd never do a workout into guys who'd never miss one.

By every conceivable marker – speed, stamina, personal satisfaction, longevity, consistency, you name it – people who sweat together, soar together. All great running cultures, from Native American tribes to Finnish track stars, built their might by mimicking hunting packs. Rarámuri ball games are as close as you can get to a hunt without an actual deer, while elite Kenyan distance runners are such believers in family-style workouts that even after they've broken through as superstars, they continue training in communal camps.

Today, Olympians no longer tremble at the names Paavo Nurmi and Hannes Kolehmainen, but back in the early 1900s they were absolute man-eaters, leading a small army of Finnish runners who dominated every middle- and distance-running event at the Games for more than a decade. And the Flying Finns' secret weapon?

Picnics.

During those long Scandinavian winters, Paavo and his pals would stuff their backpacks with fish pies and sausages and head into the forest for all-day hikes. They'd huck up hills, have themselves a big ol' lunch and a nap, then trudge back out again, often covering thirty miles. Their pace was brisk but comradely, and often for a change they'd strap on cross-country skis. Come racing season, the Finns had built not only a formidable endurance base, but a shared muscle memory of cadence and form which instinctively kicked in whenever late-race fatigue clouded their minds.

Their bodies learned from each other. The first time I experienced the same sensation was the morning when Caballo Blanco took me on that life-changing run across a high mesa in the Copper Canyons. Without even trying, I felt my back straighten and my stride shorten to match his. Later, I got to watch it unfold in front of my eyes when Barefoot Ted taught a barefoot running class in Palo Alto. About twenty or so runners were lined up on either side of Ted as they trotted back and forth across a city park. The two runners closest to Ted immediately mirrored his form … and then the two runners next to them picked it up … and onwards through the ranks, until the entire group was running identically. Ted, for once, didn't even say a word.

Only much later did I realise that Caballo had been feeding off that same body-to-body energy since he arrived in the Copper Canyons. It was the reason he'd started his ultramarathon in the first place. As a newcomer, he'd befriended only a handful of Rarámuri runners when he persuaded them to hike through the mountains with him to Urique and run back again. Caballo always described this event as a 'race', so I took it at face value and assumed he meant it the same way we do: me vs. you, *mano a mano*, each runner out for himself as he burrows through his own private pain tunnel. But then I thought about the way Caballo transferred the skills he'd learned to me, using his own body as a silent teaching tool, and I came to understand that to him – and to the Rarámuri – racing is

the Great Uniter, not a divider. It's the opportunity to spend hours and hours side by side with someone as skilled as you or better, the two or three or ten of you harmonising your feet and lungs to that time-tested rhythm.

'The reason we race isn't so much to beat each other, but to be with each other,' is how I put it in *Born to Run*, and it's become the most quoted passage in the book. It's turned up on inspirational posters and daily mileage calendars, and every year during marathon season, it's blasted out by the world's major races.

By necessity, many of our runs these days are solitary. But the opportunities are out there. Run with a shelter dog. Run with your spouse. Create an opportunity for a friend who's nervous about running. Grow your hunting pack. And you'll grow along with it.

Okay. But does any of that explain why Billy and Alyx ran so crazy fast on newborn-parent sleep and a fraction of their usual mileage?

Well, there's the raw physics: pushing a baby adds forty-plus pounds of resistance in both push and pull form, depending on whether they're using the stroller or tow cart that day, so they were subtly getting stronger.

And the biomechanics: running with a jog stroller is a self-correcting running-form instructor, because it rewards a straight back, squared hips, steady cadence and short, consistent stride. Pushing (or pulling) a stroller teaches you to pitter-pat your feet and lead with your core.

And the physiology: run too slow with a stroller and it gets heavy; too fast, and you lose control. You naturally click into a flow state you can sustain for miles, and whenever you wobble, stroller action quickly snaps you back to attention.

Any and all of those factors could have contributed to Billy and Alyx's breakthroughs, but that's not what either of them said. They're both experts on their own bodies and highly educated in exercise science (it was Billy's college major and remains Alyx's life work, after all). But when I asked them separately for their own theories, they answered like this:

Alyx: 'Maybe we raced so well because we just didn't care.'

Billy: 'Our only priority that year was being together.'

12.1
MASTERING YOUR BABY JOGGER

Eric was working Ellen Ortis hard – 'elite-level, I mean *intense*,' Ellen says – when she discovered she was pregnant. With nine fast marathons under her belt and a Boston qualifier just within reach, she had to make the not-so-easy transition from pushing her own body to pushing another one.

Note: Most doctors recommend waiting until your baby has the neck strength to support their own head at about six months before beginning jogging with a stroller. But as Whitney Heins, chief blogger for 'The Mother Runners', points out, many parents start sooner by using a stroller with a car seat attachment which supports the baby's neck and allows them to face you.

Make sure to choose a stroller designed specifically for running. Walk strollers tend to be more top-heavy and less suited for moving at speed. Quality jog strollers are expensive (expect to pay about $500), but that's what friends are for: all of your running buddies with kids probably have a great one in the basement you can borrow while you decide what you want.

Walking Warm-ups: During her pregnancy, Ellen discovered a long walk before running helped her changing body adjust to its surroundings. 'Dehydration is the number-one no-no in pregnancy,' she points out, so the extended walks allowed her to drink up and check in with herself. 'You have to listen to your body more than in any other season of your life.' After giving birth, Ellen relied on the routine for her recovery. 'If I feel good after the first mile, I try running a couple hundred metres or so to test my body. If it's cooperative, I keep going until I feel my heart rate getting higher. Then I walk and do spontaneous intervals based a hundred per cent on feel. If my body is not cooperating, I keep walking and try again at mile two. If it's a no-go at mile two, I don't push it.'

Get a Bike Bell: The sooner you can alert runners and walkers ahead of you that you're about to pass, the less likely they'll be startled and accidentally scare your baby. A little ding-a-ling helps everybody.

Get the Car Seat Attachment, Too: 'Totally worth it,' Ellen promises. 'A running mom is ready to get back at it, or at least start walking, well before babies can support themselves sitting up at around six months.' The car seat attachment gets the two of you out the door for gentle build-ups as you both get used to the stroller.

Put It on Paper: Ellen's husband knew that juggling his pick-up basketball games with Ellen's runs would take diplomacy, so before baby McCauley arrived, they agreed on a schedule. 'Three times a week I pump breast milk and he takes care of Mac while I run. Twice a week I have the stroller and use those for my forty-five-minute runs.'

The Three Best Friends You'll Hate: Meet your frenemies Take, It & Slow. If you're breastfeeding *and* training, you're putting a muscular and caloric demand on your body that constantly drains energy. 'It's a lot to give up after you worked a long time to get fast,' Ellen concedes. 'I was all *Boston Boston Boston* before Mac was born and had some near misses. But this is a long game, so my thing now is to come back healthy and patient.'

Focus on *Tall & Tap*: 'You've got this large object right in front of your knees when you're pushing the stroller, so it's tempting to lean forward and not get that full knee drive,' Ellen points out. 'So I tell myself to run tall and try to tap the back of the stroller with my knees. I never do, obviously, but it's a great model for good form.'

Virginia and Priscilla of Santa Mujeres: 'We show up in neighbourhoods that aren't used to seeing runners.'

12.2
BUILD YOUR PACK, SANTA MUJERES STYLE

'We're both very brave,' Priscilla Rojas says, 'but we've been followed, nearly hit by cars, strangers yell at us ...'

If you're a woman, this type of menace is the reality of stepping out the door for a run. If you're a person of colour, add suspicion and police harassment to the risks, and an even greater danger of being killed. 'As Black men, we had to wear masks long before Covid,' points out Jeff Davis, founder

of the Boston chapter of Black Men Run. 'Just by reason of my complexion, I'm seen as a threat. I can go on a run and I might not make it home for being Black on a Tuesday.'

As Americans, it's shameful that this national sickness hasn't been cured. But until it is, there is at least one small step you can take to help your fellow runners: join them.

'We wanted to create that safe space,' Priscilla says. 'So we formed the Santa Mujeres Running Club. Women create

THE TWO SHARED STORIES ABOUT THEIR RUNNING ADVENTURES, AND WONDERED WHY THEY'D NEVER ASKED EACH OTHER FOR HELP.

friendships in the group, so no one ever has to run alone.'

They were also tapping into the newest surge in running. Big events are dwindling, and smaller, local groups are on the rise. 'The height of racing was ten years ago. People are now finding a greater sense of community and connection from running together, rather than racing,' says Iman Wilkerson, creator of the running database The Run Down. 'Lots of self-identifying groups are popping up. I'm familiar with being the only Black woman in a space, and if you don't see a reflection of yourself, you feel like an alien. That's why there's been a tremendous surge in affinity clubs from people who decided to meet that need on their own.'

Before Priscilla and Virginia Lucia Camacho launched Santa Mujeres, neither of them had belonged to a running club. They'd never even had a running buddy, which really bugs them when they think of all the miles they missed out on together.

'We were friends from the underground music scene,' Virginia recalls.

'The Kava Lounge, Roots Factory—' Priscilla adds.

'San Diego had amazing clubs. The Adrian Younge show! That's where we met.'

'Ten years ago,' Priscilla agrees. 'Such a great time in our lives—'

'Anyway,' Virginia snaps back to focus. 'I started running in 2013 for weight loss. Priscilla noticed and was really encouraging.'

It took Priscilla four more years to try it herself, but when she did, she was *beyond* all in: before she ran her first mile, she committed to thirty-nine. She signed up for the Triple Crown: three half-marathons in one year. She googled a training plan, and began slowly learning to run on her own.

'Carlsbad was the first race,' Priscilla says. 'I was out there by myself, my pace was like 14–15 minutes, but I kept doing my thing. I cried at the end, I couldn't believe I'd done it.' Three months later, La Jolla. 'So hilly but it turned out to be my best, and I'm like, "Man, I'm going to do this!"'

Priscilla was so excited, she called Virginia to tell her she ought to sign up as well. The two shared stories about their running adventures, and wondered why they'd never asked each other for help. How many of their friends were in the same boat: nervous about starting, and not realising an entire sisterhood was out there, waiting to be connected?

'For years I wanted to be in a club, but when I looked at them I didn't see myself,' Virginia says. 'Either they're not diverse, or require entry fees, or run too fast. We wanted a place where women, especially, would be comfortable.'

In August 2020, Santa Mujeres was born. All of two friends joined them for a jog around Balboa Park in San Diego. Since then, attendance has skyrocketed. On any given Thursday, up to fifty runners now crowd the park.

'We have strollers, kids, teenagers, older people. We have fathers coming out to meet their daughters. The dad lives on this side of town, the daughter on the other, so this is where they get together,' Virginia says.

'It's a space for allies, mothers and sisters and cousins,' Priscilla says. 'For everyone to feel comfortable.'

'All of our dreams are coming true,' Virginia says.

But it wasn't by luck. 'We did our homework,' Priscilla says. They made a lot of smart choices, and discovered all kinds of invisible details that can turn two friends with a dream into a grassroots powerhouse.

1) Shrink Your Target: 'In San Diego a lot of the running clubs are white, so Latina women might not feel as comfortable,' Virginia says. So the Mujeres deliberately aimed for a demo that was so small, they might end up with no members. Turns out, science was on their side. 'There seem to be some important caveats to understanding the utility of groups, particularly in exercise settings. That is, "not all exercise groups are equal",' recommends a 2019 University of British Columbia study. The No. 1 reason people join a group and consistently show up, it found, is 'self-categorization' – seeing faces that look like yours.

'We're both first-generation Americans – our parents are from Mexico – so we came up with a name in Spanish that represents us,' Priscilla says. 'With Latina women, we can do the Spanglish thing. Our new members tell friends, "You'll love it. They're just like you."'

2) Find Your Local Iman: When Iman Wilkerson moved to California from Chicago, she found all kinds of resources for runners but most half-hidden. 'If you didn't already know about a group run, you'd never find out it was happening,' she says. So she built The Run Down app to include a breathtaking amount of information: not just the names and locations of clubs and Meetups, but their overall vibe and average pace, with neighbourhood descriptions down to the granular level of water fountains and public bathrooms.

'Iman was key for our exposure,' says Virginia. 'I found The Run Down at the beginning of the pandemic. Everything was shut down, all the parks were closed, restrooms were closed. The Run Down is such an amazing tool. It even tells you where there are streetlights so it's safe.' As soon as the Mujeres launched, The Run Down spread the word. 'Because of Iman, people who were interested could find out all about us before they came,' Virginia says. 'That was huge.'

If The Run Down doesn't cover your city yet, make sure to be as visible as possible online. Don't just post happy pictures of smiling faces; be as descriptive of your group's goals and make-up as possible. In New Zealand, the WoRM (Wellington Running Meetup) group is almost raucous in its online postings of where they'll run that week, who's going to be there, and whether one runner will be bringing his mother's almond cake to share afterwards. In London, Charlie Dark's legendary Run Dem Crew not only organises runs, but dance parties, poetry slams and youth mentorships. The Crew has a group for every speed, so by checking its website, you'll know before you arrive if you'll be more comfortable with 'Party Pace', 'Hares' or 'Greyhounds'. The more you tell beginners in advance, the more likely they'll show up.

3) Your Club Is Not Your Club: 'You have to be not selfish,' Priscilla stresses. 'You're there to support the community and meet their needs. They're not there to meet yours. So

Iman Wilkerson preps to relay from LA to Las Vegas in The Speed Project 2022 with Team Lululemon.

even as you get better as a runner, you have to keep in mind what it was like when you began.'

So the Mujeres offer two distances each week – one mile and three miles – with female run leaders directing each group. They also have a No Woman Left Behind policy, so veteran Mujeres are always circling to make sure back-of-the-packers aren't alone. 'We learn everybody's name, encourage everyone to talk about their journey,' Virginia says. 'We have physical therapists we can recommend, and if we know you've got a long run planned, we connect you with ladies who might want to join you.'

'If everyone isn't laughing at the finish, we did something wrong,' Priscilla concludes. 'It hasn't happened yet.'

Iman takes the late-night leg through the streets of LA for Team Lululemon.

4) Celebrate Your Runners: The Mujeres learned a lot from Brogan Graham and Bojan Mandaric, the astonishingly innovative founders of the all-free, all-welcome, always-happening-even-in-a-freaking-typhoon November Project (NP). Brogan and Bojan were a couple of ex-college rowers who decided one November to get back in shape, but instead of saying, 'See ya tomorrow for a run', they hocus-pocused up an air of intrigue by making it sound like they were secretly developing a nuclear bomb. They're both hard-chargers and off-the-charts competitive, but they remembered that in rowing, you're only as fast as your weakest oar. *Everyone* who shows up for a free NP workout is hugged and high-fived. They'll run through cheer tunnels, and be asked if they need water or a ride home. NP sells zero merch, but group leaders are happy to tag your T-shirt with spray paint and a stencil.

'We encourage our ladies to tell us their PRs,' Priscilla says. 'Share that joy! Bring your race medals! We let them know how proud we are.' And like NP, Santa Mujeres sell nothing: if you want a tee, you just have to show up five times.

'That's big deal to us. You've gifted us five hours of your time,' Priscilla adds. 'And they feel it – *Oh, I earned it!*'

5) Turn Out for Other Clubs: 'We do Unity runs all over town,' Virginia says. 'We're running best-friends with Black Men Run, Black Girls Run, all kinds of different groups and causes. We Run for Justice, celebrate Black women—'

'Unity runs mean *everything* to us,' Priscilla interjects. 'One reason being, it helps our members learn who else is out there. Other clubs run on different days, in different parts of town. You make these new friendships, new connections, so no one ever has to run alone.' Showing up alone for the first time at a new club can be intimidating, especially when you might be in the minority, but arriving with fourteen of your fellow Santa Mujeres is another story. 'Iman was a big part of that,' Virginia says. 'She makes sure everyone in town knows what's going on.'

In Boston, the Pioneers Run Crew decided it was time to create a marathon that truly celebrated the *city*, not the affluent suburbs that surround it. So on the day before the 2022 Boston Marathon, the Pioneers held their own '26.2

True Marathon' on a course that travelled through inner-city neighbourhoods. Lining the streets to cheer them on were TrailblazHers, Black Men Run and Black Girls Run, all of them turning out to show their support, love and presence.

6) No Matter What, Show Up: Priscilla and Virginia were invited to the November Project Summit, where Brogan and Bojan every year share, for free, the secrets of how they grew their two-man winter workouts into a booming phenomenon that has spread to fifty-three cities in nine countries. Keeping it Free is important, as are Creating Rituals and Inventing Your Own Language. 'Had we been called the "November Project Running Club", it would not have grown,' Brogan says. 'The title and how confusing it is, I cannot turn to you on a corner and explain it easily, all I can say is, "You gotta check this out for yourself."'

But none of it ever would have worked if NP hadn't developed a pathological reputation for perfect attendance. 'We had no growth plan until the right people raised their hand,' Brogan says. 'When people say, "I want to start this in Austin", we say, "No, you don't. It's too hard." We need fifty-two weeks in a row.' And you can't just arrive; you have to *show up*. You have to be ready to lead, regardless of what's waiting for you at work or falling from the sky.

'Our consistency has been a huge factor,' says Virginia. 'We're surrounded by run clubs, but one thing we noticed is clubs cancel for different reasons. Maybe it's raining, maybe someone is sick. But we never cancelled a run in 2020. The community knows that no matter what, we'll be there.'

> **"** YOU MAKE THESE NEW FRIENDSHIPS, NEW CONNECTIONS, SO NO ONE EVER HAS TO RUN ALONE. **"**

CHAPTER 12 **FAMILY: THOSE WHO SWEAT TOGETHER SOAR TOGETHER**   **201**

12.3 AID STATION: 'TO THE PROFESSOR!'

In 2007, David April found out from the guy remodelling the basement of his North Philly rowhome* that while David was at work that day, his wife had packed up and moved out. David handled it ... not well.

With nearly all the furniture gone, the echoes in David's empty house pushed him to a near panic attack. He burst out the door and ran blindly, wildly, as far as he could. That got him to the corner of his street. It was only seventy yards, but those seventy yards were seventy more than he'd run in years. Maybe ever. After he collected himself and walked back home, David realised his mad dash had actually made him feel a little better.

David still wasn't completely sold on this running thing, until his friend, Eric, took him out for a jog one afternoon and told him about an obscure study by a little-known scientist in southern Spain. The way Eric understood it, the study found that beer was as healthy after a run as water.

Eric only mentioned it because at that moment, he and David happened to be passing a bar. The two friends immediately ended their run and ducked inside for a pitcher of personal experimentation. 'And it dawned on us that we didn't really know what beer to order,' David recalls. 'What did the study suggest? Was it a lager? Was it an ale? Is it one beer? Is it two beers? And we realised that the study left many more questions unanswered than it answered.'

No, it didn't. The questions were only unanswered because: a) Eric and David hadn't actually read the study; and b) if they had, they'd have found the answers smack on the first page in a handy English version, easily findable in

approximately nine seconds of internet searching.†

'This is bigger than us!' David insisted to Eric. 'We've got to share this with the world.'

Again: No, it wasn't. And no, they didn't. What eventually made it way, *way* bigger than Eric and David was one thing:

If it wasn't a party, David wasn't interested.

'That's what makes David special,' Eric shrugs.

'Well, if I'm gonna be a runner, why not make it fun?' David retorts.

Thus, in very Philadelphia fashion, a refusal to read became a beloved institution.

'Welcome to the Fishtown Beer Runners, Responsible Running and Drinking in the Name of Science!' David shouts from his rowhome stoop. Crowding the sidewalk and spilling halfway across the street is a mob which, on any given week, can range from a few dozen to a few hundred.

'Tonight we're heading to Tattooed Mom on South Street,' David continues. That's the routine: every Thursday at 7:00 pm, come hell or hellacious weather (and he's seen both), David picks a bar and everyone sets off running.

David and Eric could only convince two friends to join them for the first Beer Run, on 20 December 2007, which is about the turnout you'd expect on the shortest day in the coldest month in the last week before Christmas. Since that dismal debut, the Beer Runners grew into a club, then a village, and now an international community. There are more than 4,000 Beer Runners worldwide and nearly a hundred chapters, not to mention twelve Beer Runner marriages (including David's) and ten Beer Runner babies. Beer Runners were at David's side when he was diagnosed with kidney cancer. And they lost their freaking minds when he recovered and made his triumphant return to the stoop.

* Terraced house.
† In case you're wondering: the study called for sixty minutes of treadmill running, followed by 22 oz/650 ml of 'common lager' with 4.5 per cent alcohol content. In short: two Bud Lights.

> **HAPPINESS IS MEDICINE. AND ON COLD, WET WINTRY DAYS, DAVID APRIL HAD FOUND A WAY TO MAKE LOTS OF PEOPLE VERY HAPPY.**

Curiously, it was *non*-runners who first signed on for these five-ish-mile jaunts across Philadelphia. 'I never actually ran before in my life,' diehard Beer Runner Mike Xander would say. 'David started talking to me one night and I thought, "Well, I like *beer*. Maybe I'll grow to like running."'

'Bars thought we were idiots, running clubs didn't think we were real runners,' David adds. 'Someone always asks, *Is it serious? Is it for real?* I remember when our first marathoner joined and I was like, "Yes! We're real now!"'

A few Philly bars got on board as well, especially when they realised it wasn't bad business to let dozens of noisy, reeking runners through the door even when you discover they've hung their sweaty tees on an improvised clothesline outside the entrance.

'If you're new here, someone will spot you and stay with you,' David shouts from the top of the stoop, continuing his weekly greeting. 'Anyone new? Any new Beer Runners?'

A few hands go up. The crowd breaks into cheers, and an interesting shift occurs: while the hands are still in the air, seasoned Beer Runners push close and surround the newcomers like protective molecules.

'Just get to the bar,' David hollers. 'Walk, run, take a cab, no questions asked. At the bar, we'll do our traditional toast to The Professor. If you don't know who The Professor is—'

Actually, there was a good long stretch before the professor himself found out who The Professor was. But from the very beginning, David always ended the evening by climbing on a chair for that special tribute.

'In the tradition of the Fishtown Beer Runners—' he'd begin, stretching the term to include a ritual that had only been around as long as the milk in his fridge, '—who believe in responsible running and drinking in the interests of science, we pay our respects to the man who brought us together.'

He hoisted a glass. 'To The Professor!'

'TO THE PROFESSOOOOOORRR!' the Beer Runners roared back.

Eventually, a bewildered physician in Spain got a baffling email from the United States. Dr Manuel Castillo Garzon had been struggling to get even his own colleagues in the School of Medicine at the University of Granada to take his beer advocacy seriously, let alone the scientific community at large. And now, out of the blue, comes a fan letter from a stranger 4,000 miles away? Who says that every week, dozens of other strangers are toasting him as a hero?

'When David sent that email, he was like a child writing to Santa Claus,' Eric recalls. 'It blew my mind when the professor wrote back.'

But there was something about The Professor they didn't know. Beer was only a sub-category of his interests. Dr Castillo Garzon was more broadly fascinated by the nearly magical medicinal power of happiness. Did you know that happy people live up to seven years longer than unhappy people, and are *half as likely* to suffer cardiovascular disease? For many scientists, these facts are uncomfortable because they're based on moods, not medicine. But they are facts. And Dr Castillo Garzon is not one of those scientists.

For whatever reason, happiness works. Happiness is medicine. And on cold, wet wintry days, David April had found a way to make lots of people very happy.

That email from David made Dr Castillo Garzon pause. For the first time in his career, he doubted his own work. Not the data – the data was rock solid – but the meaning. He'd done the right math, but gotten the wrong answer. It finally hit him that of all the drinks he could have studied, beer was unique. It wasn't just a beverage. It was a sacrament. Beer, unlike anything else, is about friendship and fun. Wine is serious, champagne is victorious, but beer – beer alone is a party in a glass.

'I realised that this toast, if it is the reason people get together, run together, have fun together, then that is worth doing the research,' Dr Castillo Garzon would say. So of course, he didn't just reply to David; he invited him to Spain, and put him in front of a packed audience of academics, and urged the Beer Runner to explain to him, The Professor, what his own study was all about.

Because it really was bigger than David and Eric. And they did have to share it with the world. They didn't reinvent running, but they did find the source of its power.

12.4
RUNNING WITH DOGS

Most of the time, Luis Escobar goes through life in a bubble of love. Most days, he's the centre of gratitude and laughter, surrounded by kids he's inspired and runners he's helped. But this ain't one of those days. This is the day after he took a bunch of teenagers out running with a gang of pit bulls.

'Oh man, some people are *pissed*,' he said when I got wind of the backlash. 'You should see the Facebook comments: *This is a bloodbath waiting to happen! You're going to get those kids killed – AND those dogs!*'

Here's what happened. Besides managing his photography business and directing his own trail race series, Luis was also cross-country coach at St. Joseph High School in Santa Maria, California. Ordinarily, he's exactly the person you want guiding your kid. He's tough enough to be nicknamed 'Sheriff', yet so kind that when a boy with autism broke down in tears after being told he couldn't play football, Luis bought him a pair of running shoes and made him a beloved and respected member of his team.

But Luis always had one problem, and it's called August. Santa Maria is a furnace in summer. Motivating kids to show up for pre-season practice and tackle hill repeats under the blazing sun, even for the Sheriff, wasn't easy. Then he had a brainstorm: instead of practice, he'd bring the team to a rescue shelter to run with the dogs. The fuse was lit:

Penned-up animals.

Teens with questionable impulse control.

Zero training.

One chaperone.

Showtime.

For both personal and research reasons, I couldn't wait to hear what happened next. At that time, I was conducting my own questionable experiment in animal partnerships, and I hoped Luis's luck was better than mine. Thanks to a chance encounter in the Pennsylvania woods that summer, and my mistake of asking my imaginative nine-year-old what she wanted for her birthday, we'd ended up with a very sick donkey in our backyard. Our friend Tanya, an animal trainer, warned me that the only way to save this donkey's life was to give it a job, some kind of daily physical challenge it would embrace as a reason to enjoy movement again. Not being a gold miner or Biblical prophet, my best idea – or worst – was to make Sherman my running partner.

I had no clue what I was doing, so I threw out a wide net for help. What I pulled in was fascinating.

I spoke with Cesar Millan, the Dog Whisperer, and Alexandra Horowitz, the Barnard College cognitive science professor who literally wrote the books on canine behaviour. I became friends with Timianne Sebright, who trains riding zebras on her Michigan farm, and spent a bitterly cold night riding a dog sled through the northern Wisconsin darkness with husband-and-wife mushers Quince Mountain and Blair Braverman. Blair would stop the sled every once in a while to change the line-up, swapping the dogs around according to split-second behavioural signals that were invisible to me but screamingly obvious to Blair and Quince.

'Why is that one yodelling all the time?' I asked.

'That's Refried,' Blair replied. 'When everything is going right, she gets so happy, she can't stop singing.'

All those tiny intuitive messages that Blair, Timianne and Alexandra had learned to read were once a mother tongue for all of us. For most of human existence, animal partnerships weren't just useful; they were a matter of life and death. Our ancestors had to understand animals, instantly and intimately, or they'd have been wiped out.

Just for fun, Danielle Kinch often takes her friends' dogs out for runs.

The best friends we made, as a species, were the wolves we used to steal from. Our ancestors learned to lope along behind wolf packs, grabbing up the leftovers once the wolves had brought down their prey and gobbled their fill. And then one day, a breakthrough: the wolves accepted us as partners instead of thieves. Very likely, it was the wolves who made the first move in this new romance. Wolves are super curious, and their ability to scent human anxiety would allow them to sniff out the safest moment to approach us.

That was a moment that would define the future: our ancestors, crouching and uncertain, watching these alpha beasts edging towards them as they decided whether to attack or accept. The wariness on both sides gradually melted because wolves, better than any other creatures, really got us. They could grasp the way we think because their brains were pre-wired with perception skills similar to ours, something naturalists like Carl Safina call 'human-like social cognition'.

Once we became a team, we were fantastic. With canines at our side, we came to be masters of the universe; these new companions were our night watchmen, our GPS guides, our first-wave assault team. From then on, we couldn't make enough animal alliances. We persuaded horses and elephants to carry us into battle, and hawks and ferrets to kill rabbits and drop them at our feet. Wildcats became tame and protected our grain from rodents.

Why do you think cuddling a cat is so irresistible? That's your inner caveman speaking, telling you that as long as that kitty is purring, nothing is trying to kill you. Our prehistoric animal partners were extensions of our own eyes and ears, using their sharp night vision and long-range hearing to alert us to danger. Now, when a tabby curls up in your lap or even when you see a cartoon of Snoopy sleeping on his doghouse roof, you're nudged by a calming ancestral instinct that says *Relax – you're safe for now*.

The partnership even worked its way into our brain chemistry. Petting a dog for a few minutes, studies show, has the same effect as a sedative: your breathing will slow, your blood pressure will drop, and your muscles will relax. Heart attack survivors who own a dog are *twice* as likely to recover from a major coronary incident, and cancer patients with

> **" WHY DO YOU THINK CUDDLING A CAT IS SO IRRESISTIBLE? THAT'S YOUR INNER CAVEMAN SPEAKING, TELLING YOU THAT AS LONG AS THAT KITTY IS PURRING, NOTHING IS TRYING TO KILL YOU. "**

some animal contact are half as likely to suffer anxiety and depression during chemotherapy. The most heart-warming magic, in my eyes, occurs between pets and children with ADHD: the animals not only help the kids perform better in class, but make them calmer, happier, more attentive and better at self-expression. The best wonder drug on the market, apparently, is 100,000 years old and furry.

Why? No one really knows.

But do we have to? The real question isn't what we get from animals. It's what we lose without them. If the animal–human bond improves our lives in every way – if the sick get stronger, the traumatised feel safer, our children learn faster, our prisons become safer – then the reverse is also true: without animals, we're weaker. We're sicker. We're angrier, more violent, more afraid. We've taken ourselves back in time, back to those desperate days when humans were alone on the planet, peering at wolves and hawks and wildcats from a distance and wishing we could somehow connect.

Once we became allies, we had it good – until we began abandoning animals, and turned our backs on the best friendship we ever had.

In Philly, one guy was trying to make things right, one lost dog at a time.

A job transfer brought Guillermo Torres to the US from

Mexico in 2015 with only his little Corgi, Patas. As a materials planner for a credit-card company, Guillermo spent long days alone in front of a screen, scouring price lists and shipping schedules. He'd often speak to no one all day, and go home feeling homesick and depressed.

'But I had to change my disposition when I came through the door, because Patas was so excited to see me,' Guillermo says. 'I had to pretend to be happy, throw the ball for a while. Being happy for him would change my attitude for real.'

Here's the thing about Guillermo: he's such a good guy, he felt guilty about receiving all that Patas love. What had he done to deserve such kindness? 'So I thought, "Maybe I can pay it to someone else. There have to be other lonely people in this city, right? This happiness he's given me, another dog can give to someone else."'

Guillermo soon found Monster Milers, a group of Philadelphia volunteers who are trained to take shelter dogs on runs. Once he got the hang of it, Guillermo came up with a scheme which, if it weren't in the service of settling his debt with Patas, would be downright diabolical: he began showing up at big group runs around the city, always with a very adoptable dog in tow.

At first, Guillermo was worried that the pit bulls he was assigned might act up around strangers, but to his surprise, he found that the bigger the group, the better the dogs behaved. 'They're more focused,' he says. 'It's very interesting to see the change that comes over them. I've never had a problem.'

Even a chihuahua named Legs got his chance. 'I thought I'd have to carry him, but he was the best!' Guillermo laughs. 'He *scritch-scritch-scritched* down the sidewalk like a little chicken and did the whole four miles. He wanted to keep going.' Legs made such an impression that within two weeks, he was adopted. It began to dawn on Guillermo that it wasn't just the running that the dogs loved, but the running group.

'It can get crazy at times in the shelter, barking twenty-four-seven,' he explains. 'But when you take the dogs out with lots of people, they sense the social atmosphere and fit right in.'

As a sales strategy, the runs were foolproof. Every time Guillermo introduced a shelter dog to a running club, someone stepped up to adopt. 'It let people see how easy it can be for dogs to learn what to do, and how fun they are to run with,' he told me. 'I had one poor dog who wasn't adopted for a hundred and eighty days. He was blind and had some problems. But we kept coming out together, and a wonderful young woman from Temple University brought him home.'

By that point, Guillermo and his project were so attached that when the student moved to Arizona, Guillermo flew down one weekend just to make sure his old buddy was settling in okay.

So – to the extent that Luis Escobar had a plan at all, that was pretty much it: take the kids to the shelter, give everyone some cuddle time, then snap on some leashes and go. For both sides, the idea was an instant hit.

'I wasn't sure who was more excited, the kids or the dogs,' Luis told me. They got everyone matched up and off they went, a band of suddenly inspired cross-country runners surrounded by a yipping crew of chihuahuas, mutts and pit bulls. One pup named Fred was too tired to keep up, so 16-year-old Josh Menusa scooped him up in his arms. By that evening, Fred was a member of the Menusa family.

Luis caught a snippet on video of Josh cradling the dog in his arms and posted it online, mostly so the kids would have a memento of the day. Two days later, he was shocked to find the view count had crashed through 20 million.

'He was just this little dog shivering in a metal cage and a few days later he's like an international cult figure,' Luis says. His fellow coaches loved the idea and reached out to Luis for more information, and celebrity chef Rachael Ray even flew Luis to New York to put him on TV and present him with a donation for the team.

Then came the backlash. On Facebook and YouTube, the keyboard cowboys had a few things to say:

ARE YOU CRAZY? These animals are traumatised and unpredictable … What if one of them erupts? What if a kid trips and triggers a pile-on? What if …

Luis could have brushed aside these cranks, since thousands of other people and a celebrity chef were calling him a hero, except in the pit of his stomach, he suspected the cranks were right. 'I've got fifteen crazy kids and

fourteen crazy dogs,' he thought. 'That's a lot of crazy.'

Someone else agreed that Luis needed help: the Dog Whisperer himself, Cesar Millan. When Cesar saw Luis's video, he was both enchanted and horrified.

'Coach, you have a fantastic idea but you have no strategy,' Cesar told Luis and me after we arrived at his Dog Psychology Center in Santa Clarita, California. We'd come for two reasons: Luis loved the idea of spreading his teen–dog running programme to shelters around the country, but could it be done safely? And I was hoping that whatever Luis learned about troublesome dogs could also apply to a damaged donkey.

'So my run is potentially dangerous?' Luis asked.

'Super dangerous,' Cesar said. 'If two little chihuahuas begin to fight, every dog will respond. And they won't be coming to help the weaker one. It will be a pack attack.'

Cesar continued ticking off worst-case scenarios, recalling the video in remarkable detail. The group was too bunched, he said, which could make a dog feel threatened. The kids were letting the dogs strain ahead instead of following, and the 'energies' were all over the place: eager and cautious teenagers were randomly mixed and matched with anxious or assertive dogs.

By the time Cesar was done, it seemed a miracle that the run hadn't ended in a ball of fangs and flying fur. That kind of analysis, he explained, is the real secret of his success.

It's been that way ever since he was a youngster in Mexico, where he was known as *El Perrero* – the Dog Boy – for his knack at taming neighbourhood strays. After he crawled through a hole in the border fence and sneaked into the United States as a 21-year-old, Cesar stayed alive in Los Angeles by knocking on doors and asking to walk dogs.

'I walked from eight in the morning till nine at night, and since I had no papers I charged very little money, just ten dollars each,' he told us. Desperately poor, he'd string together a pack of up to ten dogs, which caught the eye of a roving photographer who made the penniless Perrero a star.

'The *LA Times* ran a story about me on Sunday,' Cesar said. 'By Monday, TV producers were lining up to meet me.' Since then, he's become famous for teaching celebrities like Oprah Winfrey, Tony Robbins, Deepak Chopra, Jerry Seinfeld and even John Grogan of *Marley & Me* why they can command the respect and adoration of millions yet not the hearts and minds of their own pets.

Perhaps our worst sin as pet owners, Cesar believes, is turning naturally communal canines into solitary creatures. We pluck them from litters, then raise them alone in a house full of humans with no one to teach them how to be dogs. Often the first step for changing dangerous behaviour, Cesar believes, is to simply pair dogs so one learns how to act from the other.

'Come on, Coach!' Cesar invited Luis. 'Time for me to coach you.'

He asked an assistant to assemble his own pack, and handed Luis the leashes of eight dogs of varying breeds and sizes. But after we'd walked only a few yards, Cesar took the dogs back. 'You're too anxious,' he said.

Cesar handed the leashes to my daughter Sophie, who's never owned a dog. He gave her a few pointers (head up, arms relaxed, stay in front, walk with purpose), and we began climbing a steep dirt trail. The dogs followed quietly until Sophie glanced back and pulled the leashes a little tauter. Immediately, the dogs began scattering.

'Align yourself, sweetheart,' Cesar said. Sophie straightened her back and lowered her arms. The dogs snapped back into formation. 'You saw how a little girl did it better than you?' Cesar said to Luis. 'They're following the pack leader.'

We sat in the shade near a little garden waterfall Cesar had built for his deceased beloved pit bull, Daddy, while he sketched a plan for turning Luis's 'crazy kids' into pack leaders. As he spoke, it reminded me of something I'd been told by Alexandra Horowitz, the canine psychology expert.

'All creatures have a biological imperative: *The sun is up, so how do I fill my day?*' Alexandra said. 'By domesticating animals, we can remove their evolutionary purpose, and

> **❝ SOMEONE ELSE AGREED THAT LUIS NEEDED HELP: THE DOG WHISPERER HIMSELF, CESAR MILLAN. WHEN CESAR SAW LUIS'S VIDEO, HE WAS BOTH ENCHANTED AND HORRIFIED. ❞**

that can lead to problems.' No surprise if you've ever arrived home to discover your Springer Spaniel has stalked and eaten your dress shoes.

'The differences between us are trivial compared to the similarities,' Alexandra pointed out. So if you and I are hungry for a challenge, for some task that feels urgent and perfectly suited to our skills, why wouldn't every other creature? 'The best situation is to find a coordination of purposes.'

And personalities, Cesar was advising. First, he suggested, start with just a few teens at a time. Pick the quietly confident ones, like Josh, and match them with dogs that are not too shy, not too eager. Start with a brisk walk, eyes forward, and keep a good distance apart.

'There's only one language in the animal kingdom, and that's energy,' Cesar said. That's why you need to get your own mood in order before you begin: whatever you're feeling travels down the leash. Make sure to lead with purpose and leave the bush-sniffing for later, Cesar stressed: the walk should feel like work, not a wander.

'What you're doing is really important,' he said. 'You just have to do it right.'

12.5
DOG RUNNING
BEST PRACTICES

Darwin had a neighbour, Sir John Lubbock, who was less interested in the origins of species and more about what they could do right here, right now. After capturing a wasp in the Pyrenees, Sir John taught it to eat from his hand, and the two lived a happy life together as master and pet until the wasp passed away at the ripe old age of nine months.

Next, Sir John decided to teach his black terrier, Van, how to read. It wasn't easy; it took Sir John all of ten days to pull it off. He invited friends over to verify that when Sir John said 'Food' or 'Bone', Van would trot across the room, search a row of notecards, and fetch the right one back in his mouth. The real showstopper came when Sir John and his buds settled into conversation and forgot about Van until he interrupted, presenting the 'Water' card to indicate he was thirsty.

Van wasn't perfect. He didn't always grab the right card and, Sir John freely conceded, he couldn't do math or identify colours for crap. But that's okay, because Sir John only really cared about language; he wanted his dog to *communicate*. Van was living proof that our 10,000-year investment in creating the only man-made species had paid off. Since the Stone Age, dogs have been carefully selected and bred to do one thing and one thing alone: whatever we say.

So don't worry! No matter how feisty your pup is right now, take courage from Van, and Patas, and Legs the Cheery Chihuahua. Every genome in your dog's DNA is primed and ready to take your commands. He or she will never file your taxes or pick the right drapes, but when it comes to listening and obeying, that's their true calling. Put in the time and follow these tips, and you'll never find a better running buddy.

1) Remember the 3/3/3 Rule: Any time you bring a new dog into your home, it's arriving on an alien planet full of bewildering smells, sights and invisible dangers. This may not be the same dog you picked out because it was frisking around so happily at its original home. So as the pooch settles in, expect to see this timeline:

- **3 days on edge:** nervous, withdrawn, unresponsive, testing boundaries.
- **3 weeks to thaw:** finding its favourite places in the home; showing more energy – which is when behavioural problems can emerge.
- **3 months to feel at home:** bonding, showing trust and kinship, prone to spontaneous play and affection.

2) Know Your Breed: Alaskan huskies, Blair says, 'are fast, hard-working, loyal, have tough feet, are good eaters, get along in packs, and LOVE TO PULL'. But although they're not as furry as their Siberian cousins, they can still heat up fast. That's why during the fall, Blair and Quince only train late at night – I'm talking midnight late – when the Wisconsin temperatures drop into the forties.

So before training your dog to run, find out what limitations it may have. Short-snouted breeds, like bulldogs and English Mastiffs, are going to have less air intake, and because dogs cool off by panting, this makes them prone to overheating. Your pup may turn out to be an absolute star, no matter the breed. Catra Corbett, the trail running 'Dirt Diva', regularly puts in long miles with her two dachshunds. But she's careful, always, to watch them for any hint of distress.

3) No Running Till It's Grown Up: Puppies are cute and wriggly because it takes up to a year for their growth plates in their bones to fuse, even longer for bigger breeds. To avoid harming their development, wait till they're one and a half or two years old before starting a running programme.

4) Harness Only, No Choke Chains: If you do your job, there's no reason your pup won't learn to move confidently and calmly by your side. Now that you're approaching your first running date, it's time to invest in a quality leash and harness. Marcus Rentie rigs out Batman the Adventure Dog in Ruffwear gear, which is also the choice for top ultrarunners like Krissy Moehl and Cat Bradley. The Ruffwear Roamer is a dream set-up: it's got a leash and waist belt with a bungee tether, plus pockets for stashing pickup bags and treats.

5) Pre-game by Walking: Cesar Millan has gotten pushback from dog behaviourists who insist his 'Be the Pack Leader' approach is based on a mistaken notion that in the wild, wolf packs follow a single, dominant alpha. Cesar's response is, essentially, *Whatever, my way works*. He also points out that it's modelled on common, very observable canine behaviour: if pups aren't staying close behind the mother dog, she quickly makes sure they do.

'Leadership is not a bad thing,' Cesar says. 'It's not about punishment but about discipline, especially when you're coming from a calm, assertive energy point of view. Then dogs don't get afraid or nervous or tense. They get calm.'

So if you have a young dog, take advantage of that early development phase to practise these walking techniques:

- Pick a side and stick with it. If you're walking your dog on your left side, be consistent.
- If the dog pulls, stop walking. Wait a beat for the message to sink in that if the dog pulls ahead of you, you'll stop.
- Every few yards that the dog walks by your side, stop and reward it with a treat.
- For the first few walks, always stay in the same area to minimise distractions and strange smells.
- When you're ready to take your dog on its first runs, ease into it. Start by walking, then gradually add briskness. Continue to stop and dole out the treats if your dog stays by your side. Mix in bits of walking and jogging, until you see your dog has figured out what its job is.

6) Throw More Runners at the Problem: Our big breakthrough with Sherman, the donkey we were training to become my running partner, occurred when we gave up on coaching and just added more donkeys. We finally realised that Sherman loved following *anyone*: my daughters, a goat, our kitten, and especially other donkeys. Once my wife and our friend Zeke joined us with donkeys of their own, we were off to the races.

Long after, I got a chance to test that strategy when I was on a trail run in Charlotte, North Carolina, with Nathan Leehman, the Ultra Running Company owner. We came across a runner in the woods who was trying to run with her dog and getting nowhere. 'Can we try something?' I suggested. We positioned Nathan in front of the dog, the dog owner by its side, and me bringing up the rear. We started to run, and the dog instantly got it. For the entire mile or so back to the trailhead, the dog clicked along beautifully by its owner's side.

I'm sure that's why Guillermo's rescue-dog runs were always so successful: by surrounding his dogs with a big running club, the dog quickly got with the programme.

7) Haul Plenty of Water: When my friend Danielle brought three dogs along with us for a run on Oahu, I was surprised when she showed up with a hefty backpack. I found out why at our first rest break when she hauled out a big jug of water and collapsible dog bowls and made sure all her fellas got a good drink. Dogs can only vent heat by panting and lolling out their tongues, and that can cause them to dehydrate quickly. Whatever water you're bringing for yourself, either double it for your pup or plan your route around places where it can get a drink.

8) Check Their Feet: Even if you're in minimal shoes, you've still got a lot more protection between you and the hot asphalt than your dog does. On hot days and rocky trails, make sure to keep an eye on the terrain and check your pup's paws for sore spots or abrasions.

9) Treats Are Also Self-defence: Your dog may be a sweetheart, but you can't be sure about everyone else's. Always carry a few extra fistfuls of treats in your pouch in case you run into dogs who are out for trouble. *Drop* the treats on the ground (don't throw, because an arm swing can spook a dog into lunging), and while the other dog is distracted by the treats, make tracks outta there.

12.6
FAMILY: **ACTION ITEMS**

Mike's Block Run: Eric Orton bumped into an old high-school buddy at their thirtieth reunion who confided that as a single dad, he was overworked and out of shape and feeling down about life. So Eric said, 'Let's start super simple. Why don't you cut out sugar, and run around the block every evening? That's all. Just one block.' Eric then sent out a message to all their mutual friends, inviting them to join Mike for a one-block run every Wednesday. 'Everyone looks forward to the weekend. I wanted them to look forward to hump day,' Eric says. Mike's Block Run quickly caught fire. Mike began blogging about his progress, and made so many online friends that one follower in Australia detoured to New Jersey to run with Mike during a visit to the US. Since then, Mike has progressed from one block a day to fifty miles nonstop. When a friend was diagnosed with cancer, Mike's Block Run became Kevin's Run: every Wednesday, Mike and his pals ran to Kevin's house to spend time with him during his treatment. So if you don't belong to a running club, all you need is a friend in need and you're on your way.

Caballo Blanco leads the original 'Born to Run' *Más Locos* into the Copper Canyons.

Final Lesson from the White Horse: Run Free, Caballo

13

I was a little weirded out when I arrived for a speaking event at a public library in Agoura Hills, California, on a Thursday evening in March 2012, and a stranger came barrelling at me across the parking lot.

'Thank goodness you're here!' he said. 'Maria has been trying to reach you.'

I had no idea who, or what, he was talking about.

'Am I late or something?' I asked

'No, it's not that,' he said. 'We've been getting urgent calls from your friend Maria. She sounds very upset.'

Still no clue. My phone had died sometime between my arrival that morning at LAX and the long drive through the Los Angeles canyons, so I hadn't gotten any messages for a while. To the best of my recollection, I hadn't gotten an urgent call from anyone named Maria since a Greek journalist friend ran out of cilantro while cooking Thanksgiving dinner in 1998.

The stranger, who turned out to be the library director, hit REPLY and handed me his phone. The woman who answered immediately launched into a story about someone's dog and New Mexico, until I had to cut her off. 'I'm sorry,' I interrupted. 'Who is this?'

'Maria.'

'Maria …?'

'Mariposa.'

Suddenly, a little fist of fear gripped my stomach. I didn't know what was going on, but as soon as I heard that name, I knew who was involved and it had to be bad. Maria – 'La Mariposa' – was Micah True's girlfriend. We'd never spoken on the phone before, and the fact that she was not only calling me out of the blue, but had tracked down the cell number of a California library director meant something very, very strange was going on.

Two days earlier, Maria told me, Micah had set off for a

run in the Gila Wilderness, New Mexico, and hadn't been seen since. It was Thursday now, and I heard Maria's distress, but the panic-grip in my belly began to ease. After all, it was Caballo Blanco we were talking about, the wandering White Horse of Mexico's Copper Canyons. For decades now, the Horse had been roaming some of the trickiest and most inhospitable terrain in North America, and no matter what kind of trouble his restless eye got him into, his legs always got him back out again. If Caballo wasn't lost, he wouldn't know where he was.

In fact, he'd just gotten lost on the day I met him in 2005. He'd set off for an easy hike that morning from Creel, a Mexican town on the fringe of the canyons, but got sidetracked by a tasty trail, started running, and ended up bushwhacking the Copper Canyons outback until he finally got his bearings just before nightfall. 'I'm always getting lost and having to vertical-climb, water bottle between my teeth, buzzards circling overhead,' Caballo told me. 'It's a beautiful thing.'

That's been the story of his life, stretching from his discovery of running during his backroom fight-club days in the 1980s – the same era when a fellow-wanderer named Smitty found him roaming the Hawaiian rainforests and showed him a secret cave he could make his home – right up to the present, when he'd recently pissed off some bandit named Jorge down in the Copper Canyons and had to blaze a new route along the edge of a cliff to avoid him.

I knew that this time, Caballo must have gotten an urge to spend a few nights in the Gila cliff dwellings, or had strayed out of the wild and onto the highway and was hitchhiking back to the lodge at that very moment, or was behind bars after locking hard heads with a park ranger and was too stubborn to phone for help, and I was about to tell Maria so when she said:

'I just wish Guadajuko was with him.'

Uh-oh.

'He left him tied to a porch post.'

My heart sank. Guadajuko, the 'ghost dog', was a half-wild Mexican mutt that Caballo had adopted down in the canyons three years ago after rescuing him from a river. They'd been inseparable ever since. The last time I saw Caballo, in Boulder, Colorado, Guadajuko had a cast on

> " TEXTING WHILE HE DROVE, FIGHTING HIS WAY THROUGH RUSH-HOUR TRAFFIC, LUIS WAS STEERING WITH HIS KNEES WHILE COORDINATING AN ALL-POINTS BULLETIN WITH HIS THUMBS. "

his leg from getting clipped by a bus. Caballo was carrying him around like a baby, even into a chic brew pub where Guadajuko proceeded to snarl and try to snatch a burger out of Caballo's hand. No way Caballo would dither in the woods if Guadajuko was waiting for him.

'Have you talked to Luis?' I asked.

'Yes. He's waiting to hear from you.'

'What's that crazy guy up to now?' Luis shouted when I got him on the phone.

It was amazing and almost reassuring to hear Luis now sounding so calm and light-hearted, because his first reaction after talking to Maria, he told me, was to grab the keys of his wife's Chevy Tahoe, tell her, 'I'm going', and start barrelling south from Santa Barbara, California, on a 700-mile rescue mission. Texting while he drove, fighting his way through rush-hour traffic, Luis was steering with his knees while coordinating an all-points bulletin with his thumbs.

I calculated his drive time, and realised I'd have just enough time to give my talk and get to LAX to cancel my flight and dump my rental car. When Luis picked me up at the airport three hours later, two other volunteers were already in his truck and a third – beer-mile champ Pat Sweeney – was waiting for us to get him.

Soon, we had to pull Luis out of the driver's seat and stick him in the back, because his cell phone kept pinging all night with fresh offers of help. Kyle Skaggs – the Hardrock 100 record-holder who barely knew Micah – was already on the road from his farm in New Mexico. When we stopped around midnight to fill the tank somewhere in Arizona, it was free; a woman in Colorado had insisted on PayPal-ing us gas money.

'I keep thinking we'll burst in on him somewhere peaceful in the woods, and he'll give us that grin of his,' Luis said as we drove through the night. 'The one where you can tell he's thinking, "You're such a dumbass."'

But Luis was still anxious enough to keep his ear to his iPhone and his Tahoe hurtling down the highway and into the wilderness.

Ever since the *Born to Run* crew first met at an El Paso hotel and journeyed on for that race of a lifetime, we've yoyo-ed in and out of each other's lives, with Caballo often the string that held us together. Caballo and Guadajuko would shack up at Luis's house whenever they drifted through California, while Jenn, Billy, Barefoot Ted and I crewed for Luis at the Badwater ultra. Barefoot Ted and I became lifelong friends during a magical night when I paced him to the finish of the Leadville Trail 100 wearing a pair of homemade sandals he'd given me.

Earlier, Caballo had spent a week in Leadville with me and Eric Orton. We ran trails all day and told stories over beer and jalapeño pizza at night, seeing a warm and fun-loving side of Caballo that had been eclipsed during the chaos of the Copper Canyon race.

So it wasn't surprising we remained friends; the real shocker was the way Caballo was transformed almost overnight from a lifelong loner into the field marshal of an international army of online amigos. For decades, he'd lived like a wanted man; he'd bust his hump as a vagabond furniture mover for a few months in Boulder, then drop off the planet the second he'd saved enough for a year's frijoles. He'd disappear into the Guatemalan highlands or

> ❝ CABALLO WAS TRANSFORMED ALMOST OVERNIGHT FROM A LIFELONG LONER INTO THE FIELD MARSHAL OF AN INTERNATIONAL ARMY OF ONLINE AMIGOS. ❞

Mexican canyons, spending his days rattling around the hills and inside his own head. Until he was nearly sixty years old, Caballo split his time between a one-room hut in Rarámuri territory and a sleeping roll in the back of a pickup in Boulder. The Rarámuri were his ideal companions: they ran a lot, spoke little, and never said no to a brew.

But after *Born to Run*, Caballo was the man in demand. Suddenly, he was jetting off to speaking engagements in London and Stockholm and signing autographs at standing-room-only events. He became an accidental icon, and I loved the way it didn't soften his raw edges a bit. Minimalist movement? He couldn't care less, even though he'd been moving minimally for forty years and had adopted the Rarámuri taste for toe-freeing sandals long before the name FiveFingers was associated with anything besides shoplifters.

He remained searching and sceptical, sunny and surly, a true cowboy who picked his own name, went his own way, and was his own horse. When The North Face offered in 2007 to finance the Copper Canyon Ultramarathon he was struggling to keep alive with his own cash, Caballo turned them down, afraid his funky festival in the middle of nowhere would become a corporate-bannered monstrosity with its heart hollowed out by expo booths. His reply summarised his life and became his public identity: 'Run Free.'

But right when the rest of us were catching up to him, Caballo disappeared.

The more Search and Rescue (SAR) found out about his last known movements, the more bewildered they became.

Caballo left Mexico on 23 March, driving north in his old pickup towards Phoenix, Arizona, to see Maria. He'd stopped off along the way to visit friends and kick back a little at Gila Wilderness Lodge, a place he'd been many times. Caballo was overdue for some downtime; he'd just pulled off a masterpiece of a race, somehow managing logistics for a field of more than 400 Rarámuri and eighty-some American and international runners at the latest edition of the Ultra Maratón Caballo Blanco, beginning on 4 March. Afterwards, everyone headed home while Caballo spent the next two weeks barnstorming the canyons, making sure that the

sacks of corn the Rarámuri winners had earned as prizes made it to their villages.

On his first morning at the Gila Wilderness Lodge, Caballo set off on one of his epic, six-hour trail runs. The next day – Tuesday – he told his buddies at the lodge he only had time for a little twelve-mile leg-stretcher before hitting the road to Phoenix. Guadajuko's paws were sore from the day before, so Caballo left him tied to the porch and said he'd be back in a couple of hours.

SAR was certain he then ran three miles right down the centre of Route 15 towards the Gila Visitor Center, because drivers remembered swerving around him.

So, the good news: that left only three more miles before he would have turned around to finish his twelve-mile out-and-back.

And the bad: after scouring that three-mile perimeter by day with dogs, horseback patrols and helicopters, and by night with infrared heat-seeking surveillance planes, they'd turned up nothing.

'It's like your friend just vanished from the face of the earth,' a Gila Park volunteer told me. 'This is the most intense search I've ever seen, and we're not getting anything. Not even a scent.' While we were being briefed, one of the search directors paused to stare at my feet. I'd only planned to be in LA for two days, so the only shoes I had were a pair of Barefoot Ted's huaraches. 'Okay, I'm not allowed to see those,' he said. 'You should get going before I do.'

We grabbed light backpacks and water bottles and were assigned to a team. Two SAR veterans from Roswell, New Mexico, took me, Luis and Pat Sweeney. Kyle Skaggs was already out with a team that included Nick and Jamil Coury, trail running brothers from Arizona who have gone to Caballo's race every year since 2009. Our two teams would start from opposite directions and criss-cross in the middle, so we'd cover the same ten-mile loop twice and from both sides. We began scrabbling through gullies and juniper brush, hollering and yodelling as we climbed towards a mesa at 8,000 feet.

'CABAAAY-YOOOOEEE …'

'MICAH TRUUUUUUUEEEE …'

'Ca-BAAAAA-YOOO, you pain in the aaaaaaasssss! Where the hell are you?'

Now that fast legs like Sweeney, Skaggs and the Courys were on his trail, we were sure we'd find Caballo by dark. When we didn't, when we were trudging back defeated that evening, we were so baffled and dispirited that weird speculation didn't sound so weird any more. One searcher began wondering if a drug cartel had contracted a hit on

Caballo, planning it for his home turf to avoid detection. Barefoot Ted left me a message hinting that maybe it was no accident; after all, Gila was Geronimo's hideaway and Caballo always said he wanted to end his days Apache style with one final walk into the wilderness. Someone I'd never met emailed to remind me of the opening epigraph in *Born to Run*: 'The best runner leaves no tracks.'

Yeah, right; Luis wanted action, not melodrama. As soon as we reached base, he went in to see the search director. 'Look, you've got some of the best trail runners in the country right outside your door,' he said. 'They're an unbelievable resource. You ought to hear what they have to say.'

To his tremendous credit, the director grabbed a clipboard and was soon standing in a circle of ultrarunners, fielding suggestions.

'Did you take Caballo's dog out?' Luis asked.

'Yes.'

'Did you walk him, or run him?'

'We walked him. He got a scent, but it turned out he was tracking a deer.'

'That's because you walked him,' Luis said. 'Dogs behave differently when they're running. They're moving too fast to get distracted. If he's running, out of habit he'll go where Daddy went.'

'Okay,' the search director said. 'So how far could Micah go?'

'He had huge range,' Luis said. 'If he felt like it, he could turn twelve miles into thirty.'

So instead of walking a grid where Caballo might be, why not let us run the trails where he *had* to be? The Gila is so steep and scrabbly, Kyle and Pat Sweeney could cover more ground in a day than a horse. The search director promised he'd think it over, but by the next morning, Luis and Kyle had come up with plans of their own.

It was Saturday, and more of Caballo's friends and fans had arrived, bringing the number of volunteers at the pre-search briefing up to about fifty. Simon Donato, the Canadian geologist who'd helped search for the missing balloonist Steve Fossett, had come in from Calgary; with him were Caleb Wilson and Tim Pitts, two fellow ultrarunners he'd met at Caballo's race.

With that many searchers, Luis figured we could slip away without being noticed. He wanted to go back to the lodge, put a leash on Guadajuko, and do his best to mimic Caballo's running style to see where Guadajuko would lead him. Meanwhile, Kyle motioned for me and another trail runner to quietly follow him.

'They might ban us from the search after this,' someone pointed out.

'It's Day Five,' Kyle said. It was below freezing at night and scorching by day. Without warmth or water, Caballo might not have a Day Six.

Our little secret ops group set off shortly after daybreak on a twenty-mile loop that would climb Little Bear Canyon and circle back down along the river. Kyle could only envision two scenarios: either Caballo had taken a hard fall while heading for water, or he'd mis-stepped on a switchback and gone over the cliffs. Nothing else made sense. We started at a fast hike, then broke into a run, splitting into two-man teams whenever the trail forked, finding each other and regrouping with hollers and whistles.

By noon, we'd gone double the distance of Caballo's turnaround point and hadn't seen a thing: not a footprint, not a blood smear, not even a hidden trail or gully. We'd been going hard on a hot day, climbing steadily till we'd hit 8,000 feet, so we stopped to cool down and water up. We passed around bags of dates and nuts, resting in the thin shade of scrub junipers. We checked the sky, but no help there; it was too early in the spring for buzzards.

'So, how are the fresh kicks working out?' someone asked me. That morning, an SAR volunteer from Albuquerque had turned up with an extra pair of trail shoes in my none-too-common size 14, allowing me to swap out for the Barefoot Ted huaraches I'd worn the previous two days.

'A lot more shoe than I'm used to, but not bad,' I replied.

Looking back, that was The Moment. That's when I knew the search was over. We didn't ease up – we soon got back on the trail and kept beating the brush until daylight faded – but the adrenaline charge which had kept us hammering for three days had been subtly rechannelled from urgency into potency. No one said it, but we'd begun to enjoy the run, to the point where it felt less like a rescue and more like a tribute. I kept catching myself thinking, 'I never would have known these guys without Caballo. I never would have even attempted a run like this before I met him.'

We'd lost Caballo – we could feel it – but the Caballo-feeling was taking over.

Simon Donato and his friends must have felt it as well, because that evening, they did exactly what Caballo would have done. They'd finished their search assignment and it was getting dark, so the only smart play was to get into their sleeping bags, rest up, and avoid getting lost themselves.

But since Caballo had to be somewhere north – dead certain, no doubt about it – they went back out and headed south. Soon, they ran into Ray Molina, who'd known Caballo longer than any of us. Ray and his partners had gone even further in the wrong direction … and there, looking so peaceful, was Caballo, lying along the banks of a creek with his legs still in the water.

Ray immediately screamed '*MICAH!*', thinking he could wake him up. But it was far too late.

They built a fire, and spent one final night out in the wild with their friend. By early morning, SAR was able to get a horse – a white one – down into the canyon to carry Caballo's body out. His hands and knees were scuffed, making it appear he'd taken a fall while following the creek out of the woods. Donato wants people to know that.

'The creek would have led him back,' Donato said. 'He knew what he was doing.'

To this day, no one really knows what killed Caballo. The most credible theory I've heard is Chagas disease, a tropical parasitic infection that gradually weakens the heart. Caballo had told me about weird fainting spells he'd had over the years, and not long ago he'd felt so listless and feverish that he thought he'd contracted West Nile virus.

Both symptoms could indicate Chagas, and it's plausible that the stress of organising his race and all the hard, hot miles he'd put on his body were too much for his secretly withering heart. But just writing those words makes me feel pompous and stupid, because it's exactly the kind of thing that would make that cut-the-crap grin creep across Caballo's face.

'McOso, who cares how Geronimo died?' he'd say. 'Let's just talk about how he lived.'

So I will.

Micah True was a strong, smart, very tough man from the richest nation in history who decided to turn his back on all that and, instead, follow the example of the most peaceful, sharing people on the continent.

When he did, he set the wheels in motion for maybe the greatest revolution in running in our lifetime. He was bewildered – and outraged – that the rest of the world didn't see what was so gloriously obvious to him: the Rarámuri were custodians of an ancient skill that could make everyone on the planet stronger, happier, healthier and kinder.

But skill can't be bought. It can't be life-hacked or hurried. You can throw all the money and gear you want at a skill, and you'd be throwing it away. No wonder a rebel like Caballo loved running so much. If you were humble enough to go back to basics, and learn from the quietest teachers in the world, you could soar.

Micah True opened that door for me, and for everyone who's been inspired by *Born to Run*. That's why this book is dedicated to his memory. But there's a better way to honour his life:

Follow in his footsteps.

Run free.

Part 3:
THE 90-DAY RUN FREE PROGRAMME

Living the Caballo motto in the mountains of Hawaii.

14

The Plan

Once you cross this bridge, there's no turning back.
So if you come with me, you've got to take this vow.
Raise your right hand:

If I get hurt, lost or die,
it's my own damn fault.

—*Caballo's oath of adventure*

HOW TO EXECUTE
THE 90-DAY PROGRAMME

Download the 90-Day programme app by using your phone to scan the QR code at the end of the book. The training app will keep track of your progress, and automatically pull up each day's workout. You'll also find instructional videos and training tips from Coach Eric to remind you how all the Run Free skills are performed.

DAILY SEQUENCE:

- Make sure to do the skills in order. The strength and form exercises build on each other, and also serve as a warm-up for the run. The run always comes last.
- Every workout has a specific purpose, so do your best to stick with the weekly sequence. This will allow you to get rest when needed and progress steadily. If you miss a workout, it's best to just skip it and move on, keeping with the weekly sequential order.

DAILY RUNS:

- Each run is assigned by either time duration or interval sets. Be smart about this! Don't push up your miles until you feel ready. *Frequency* is our gold standard, so be patient. It's better to do a little less each day and come back strong the next.

CALCULATING YOUR 'BIG DEAL' DISTANCE:

- You'll be training your body to feel differences in cadence, pace and effort. The same holds true with distance. Instead of being assigned the same long run as everyone else, you'll customise your own ideal range. It's based on a simple calculation: What do you consider a Big Deal?
- Imagine your friend texts and asks, *Hey, up for 15 tomorrow?* What's your gut reaction? 'I'm in!' or 'Whoa, that's a big deal'? If you're used to a casual eight miles every Saturday with your buddies, bumping it to twelve is a Big Deal. If your longest race is a half-marathon, then twenty miles will feel like a lot.
- True, this is a very subjective measure that varies with your mood and current fitness – *but that's the point*. You don't build strength and self-awareness by forcing your body to meet a cookie-cutter standard. Your greatest gains in performance and confidence will come from mastering your internal odometer and dialling in your own ideal distance range.
- Every week, you'll determine your long run based on some percentage of your Big Deal distance.

RUN SPEED/INTENSITY:

- The One-Mile Test will allow you to calculate your 'gears', or personal training speeds.
- Everything you do is a customised approach based on *your* ability, so it's important to remain with these ranges.
- Remember, we're aiming to build a stronger foundation, so it may feel as if you're running faster or slower than you're used to. Embrace the change, because that is the first sign that you're expanding your fitness base.

TRAIL RUNNERS:

- Smooth roads are easier than trails, so naturally you're going to run more slowly in the woods. Therefore, don't worry about miles-per-minute pace. Instead, focus only on how each gear should feel.
- Keep that long-run effort feeling easy, hiking when necessary on hilly terrain.
- Running trails and mountains is great for strength, but not for generating speed. So it's best to do your Strength/Form runs on flat terrain, as well as some of your weekly long runs.

The 90-Day Run Free
Programme

Lenaiya Flowers and Stella Woy were surprised how much they enjoyed their first day of Run Free skill drills.

' = minutes   " = seconds   RI = rest interval

WEEK 1

WORKOUT	DAY 1	DAY 2	DAY 3	DAY 4	DAY 5	DAY 6	DAY 7
FOOD	Two-Week Test	Two-Week Test	Two-Week Test	Two-Week Test	Two-Week Test	Two-Week Test	Two-Week Test
FITNESS	2 Sets of Foot Core	OFF	1 Set of 100 Up Minor & 3 Sets of Wall Squat	2 Sets of Foot Core	OFF	1 Set of 100 Up Minor & 3 Sets of Wall Squat	2 Sets of Foot Core
FORM	Complete the Five-Minute Fix (p. 114) to emphasise your run form craft.	Running Logs Part 1	OFF	Running Logs Part 1	OFF	Running Logs Part 1 + 5 x 6–8 Skipping for Height	3 x 2' barefoot running in place to music playlist
FOCUS RUN	10–30' in Gear 1. Stay patient with your effort and keep good awareness to foot strike. This is strength training.	20–40' in Gear 2 with a focus on visualising running logs while running.	20–40' in Gear 2	OFF	10–30' in Gear 1. Stay patient with your effort and keep good awareness to foot strike. This is strength training.	Today's run distance/time should be 65% of your Big Deal. Gear 1–2 staying patient and keeping things feeling good. Train, Don't Strain.	OFF

WEEK 2

WORKOUT	DAY 8	DAY 9	DAY 10	DAY 11	DAY 12	DAY 13	DAY 14
FOOD	Two-Week Test	Two-Week Test	Two-Week Test	Two-Week Test	Two-Week Test	Two-Week Test	Two-Week Test
FITNESS	2 Sets of Foot Core	OFF	1 Set of 100 Up Minor & 3 Sets of Wall Squat	3 Sets of Foot Core	OFF	1 Set of 100 Up Minor & 3 Sets of Wall Squat	OFF
FORM	OFF	Running Logs Part 1 + 5 x 6–8 Skipping for Height	OFF	4 x 2' barefoot running in place to music playlist	OFF	OFF	Running Logs Part 1 + 5 x 6–8 Skipping for Height
FOCUS RUN	20–40' in Gear 1. Stay patient with your effort and keep good awareness to foot strike. This is strength training.	20–40' in Gear 2 effort with a focus on visualising running logs while running.	20–40' in Gear 2 effort + 5 x 30" accelerations building speed to Gear 7 by the end of each with 1' RI.	OFF	20–40' in Gear 1. Stay patient with your effort and keep good awareness to foot strike. This is strength training.	Today's run distance/time should be 70% of your Big Deal. Gear 1–2 staying patient and keeping things feeling good. Train, Don't Strain.	OFF

WEEK 3

WORKOUT	DAY 15	DAY 16	DAY 17	DAY 18	DAY 19	DAY 20	DAY 21
FITNESS	3 Sets of Foot Core	3 Sets of Leg Stiffeners	2 Sets of 100 Up Minor & 4 Sets of Wall Squat	3 Sets of Foot Core	OFF	1 Set of 100 Up Minor & 3 Sets of Wall Squat increasing reps	2 Sets of Foot Core
FORM	OFF	Running Logs Part 1 + 5 x 6–8 Skipping for Height	OFF	4 x 2' barefoot running in place to music playlist	5 x 30" Running in Place + 5 x 6–8 Skipping for Height	OFF	5 x 1' barefoot running in place to music playlist
FOCUS RUN	20–40' Strength/ Form running in Gear 1 with a focus on foot strike and cadence. Stay patient with your speed.	30' in Gear 2 + 5 x 30" in Gear 6 with 90" RI.	20–40' in Gear 2 with a focus on visualising running logs while running.	OFF	20–40' Strength/ Form running in Gear 1 with a focus on foot strike and cadence. Stay patient with your speed.	Today's run distance/time should be 75% of your Big Deal. Gear 1–2 staying patient and keeping things feeling good. Train, Don't Strain.	OFF

WEEK 4

WORKOUT	DAY 22	DAY 23	DAY 24	DAY 25	DAY 26	DAY 27	DAY 28
FITNESS	2 Sets of Foot Core. Increase challenge by adding more time/reps or with less balancing aid.	2–3 Sets of Leg Stiffeners + 3 Sets of Wall Squats	OFF	Complete Day Off. Remember, recovery is when you get stronger.	2 Sets of Foot Core	2 Sets of 100 Up Minor & 2 Sets of Wall Squat increasing reps	Complete Day Off. Remember, recovery is when you get stronger.
FORM	OFF	4 x 6–8 Skipping for Height. Focus on being more powerful.	Running Logs Part 2. Feel the force applied into the ground as logs get further apart.	OFF	Complete the Five-Minute Fix (p. 114) to emphasise your run form craft.	OFF	OFF
FOCUS RUN	20–40' Strength/ Form running in Gear 1 with a focus on foot strike and cadence. Stay patient with your speed.	30' in Gear 2 + 7 x 30" in Gear 6 with 90" RI.	20–40' in Gear 2 with a focus on feeling the force applied into the ground to run forwards.	OFF	30–50' in Gear 2 + 4–6 x 20" hill repeats with hands behind your head/elbows wide. 3–4 x 20" hill repeats with normal arms.	Today's run distance/time should be 50% of your Big Deal. Gear 1–2 staying patient and be OK with the reduced run today. Recovery is when you get stronger.	OFF

WEEK 5

WORKOUT	DAY 29	DAY 30	DAY 31	DAY 32	DAY 33	DAY 34	DAY 35
FITNESS	3 Sets of Foot Core + 2 Sets of Run Lunge	1 Set of 100 Up Major & 4 Sets of Leg Stiffeners	OFF	3 Sets of Wall Squats + 2 Sets of Run Lunge	3 Sets of Foot Core	OFF	3 Sets of Wall Squats + 2 Sets of Run Lunge
FORM	OFF	3 x 6–8 Skipping for Height + 2 Sets of Sticky Hops	OFF	OFF	3 x 3' barefoot running in place to music playlist	Running Logs Part 1 & 2	OFF
FOCUS RUN	30–50' in Gear 2. Stay patient with speed and focus on form and getting into a steady groove.	10–20' in Gear 2 + 3 x 1' in Gear 7 with 90" RI + 3 x 4–5' in Gear 5 with 2' RI.	15–30' Strength/Form running in Gear 1 with a focus on foot strike and cadence. Visualise running over logs.	20–30' in Gear 2 + 6–8 x 20" hill repeats with hands behind your head/elbows wide. 4–6 x 10" hill repeats with normal arms.	OFF	75% of your Big Deal Distance/time in Gear 1–2 + 6 x 30" flat repeats building speed to Gear 7 by the end of each with 90" RI.	25–45' Strength/Form running in Gear 1 with a focus on foot strike and cadence. You are strength training and developing muscle memory; stay patient with your speed.

WEEK 6

WORKOUT	DAY 36	DAY 37	DAY 38	DAY 39	DAY 40	DAY 41	DAY 42
FITNESS	3 Sets of Foot Core + 3 Sets of Wall Squats	1 Set of 100 Up Major & 3 Sets of Leg Stiffeners	OFF	2 Sets of Wall Squats + 3 Sets of Run Lunge	3 Sets of Foot Core	OFF	3 Sets of Wall Squats + 2 Sets of Run Lunge
FORM	OFF	3 x 6–8 Skipping for Height + 4 Sets of Sticky Hops	OFF	OFF	5 x 2' barefoot running in place to music playlist	Running Logs Part 1 & 2 + 2 Sets of Sticky Hops	OFF
FOCUS RUN	30–50' in Gear 2. Stay patient with speed and focus on form and getting into a steady groove.	10–20' in Gear 2 + 4 x 1' in Gear 7 with 90" RI + 4 x 4–5' in Gear 5 with 2' RI.	15–30' Strength/Form running in Gear 1 with a focus on foot strike and cadence. Visualise running over logs.	20–30' in Gear 2 + 6 x 30" hill repeats with hands behind your head/elbows wide. 5 x 30" hill repeats with normal arms.	OFF	80% of your Big Deal Distance/time in Gear 1–2 + 7 x 30" flat repeats building speed to Gear 7 by the end of each with 90" RI.	25–45' Steady in Gear 2 with relaxed form. Start to feel good and bad form, and adjust as you run.

WEEK 7

WORKOUT	DAY 43	DAY 44	DAY 45	DAY 46	DAY 47	DAY 48	DAY 49
FITNESS	3 Sets of Foot Core + 3 Sets of Run Lunge	1 Set of 100 Up Major & 3 Sets of Leg Stiffeners	OFF	3 Sets of Wall Squats + 2 Sets of Run Lunge. Increase reps to continue to add challenge.	3 Sets of Foot Core. Increase challenge by adding more time/reps or with less balancing aid.	OFF	2 Sets of 100 Up Minor + 3 Sets of Run Lunge
FORM	OFF	3 x 6–8 Skipping for Height + 4 Sets of Sticky Hops	OFF	OFF	3 x 3' barefoot running in place to music playlist	Running Logs Part 1 & 2 + 2 Sets of Sticky Hops	OFF
FOCUS RUN	30–50' in Gear 2. Stay patient with speed and focus on form and getting into a steady groove.	10–20' in Gear 2 + 5 x 30" building speed to Gear 7 with 90" RI + 3 x 6' in Gear 5 with 2–3' RI.	15–30' Strength/ Form running in Gear 1 with a focus on foot strike and cadence. Visualise running over logs.	20–30' in Gear 2 + 4 x 20" hill repeats with hands behind your head/elbows wide. 8 x 30" hill repeats with normal arms.	OFF	85% of your Big Deal Distance/ time in Gear 1–2 + 8 x 30" flat repeats building speed to Gear 7 by the end of each with 90" RI.	25–45' Steady in Gear 2 with relaxed form. Start to feel good and bad form, and adjust while running.

WEEK 8

WORKOUT	DAY 50	DAY 51	DAY 52	DAY 53	DAY 54	DAY 55	DAY 56
FITNESS	Complete Day Off. Remember, recovery is when you get stronger.	2 Sets of Foot Core + 2 Sets of Run Lunge	OFF	OFF	2 Sets of Foot Core + 2 Sets of Run Lunge	3 Sets of Wall Squats	Complete Day Off. Remember, recovery is when you get stronger.
FORM	OFF	OFF	Running Logs Part 1 + 4 x 6–8 Skipping for Height. Be relaxed to get height.	OFF	3 x 2' barefoot running in place to music playlist	Running Logs Part 1 & 2 + 3 Sets of Sticky Hops	OFF
FOCUS RUN	OFF	30–50' in Gear 2. Stay patient with speed and focus on form and getting into a steady groove.	OFF	20–30' in Gear 2 + 5 x 20" hill repeats + 3 x 1' flat intervals in Gear 7 with 2' RI	OFF	40–60' in Gear 2. Good recovery.	OFF

WEEK 9

WORKOUT	DAY 57	DAY 58	DAY 59	DAY 60	DAY 61	DAY 62	DAY 63
FITNESS	2 Sets of Foot Core + 4 Sets of Run Lunge	1 Set of 100 Up Major & 2 Sets of Leg Stiffeners	OFF	4 Sets of Wall Squats + 2 Sets of Run Lunge	3 Sets of Foot Core + 2 Sets of Leg Stiffeners	OFF	2 Sets of Foot Core
FORM	OFF	4–5 Sets of Sticky Hops + 2 Sets of Skipping for Height	5 x 1' barefoot running in place to music playlist	OFF	3 x 3' barefoot running in place to music playlist	4 Sets of Sticky Hops	OFF
FOCUS RUN	35–60' in Gear 2. Stay patient with speed and focus on form and getting into a steady groove.	15–30' in Gear 2 + 4–5 x 3' in Gear 7 with 3' RI. Use all of the RI.	20–45' Strength/ Form running in Gear 1 with a focus on foot strike and cadence. Visualise running over logs.	20–30' in Gear 2 + 3–4 x 6' in Gear 5 with 2' RI.	OFF	85% of your Big Deal Distance/ time in Gear 1–2. Focus on spending a lot of time steady in Gear 2 + 5–7 x 20" moderately fast downhill repeats with a focus on good foot strike. Slow down enough so you do not heel-strike.	20–45' Strength/ Form running in Gear 1 with a focus on foot strike and cadence. Visualise running over logs.

WEEK 10

WORKOUT	DAY 64	DAY 65	DAY 66	DAY 67	DAY 68	DAY 69	DAY 70
FITNESS	2 Sets of Foot Core + 4 Sets of Run Lunge	1 Set of 100 Up Major & 2 Sets of Leg Stiffeners	OFF	2 Sets of Wall Squats with increased reps + 4 Sets of Run Lunge	3 Sets of Foot Core + 2 Sets of Leg Stiffeners	OFF	2 Sets of Foot Core
FORM	OFF	4–5 Sets of Sticky Hops + 2 Sets of Skipping for Height	5 x 1' barefoot running in place to music playlist	OFF	3 x 4' barefoot running in place to music playlist	5 Sets of Sticky Hops	OFF
FOCUS RUN	35–60' in Gear 2. Stay patient with speed and focus on form and getting into a steady groove.	30' in Gear 2 + 4–5 x 3.5' in Gear 7 with 3' RI. Use all of the RI.	20–45' Strength/ Form running in Gear 1 with a focus on foot strike and cadence. Visualise running over logs.	15–30' in Gear 2 + 8'/6'/4' in Gear 5 with 2' RI.	OFF	90% of your Big Deal Distance/ time in Gear 1–2 + 7 x 20" moderately fast downhill repeats with a focus on good foot strike. Slow down enough so you do not heel-strike.	OFF

WEEK 11

WORKOUT	DAY 71	DAY 72	DAY 73	DAY 74	DAY 75	DAY 76	DAY 77
FITNESS	2 Sets of Foot Core + 3 Sets of Wall Squats	3 Sets of Leg Stiffeners	OFF	1 Set of Wall Squats with increased reps + 5 Sets of Run Lunge	3 Sets of Foot Core + 2 Sets of Leg Stiffeners	OFF	2 Sets of Foot Core
FORM	OFF	2 Sets of Sticky Hops + 2 Sets of Skipping for Height	OFF	OFF	4 x 2' barefoot running in place to music playlist	Running Logs Part 1 & 2 + 3 Sets of Sticky Hops	OFF
FOCUS RUN	35–60' in Gear 2. Stay patient with speed and focus on form and getting into a steady groove.	30' in Gear 2 + 4–5 x 4' in Gear 7 with 4' RI. Use all of the RI!	20–40' Strength/ Form running in Gear 1 with a focus on foot strike and cadence. Visualise running over logs.	35–60' in Gear 2. Stay patient with speed and focus on form and getting into a steady groove.	OFF	20–30' in Gear 2 + 3 x 8' in Gear 5 with 2' RI	40–70' in Gear 2

WEEK 12

WORKOUT	DAY 78	DAY 79	DAY 80	DAY 81	DAY 82	DAY 83	DAY 84
FITNESS	Complete Day Off. Remember, recovery is when you get stronger.	1 Set of Leg Stiffeners	2 Sets of Foot Core	2 Sets of Wall Squats with increased reps + 2 Sets of Run Lunge	Complete Day Off. Remember, recovery is when you get stronger.	OFF	Complete Day Off. Remember, recovery is when you get stronger.
FORM	OFF	3 Sets of Skipping for Height	OFF	2 Sets of Sticky Hops	OFF	3 Sets of Skipping for Height + 2 Sets of Sticky Hops	OFF
FOCUS RUN	OFF	30' in Gear 2 + 3 x 3' in Gear 7 with 3' RI. Then finish with 8' between Gear 4–5 (you can estimate Gear 4 by feel).	20–40' Strength/ Form running in Gear 1 with a focus on foot strike and cadence. Visualise running over logs.	35–60' in Gear 2	OFF	100% of your Big Deal Distance in Gear 1–2.	OFF

WEEK 13

WORKOUT	DAY 85	DAY 86	DAY 87	DAY 88	DAY 89	DAY 90
FITNESS	2 Sets of Foot Core + 3 Sets of Wall Squats	OFF	2 Sets of Wall Squats + 3 Sets of Run Lunge	2 Sets of Foot Core	OFF	OFF
FORM	OFF	2 Sets of Skipping for Height + 2 Sets of Sticky Hops	OFF	2 Sets of Sticky Hops	OFF	2 Sets of Skipping for Height + 2 Sets of Sticky Hops
FOCUS RUN	20–30' Strength/Form running in Gear 1 with a focus on foot strike and cadence. Visualise running over logs.	30' in Gear 2 + 3 x 2' in Gear 7 with 4' RI. Pay attention to how this feels to help you pace for the retest on Day 90.	20–40' in Gear 2. Stay patient so you are fresh for the test.	OFF	20–30' Strength/Form running in Gear 1.	One-Mile Test on the same course used at the beginning of the programme.

Note: Even if you're not currently in pain, try all of these Flat Tire exercises. They're a terrific diagnostic tool for revealing hidden hot spots.

Injuries: Fixing Your Flat Tires

15

If you're hurt, we've got good news:

You won't be for long. And you may never be again.

Running injuries aren't caused by your body. They're caused by your behaviour. They have nothing to do with your age or weight, your 'pronation pattern' or 'leg-length discrepancy'. If you're struggling with plantar fasciitis, Achilles tendinitis, or any of the other run-related usual suspects, there is nothing wrong with you that can't be cured by changing the way you move. As runners, we need to be more like swimmers and martial artists who constantly rehearse their movements until they can instantly feel a bad movement and correct it. Imbalance is the problem. Skill is the solution.

Coach Eric doesn't even use the word 'injury'. He insists on 'dysfunction', because you're not broken. You're not even really hurt. Your body is complaining because you made it function in an awkward position, same as it would if you slept all night with your head cocked funny. Fix your form, and in nearly every case, you'll fix your problem.

'Everyone thinks they're a special situation, but functionally, we're all very similar,' Eric explains. 'Take away the extremes on either end, and most of us are right in the middle, with bodies that are designed to move the same way.'

That's why the standard treatments – rest, ice, ibuprofen, static stretching and orthotics – don't work. They can provide some short-term relief by easing the symptoms, but long term, they set you back by ignoring the actual dysfunction. You can numb a broken leg, but that's not setting the bone. But once you learn to run properly, you get a double pay-off: every step you take with good form is a strengthening exercise in itself. You're not only correcting your imbalances, but simultaneously building the muscles which make it easier to run.

You're reversing the cycle of:

Poor form ▶ Weakness ▶ Tightness ▶ Pain

By turning it into an endlessly recharging battery of:

Good form ▶ Increased strength ▶ Longer good-form runs ▶ Even greater strength

Feeling hopeful? You haven't even heard the best part:

Everything you need, you already have.

The Fitness, Form and Movement Snacks exercises you've been learning are a complete tool kit for easing your pain and correcting the root cause. They're also a great diagnostic tool: none of the exercises will make you feel worse, and if they don't make you feel better, that's a sign you could have a different underlying cause and may need to see a specialist. Sadly, we've been led to believe that soreness and tightness are normal for running, when they're actually red flags for dysfunction. Most of us have no idea how great running can feel if we speed up our cadence, flatten our foot strike, and add Eric's movement exercises to our routine.

Tightness is not a flexibility issue! 'So many runners try to address tightness with stretching and yoga, but it's really a tug and pull from muscle imbalances,' Eric says. 'Stretching won't help. But form and strength will change everything.' Even if you don't think of yourself as injured, the tightness you accept as normal could actually be a slowly leaking tire on its way to a blowout.

These skills are also a terrific way to introduce you to your body. Most of the time, our lower extremities are out of sight and out of mind until they start causing trouble. When was the last time you had a good look at your arches? Have you ever run your fingers down your Achilles or calves and been surprised to discover they're kind of knotty? Could you take a finger right now and, with any degree of certainty, trace the path of your plantar fascia? Usually, all of our parts below the knee are distant cousins we rarely visit until they start complaining of neglect.

Recently, Eric worked with a pro athlete who came in with pain along the top of her foot. Whenever she tried to run, a fiery stab shot from her ankle to her big toe. Eric bypassed the top of her foot and worked underneath until he reached the arch. As he suspected, 'she nearly shot through the roof'. It wasn't hard for him to figure out what was going on. Rarely is the painful area the source of the issue. More often, it's a consequence of a weak link further up the chain.

'Your body tells the story. Follow the story,' Eric says. Your foot is actually a pretty simple apparatus, he explains. It's a shock absorption system designed to cushion and stabilise your landings. So if your landings hurt, the first move is to check the suspension. The second is to figure out why it's not working. Eric looked at the athlete's shoes, and found they were top-of-the-line models with a 'stability correcting' insert and a hard rubber outsole. Because it was mid-winter, the freezing cold was stiffening the shoes more than usual, turning them into hard platforms with zero room for the athlete's arches to flex. Eric ran her through some 'Remedy Snacks' and some basic stability exercises to work on, and she walked out the door pain-free.

But here's the point: this pro athlete had already seen doctors and therapists. None of them said, 'Let's assume your foot is fine. How about we just flick the light switch to see if the power is on?' For foot mobility, the light switch is the arch. Rather than freeing it, the most common therapeutic response is to immobilise it. The athlete was such a stranger to her own feet, she had no idea her arches were deactivated until Eric pressed on them.

To remedy these dysfunctions, Eric provides a two-part approach:

- First, a 'Remedy Snack' to relieve discomfort.
- Second, a long-term strategy to work on the source of the problem, with exercises to do a few times a week until full mobility is restored. Afterwards, repeat these exercises whenever you feel a twinge or tightness coming on.

So consider this your owner's manual. You're about to become a master mechanic of your own body.

PAIN IN THE BOTTOM OF THE HEEL (PLANTAR FASCIITIS)

HOW IT FEELS

Pain in the bottom of the heel that's worse in the mornings and after walking and running.

CAUSES

- The plantar fascia is the thick band of tissue which runs beneath your foot, connecting your heel to your toes. Plantar fasciitis usually originates from a tight calf, which reduces range of motion in your lower leg. With no ability to flex, your leg pulls harder and harder on the plantar tissue.
- Contributing factors are anything which overloads your calves, like hill running; overstriding; poor hip flexor mobility; or poor body weight shift from slow cadence.
- Any drastic change to footwear can cause your calves to tighten protectively. That's why many runners who adopt barefoot-style shoes pay the price if they don't decrease their miles and transition gradually.

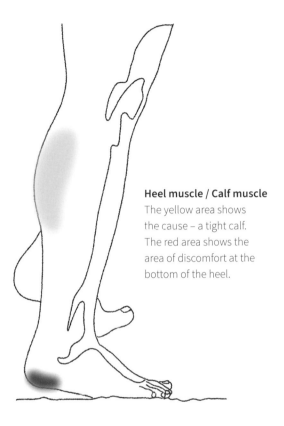

Heel muscle / Calf muscle
The yellow area shows the cause – a tight calf. The red area shows the area of discomfort at the bottom of the heel.

◀ Notice the way Karma has to lean forward because her hip flexors are too tight. She's forced to push off and drive from her ankles, overloading her calf. Very common among runners who maintain the same slow pace every day.

▲ Overstriding, or reaching out with the front leg, puts excess strain on your calves by increasing ground contact time. Notice Karma has almost no knee drive.

▲ Two quick tests for plantar fasciitis vulnerability are Ninja Jumps and Deep Squats. Karma struggles to compress, indicating limited range of motion in her calves.

▲ **When good things go wrong:** Runners who are trying to quit heel-striking can overcorrect the other way. Instead of letting their feet land and flatten naturally, they'll force themselves to stay on their toes. First-time minimal runners also tend to run slowly with little leg movement, all of it placing stress on their calves.

REMEDY SNACK

To break up the adhesion in the calf and allow it to lengthen, do a combination of massage first and then stretch after, 2–3 times per day when you can. The goal is to get past the tightness in the calf so you begin to feel a burning/stretching sensation in your heel. When you reach this point, you'll be stretching and lengthening the painful fascia at the heart of the problem.

Be patient. Getting past the calf tightness before reaching the heel might take 7–10 days of massage and stretch cycle. When you get there – you will know it when you feel it – you should start to feel immediate pain relief.

1) Running

- Taking time off from running will typically ease the pain, but not the problem.
- The more you run during this treatment, the slower you'll make the process by tightening your calf, so it's best to reduce your miles and avoid hills.

2) Massage

Lie face down on the floor and have a partner massage your calves, going deep into the muscles. The massager should use their fingers and thumbs to feel for knots. When tender knots are detected, the massager should work these areas by pressing firmly, isolating on the spot with good pressure and no movement.

You can self-massage by sitting in a chair and working your way down your calf with your hands.

Note: Be sure to use your hands, not massaging tools like foam rollers. Your hands allow you to precisely locate and work the knots.

3) Leaning Calf Stretch

- After massaging the knot thoroughly, stand up for this stretch. Always massage first and stretch after, so you are breaking up the adhesion in the calf and allowing it to lengthen.
- Place your arms against a wall and straighten the affected leg behind you.
- Gradually lower your heel to the floor until you feel good, taut resistance in your calf.
- Stretch the calf in a MODERATE manner, only to the point where you can sustain the stretch for 2–5 minutes.
- If you can't hold the stretch that long, you are making the stretch too intense. Back off a little and be patient.
- Perform this sequence 2–3 times per day when you can.
- The goal is to eventually get past the tightness in the calf so you begin to feel a burning/stretching sensation in your heel.
- When you reach the point where you feel the stretch in the heel, you'll be stretching and lengthening the painful fascia at the heart of the problem.

LONG-TERM STRATEGIES

- Foot Core and Run Form exercises for foot strike/overstriding (see pages 96 and 114).
- Barefoot cadence running in place to 'Rock Lobster' or other 90-bpm music (see page 121).
- Easy running with short-stride good form.
- When pain-free, begin Pogo Hops (see page 99).
- Posterior Floss: the traditional touch-your-toes stretch. Stand tall and keep your legs straight. Reach down towards your toes, keeping your knees locked (or slightly bent if you're feeling a lot of resistance). Don't push too far; the goal is to find the point of tension and hold there a few moments. The farther in front of your feet you reach, the more you'll stretch your calves.
- Wall Squats/Run Lunge (pages 102–103).

TIGHT/PAINFUL CALVES

HOW IT FEELS

Calf pain is either **acute** or **chronic**.

If you felt the pain while running and had to stop, or your calves became very sore after running uphill or very fast, you have an **acute** dysfunction.

Pain that develops gradually over time, persists throughout the day, and isn't triggered by an acute event, like running hills, is **chronic**.

CAUSES

Acute calf pain often comes from:

- A change in running form or foot strike while transitioning to a more minimal shoe.
- Running more, faster or steeper than usual.

Chronic calf pain comes from:

- Bad form/strength.
- Overtraining uphill repeats and speed.
- Poor/low cadence and running slow all of the time.

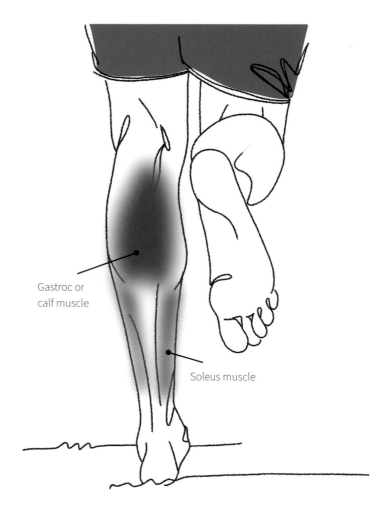

Gastroc or calf muscle

Soleus muscle

Doing more hills or more volume can cause both acute and chronic soreness, as can keeping the heel elevated when running.

Sometimes runners focus on having a forefoot strike but are still overstriding, which causes them to point the toes to land on the forefoot and overload the calf.

REMEDY SNACK

- Acute soreness: Active rest, like gentle walking, while pain subsides.
- Acute and chronic: Hand massage of the calves. Don't use a foam roller, which blocks awareness of knots in your muscles. When massaging, be aware of any tender spots and work on these areas with your fingers to break up the adhesion and muscle tightness. THEN do a light calf stretch following your massage.
- Acute: Resume gentle, pain-free running, but reduce volume as you transition your calves back to bearing load.

LONG-TERM STRATEGY

- Daily calf massaging and calf stretch.
- Walking, and rest from running if limping.
- Self-reflection on what might be new/too much/ bad form.
- Movement Snacks: Bear Crawl with legs straight for calves (see page 51).
- Posterior Floss (traditional touch-your-toes stretch): 2–3 sets of 30–45 seconds.
- Fitness Exercises: Foot Core (see page 96) and, when pain-free, Leg Stiffeners (see page 98).

SHIN PAIN (SHIN SPLINTS)

HOW IT FEELS

Pain along the shin bone (or tibias muscle), running along the front of the leg from knee to ankle.

CAUSES

- Heel-striking/overstriding/poor strength and stability are all big culprits in shin splints.
- In concert with this or separately, too much ground contact time/low cadence.
- Common in young, school-aged runners who do not run consistently throughout the year, but suddenly ramp up for sports in a very short period of time.

Shin splints

Overstriding causes more ground contact time.

Notice the position of the knee over the toes and the excessive ankle dorsiflexion. This causes increased ground contact time, which sends added stress to the shins.

REMEDY SNACK

- First try the Tight Calves remedies. Loosening you calves might provide immediate relief and a long-term remedy.
- If your shin pain persists despite the Tight Calves protocol, time off from running is best to help things calm down.
- During your time off from running, follow the Foot Core protocol (see page 96).

LONG-TERM STRATEGY

- Fitness Exercises: Foot Core, Wall Squats and Run Lunge protocol (see pages 96, 102 and 103).
- Form: Skills practice for foot strike/overstriding (see pages 116–19).
- Barefoot cadence running in place to 90-bpm music (see page 121 for song suggestions): 5 x 1–2 minutes.
- Focus: Easy Gear 1 running with short stride and good form (see page 130).
- When pain-free, try Leg Stiffeners (see page 98).
- Posterior Floss by doing traditional touch-your-toes stretch with legs straight: 2–3 sets of 30–45 seconds.

ACHILLES AND SOLEUS PAIN

HOW IT FEELS

You'll feel pain in the Achilles, the tendon on the back of the heel that attaches to the heel bone, or in the soleus muscle, which runs along back of the lower leg. Sometimes you'll feel it in one or the other, other times the pain will be in both areas.

CAUSES

- Excessive ground contact time from slow cadence. Ground contact time allows the leg to wobble and overload the Achilles and/or soleus.
- Increase in hill running.

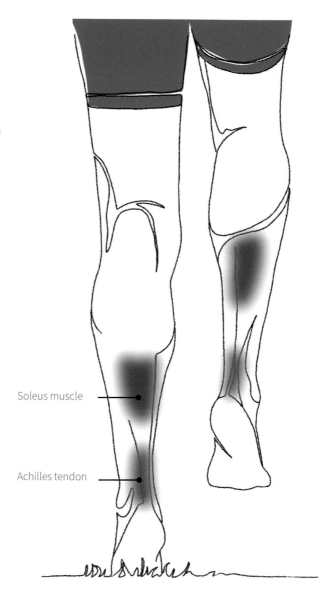

Soleus muscle

Achilles tendon

Any time your knee flexes too far over your toes, whether from poor form, slow cadence or muscle imbalance, you're loading stress on your Achilles. You're also at risk of other injuries, because your thighs are carrying too much load and your glutes aren't engaged.

Hills can be hell on an ailing Achilles.

REMEDY SNACK

- Rest until pain-free.
- Massage the area to gauge the level of soreness and feel how it is healing.

LONG-TERM STRATEGY: WHEN PAIN-FREE

- Movement Snacks: Bear Crawl with legs straight for calves (see page 51).
- Posterior Floss by doing traditional touch-your-toes stretch: 2–3 sets of 30–45 seconds. This simple movement resets everything and gives you the floss where you need it.
- Fitness Exercises: Foot Core, Leg Stiffeners, Wall Squats and Run Lunge protocol (see pages 96, 98, 102 and 103).
- Form: Skills practice (see pages 116–19).
- Faster running/accelerations can help reduce ground contact time and knee flexion. Try it 4–5 x 10–20 seconds.
- Barefoot cadence running in place to 90-bpm music (see page 121): 3–5 x 1–2 minutes.

BACK OF HEEL PAIN

HOW IT FEELS

Pain in the back of the heel bone (not the Achilles or bottom of the heel). It's a bruised, tender feeling right on the bone, not an irritation or friction like a blister.

CAUSES

- Overstriding, often by landing on the outside of your foot and rolling in, putting torque on the heel.
- Wearing shoes that are too short or tight, inhibiting foot movement.
- Wearing shoes with very high stack height and mushy cushioning, which causes the foot to have a lot of lateral torque/ movement at foot strike.

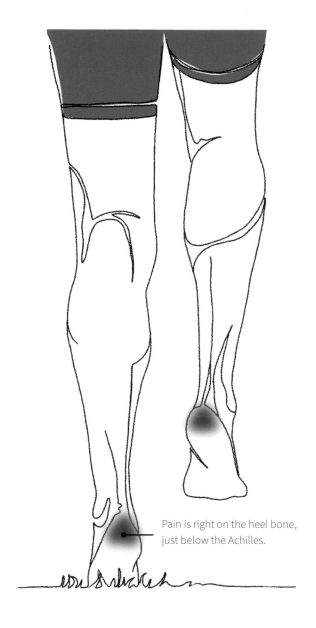

Pain is right on the heel bone, just below the Achilles.

Note how the lead runner is reaching out with his right foot, causing him to land on the extreme outside edge and roll inward. All that torque puts tremendous stress on the heel and leads to pain.

REMEDY SNACK

- Check if your shoes are too snug without enough space for your toes to move. If so, try a longer pair with bigger toe box.
- Pull out the insoles of your shoes and go for a light run. Just that small amount of extra space could provide immediate relief.
- Experiment with a lower-platform shoe to have more stability when striking the ground.
- Focus on striking the ground closer to your body, rather than reaching in front with your lead leg. This will keep your foot strike more stable.
- If neither of these help, follow the Calf/Achilles remedies (see pages 245 and 249).

LONG-TERM STRATEGY

- Posterior Floss (traditional touch-your-toes stretch): 2–3 sets of 30–45 seconds.
- Fitness Exercises: Foot Core protocol (see page 96).
- Form: Skills practice (see pages 116–19).
- Barefoot cadence running in place to 90-bpm music (see page 121): 3–5 x 1–2 minutes.

FLAT FEET

HOW IT FEELS

Low arch where the foot appears to be flat.

CAUSES

- Flat feet aren't a dysfunction, but by training them you can add some height to your arch and gain extra strength and shock absorption.
- Just like building other muscles, flat feet will respond to strength work.
- Because our feet are the first line of defence when it comes to stabilisation, strengthening your arch will reduce pressure on your glutes and calves.

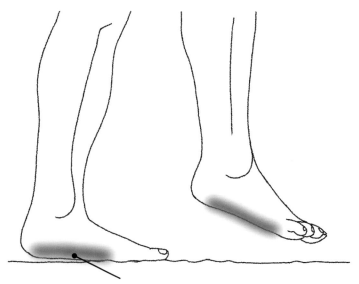

The arch is collapsed and 'flat'.

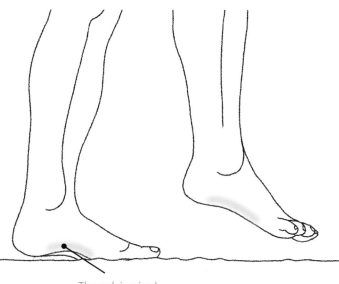

The arch is raised.

REMEDY SNACK

- Walk barefoot as much as possible in your daily life.
- Strength runs in minimal shoes.

LONG-TERM STRATEGY

- Fitness Exercises: Foot Core and Leg Stiffeners
  (see pages 96 and 98).
- Form: Forefoot run (see page 114).
- Barefoot cadence running in place to 90-bpm music
  (see page 121): 3–5 x 1–2 minutes.

PAIN ON THE OUTSIDE OF KNEE OR LEG (ILIOTIBIAL BAND (ITB) PAIN)

HOW IT FEELS

Irritation and pain on the outside of the knee, generally about ten minutes into a run, depending on severity.

CAUSES

- The ITB is a band of thick fibres that run from your hip to the outside of your knee. Friction of the band against your knee can cause irritation and pain on the outside of the knee.
- Where you feel it is typically not the source of the problem. Pain presents in the knee, but is caused by weaknesses higher up the chain in your hips and glutes.
- Heel-striking and overstriding are the main culprits. When we heel-strike, we're not able to utilise our feet as the first stabiliser. That sets off a reaction up the stability chain to your ITB, quads and hip flexors.
- Hip flexors get tight from being overworked from poor glute stability. This tightness pulls on the leg, causing tightness to the quad and ITB area.
- Heel-striking also makes your quadriceps work harder, shutting off your glutes.
- Shoes with high stack height and mushy cushioning contribute by causing poor stability and weakening your feet.

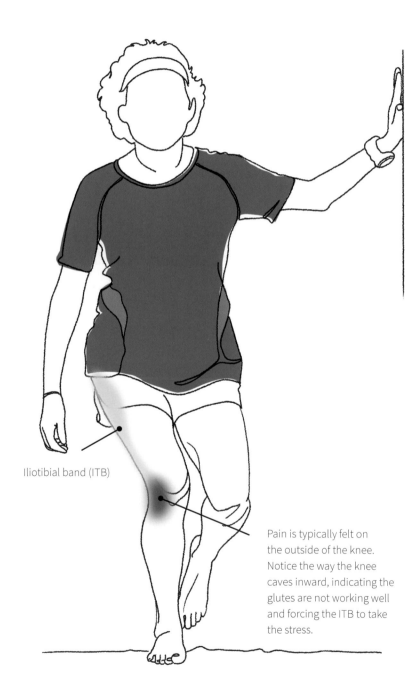

Iliotibial band (ITB)

Pain is typically felt on the outside of the knee. Notice the way the knee caves inward, indicating the glutes are not working well and forcing the ITB to take the stress.

Manny keeps his stance leg too bent at take-off, forcing his quads to overwork and his glutes to shut down.

Heel-striking puts too much stress on the quads and too little on the glutes, causing stress to the ITB.

Knees caving during a Deep Squat shows quad dominance and poor glute stabilisation, leading to knee pain.

REMEDY SNACKS

- You DO NOT want to foam roll or stretch the ITB. The ITB is a very thick fibrous band that can't be stretched very well. Rolling just keeps it irritated. It might feel good immediately after, but since you are not treating the source, this is a fleeting 'feel good' that doesn't last, just like most stretching protocol.
- Instead, massage the quad to help break up adhesion and tender spots.
- Then try some Movement Snacks – Shin Box and Three-Point Crab will help elongate your hip flexors and ITB attachment muscles (see pages 49 and 52).

LONG-TERM STRATEGY

- Heel-striking is a primary form issue that can cause ITB pain, so form work is key.
- Foot Core strength will also provide a huge benefit, creating the natural stabiliser in our arch that helps stabilise the knee and activate the glute.
- Building glute strength and muscle equilibrium with Wall Squats and Run Lunges takes stress off the hip flexors.
- Form: Skills practice (see pages 116–19).
- Fitness: Do the Foot Core, Leg Stiffeners, Wall Squats and Run Lunge exercises (see pages 96, 98, 102 and 103).
- Focus: 5–6 x 20–30 seconds Gear 7–8 accelerations (see page 130).
- Movement Snacks: Shin Box, Three-Point Crab and Deep Squats (see pages 49, 52 and 48).
- Posterior Floss (traditional touch-your-toes stretch): 3–5 x 30–45 seconds.

TIGHT/PAINFUL HIP FLEXORS:

HOW IT FEELS

- Pain or tightness in your hip flexor muscles, which are located on the front top of your quads in your pelvic region.
- Hip flexors do the heavy lifting when your leg comes up for each stride. When they're tight, you'll not only feel tension in your hips and glutes but often discomfort in your lower back and hamstrings.
- Can you stand in the 100 Up position with your stance leg straight and the other knee high? If not, your hip flexors are too tight.

CAUSES

- Excess sitting, causing tightness/ weakness and shutting down of the glutes.
- Poor glute strength.
- Poor form.

Tight hip flexors

Healthy hip flexors allow you to 'run tall', with an upright torso and a straighter leg at push off. The hip flexors are on stretch, pulling back the 'rubber band' to spring forward.

Tight hip flexors keep the leg too bent and/or inhibit hip flexion, causing a runner to lean forward at the waist.

REMEDY SNACK

- Test your hip flexor flexibility with the 100 Up. If you're struggling to get your knee high and keep your leg straight, you could use some loosening.

LONG-TERM STRATEGY

- Fitness Exercises: Foot Core, Wall Squat and Run Lunge to help activate glutes (see pages 96, 102 and 103).
- Form: Skills practice (see pages 116–19).
- Skipping for Height to help lengthen hip flexors.
- Movement Snacks: Shin Box and Three-Point Crab to lengthen hip flexors/quads (see pages 49 and 52).
- Uphill repeats with hands behind head to get leg/hip extension: 5–8 x 10–20 seconds.
- Fast, Gear 7–8 accelerations to get good hip flexor extension: 5–8 x 20–30 seconds (see page 130).

KNEE PAIN (RUNNER'S KNEE):

HOW IT FEELS

- Pain around the knee, specifically on the inside of the knee, the top of the kneecap, or below the kneecap.

CAUSES

- Runner's knee is typically caused by quad tightness, causing the knee to track poorly and resulting in irritation around it.
- The main culprit tends to be the sartorius muscle, which runs from the top of the quad and hip flexor attachment and attaches to the inside of the knee. This is a very long muscle that can get tight and pull on the knee, causing poor tracking and pain.

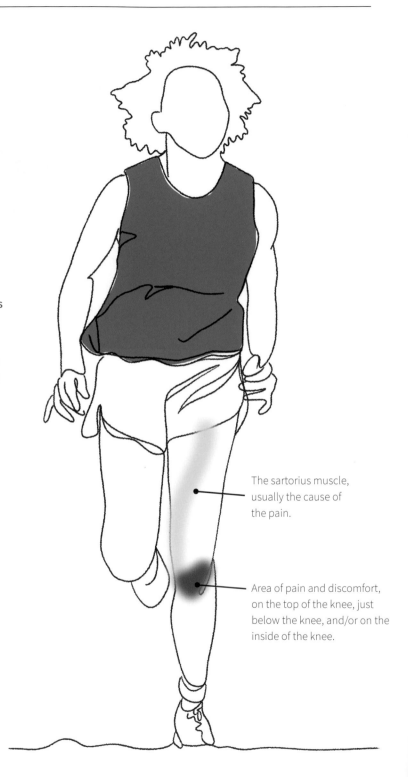

The sartorius muscle, usually the cause of the pain.

Area of pain and discomfort, on the top of the knee, just below the knee, and/or on the inside of the knee.

Heel-striking and overstriding stresses the quads too much with poor general stability, causing tightness that leads to knee pain.

Too much knee action, where the knee pitches forward and inward, places stress on the quads and destabilises the glutes. This also contributes to lower cadence and increased ground contact time. No different than having trouble when doing Ninja Jumps or Deep Squats (see pages 242 and 255).

REMEDY SNACK

- To immediately help with the discomfort and pain, massage the quad all over using fingers/thumbs and a massage stick, but NOT a foam roller.
- Be on the lookout for a tender spot or knot in the middle of the sartorius, about halfway down the quad and slightly inside, where the sartorius begins to wrap towards the inside knee. Follow this path from the top of the quad to the inside of the knee with your massage to find tender spots.
- If this area is tender, massage it and apply pressure with your thumb, holding and breathing deep for 20 seconds to help release it. You may even try flexing the knee back and forth as you apply this pressure.
- After the massage session, perform the Movement Snacks listed right to help elongate the quads.
- Do a Common Quad Stretch: lie on your side, grab your foot of your top leg and pull your leg behind you to feel a gentle stretch in your quad. Hold the gentle stretch for about 60 seconds at a time.

- This massage/stretch cycle should help with the quad tightness and should immediately relieve the knee pain to allow you to run.
- If your knee protests during a run, stop and massage above the knee and do a quad stretch.

LONG-TERM STRATEGY

- Form: Exercises working on leg extension, running logs and foot strike (see pages 116–19).
- Fitness Exercises: Foot Core, Leg Stiffeners, Wall Squat and Run Lunge protocol (see pages 96, 98, 102 and 103).
- Movement Snacks: Shin Box and Three-Point Crab (see pages 49 and 52).
- Flat and hill interval training in Gear 7–8: 5–8 x 10–20 seconds (see page 130).

TIGHTNESS OR PAIN, HIGH HAMSTRING

HOW IT FEELS

- Tightness and a pulling feeling high in your hamstring, just under the glute at the hamstring/glute attachment. This might impede range of motion when running, especially at faster speeds.

CAUSES

- Even though it feels like a hamstring issue, the cause is tight glutes which pull at the hamstring attachment.
- A major culprit is too much sitting/driving that causes the glutes to get tight.

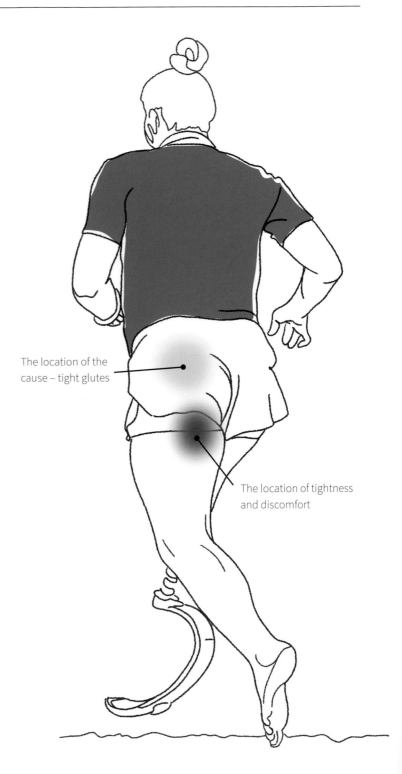

The location of the cause – tight glutes

The location of tightness and discomfort

REMEDY SNACK

- The key is to break up adhesion and tightness first, and then add strength and range of motion.
- Start by rolling the glutes with a hard, softball-sized ball to break up tightness.
- Then perform the Wall Squat (see page 102) to increase strength and stabilisation, with good range of motion.

Note: Stretching the hamstring itself will not help and could make it worse.

LONG-TERM STRATEGY

- Fitness Exercises: Wall Squats and Run Lunge (see pages 102 and 103).
- Posterior Floss (traditional touch-your-toes stretch): 3–5 x 1–2 minutes.
- Movement Snack: Shin Box and Deep Squats (see pages 49 and 48).

THE BIRTH OF *BORN 2*
(AKA, OUR GRATEFUL ACKNOWLEDGEMENTS)

You don't end up as a remote coach high in the Tetons or, in my case, living on a farm with more goats than neighbours unless you and the world at large have mutually agreed it's best for you to work alone. So right off the bat, Eric and I would like to acknowledge the minor miracle that somehow, despite a shared rap sheet of Doesn't Play Well With Others, we've remained great friends and collaborators for more than a decade. Eric was a dream partner on this book, not least because without him there would be no book. All the smart training stuff, all the *ah ha!* revelations about ancestral fitness – all Eric. But above and beyond his brain power, the guy is Cool Hand Orton. He doesn't rattle. Even when we discovered that maybe our only chance of pulling off a photo shoot in the middle of a pandemic meant persuading runners we'd never met to gather at a nudist ranch populated by wild donkeys somewhere in the desert, Eric calmed my fretting by never doubting we'd manage it.

Eric and I would also like to acknowledge something about the title:

Nobody likes it.

Everyone warned us that *Born to Run 2* was a terrible idea, just a real bonehead move that every other author in history has been smart enough to avoid. *No one* numbers their books like they're Vin Diesel vehicles, not even if they're cranking out an eight-part kid wizard saga. So yeah; if *Born 2* turns out to be a disaster, that one's on us.

Fortunately, we've had superb guidance to otherwise protect us from our worst instincts. For the first time in my career, I reached out to a publisher in the middle of writing a book to gush my gratitude for the editor I'd been assigned. Cindy Chan at Profile Books is really the third creator of this project. Her input was crucial for establishing the tone and direction, and the gorgeous art and layout she skippered were beyond our hopes. Edward Kastenmeier at Knopf has been my editor now for fourteen years and four books, and I couldn't ask for a

better champion in public or taskmaster in private. Richard Pine at Inkwell Management Literary Agency is the very best kind of friend, always cheering us on and pushing us to be better. As copy-editor, Patrick Taylor somehow knew our minds better than we did, repeatedly surprising us by showing us what we really wanted to say. As designer, Louise Leffler blew past our imaginations, transforming this project into a work of art that's left us giddy.

One of our first best moves was reaching out to Luis Escobar, our old 'Born to Run' compadre, at the very beginning to help set up a photo shoot. We wanted every reader who opened this book to see someone who looked just like them, so we asked Luis if he could not only find us athletes spanning a range of ages, gender identities and ethnicities, but also talk them into travelling to Colton, California, from as far away as Birmingham, Alabama, for a weekend of running-form drills.

It was too big a job for us. It took Luis about an hour.

The crew he assembled was so fun and friendly and fascinating that we've been wondering ever since if we just got lucky, or whether there's something uniquely big-hearted and self-selecting about trail runners. Luis's model pool ended up affecting the book so profoundly that we'll always think of them as *Born 2*'s beloved 'Original Cast':

Iman Wilkerson, Emmanuel Runes, Karma Park, Zachary Friedley, Alejandra Santos, Jenna Crawford, Challis Popkey, Patrick Sweeney, the ace canine trainers Geoff Clinton and his daughter, Olivia, and that distance-running duo, Marcus Rentie and Batman the Adventure Dog.

But great as Luis is, our Hawaiian photographer Mahinahokukauikamoana Choy-Ellis one-upped him by handing off the camera and jumping in front of the lens herself. We wanted to remind the rest of the world that Pacific Islanders have a trail running tradition that's even more important to their history than surfing. So in Hawaii, Mahina made it happen by first recruiting a terrific team, then scouting locations by hucking through mud in flip-flops (her choice) and switch-hitting as both model and lead photographer of our Born 2 Hawaiian Island All-Stars:

Sienna 'Big Sienna Energy' Akimo, Sky Kikuchi, Kaimana Ramos, Daniel Gutowski and Danielle Kinch.

Barefoot Ted McDonald had urgent family business to deal with when I asked him to join us in Colton, but he didn't say a word about it until *after* he'd spent six hours on a train to get there and made each member of the Original Cast a custom pair of Luna Sandals. I'm never really in sync with Ted's Astral Monkey brain, but I have no doubt about his oversized heart. Same with Billy Barnett and his wife, Alyx. The Bonehead lives to the beat of his own savage drums, but when I asked him and Alyx for help with On the Run recipes and training advice for new parents, they were quick to step up and fantastically knowledgeable, as was new mama Ellen Ortis, whose baby jogger knowledge deserves its own YouTube channel.

Down in the Copper Canyons, we were lucky to learn from Arnulfo Quimare, Silvino Cubesare, Manuel Luna and the rest of Caballo's Rarámuri buddies. But that was just the beginning of our education. Bucky Preston and Dennis Poolheco took me out for a long run one evening on the high mesas of Hopi tribal land, and as the moon rose and coyotes barked in the distance, they suddenly and permanently changed my thinking by introducing me to prayer runs, the ancestral tradition of turning your run into an act of selflessness. Dennis Poolheco was a warm-hearted and purely self-taught champion, and not long after that night, he died too soon. Since his passing, we've been fortunate to continue learning from Jordan Marie Brings Three White Horses Daniel (who was still answering my questions the same week she was about to give birth) and Native American wellness researchers Chelsey Luger and Thosh Collins, who were kind enough to give me an early read of their own magnificent book: *The Seven Circles: Indigenous Teaching for Living Well*.

Dr Irene Davis has been our hero for years, and not just because of the way she held her own on-air with Neil deGrasse Tyson. Irene had the courage and professional integrity to re-examine decades of her own work in biomechanics when she got wind of the benefits of the barefoot movement, and since then, she has led the rebel resistance against the mass hypnosis of running shoe marketing. Her research has been fundamental in shaping our understanding of footwear and form, as has the brilliance and self-experimentation of Golden Harper, Curt Munson, Kelly and Juliet Starrett, Nathan Leehman and Amy Stone.

Likewise for Dr Phil Maffetone. For a person with his extraordinary knowledge and achievement, Phil Maffetone has never lost that inner light of the lifelong hippy. We've been thrilled to have Phil and his wife pull up in their RV to our home in Peach Bottom for impromptu visits during their cross-country rambles and take over our kitchen, treating us not only to their friendship and wisdom but also some mighty fine meals. Phil was also the one who first connected me with Rick Rubin. Just before I was supposed to meet Rick for a breakfast interview, I had to cancel because I got word that Caballo was missing. It took nearly ten years for Rick and I to reschedule, and when it happened – wow. Everything you've heard about Rick Rubin being a bold, generous, breathtakingly brilliant brainiac is an undersell by 50 per cent.

Despite Rick Rubin's formidable reputation, our new friend Lady Southpaw (aka, Erin Molloy) wasn't afraid to debate him on the subject of running with music (indirectly, but still! It's Rick Rubin!). Lady Southpaw then put her argument into action by writing and recording her song, 'Born to Run Too' – *our very own rock anthem!*

Callie Vinson, Margot Watters (with assistance from husband Tim) and Lucy Bartholomew not only turned their kitchens into Born 2 Test Labs, but were brave enough to share personal stories about their own struggles with injury and mental health. I once heard Lucy speak in person at an event in France, and I've vowed ever since to read every word she writes. Ultrarunning stardom is the least interesting thing about her; she's also a gifted storyteller with tremendous guts and wit.

Julie Angel made her bones as a film-maker, crafting three of the best Parkour shorts I've ever seen, but she's since shifted from observer to teacher by teaming up with Jared Tavasolian to create Movement Snacks. Movement Snacks are so perfect for runners that I had a low-grade cardiac episode before asking Julie if we could include them in *Born to Run 2* because I was afraid she'd say no – but Jules being Jules, she not only agreed in a blink but recruited Jared to join her in teaching Movement Snacks to our Born 2 San Diego crew:

Jonathan Milnes, Zachary Friedley, Iman Wilkerson, Steven Henriquez, Sonia Ludon, Todd Barnett and Lesford Duncan.

I tried my own hand at film-making for our Born to Run app, which meant my brave volunteers did endless retakes of Rock Lobster drills and wall squats while I fumbled around with a GoPro. Amazingly the videos turned out great, and it was all thanks to the relentless good spirits of the Born 2 Lancaster Squad:

Lenaiya Ivan Flowers, Elias Destin Aviles, Stella Woy, Christine Le, Ashton Clatterbuck, Geordonn Robinson and Ruby Rublesky.

Between video shoots, I was also able to hit the trails and catch up with *Vella Shpringa*, my Amish country running buddies who, along with David April and the Fishtown Beer Runners, are my personal inspiration for what a local running club is all about. We're also indebted to Justin Wirtalla, whose film *Beer Runners* is the best movie about the transformative power of running ever made. *Chariots* can pound sand.

Iman Wilkerson is founder of The Run Down, and she's the one who opened my eyes to a revolution that's quietly changing the face of running. Instead of waiting for the industry to stop ignoring them, LGBTQ runners and runners of colour are forming their own support systems and taking to the streets. We've been blown away by the joy and dedication we've found in clubs like Santa Mujeres, Run Dem Crew, FrontRunners, TrailblazHers, Pioneers, Black Men Run, Black Girls Run, Latinos Run, Swaggahouse, Riot Squad and Eight Six Go who turn out every week, in all kinds of weather, to provide a family for first-timers and show that community is more important than competition.

That's the real runner's world.

And it's long overdue.

If you want to strain your own family, write a book. Take it from us. Your loved ones will be subjected to months of whining and self-pity, and no snack in the house will be safe at any hour. I'm not kidding: we're insufferable. That's why we're grateful beyond words to our lifelong trail companions for setting off with us once again on this adventure. To Michelle Rooks and Angel Rooks Orton, Mika and Maya and Sophie McDougall, thank you for making every moment, every memory, every step along the way a joy.

INDEX

Page references in *italics* indicate images.

PHOTO CREDITS

Front and back cover, 6–7, 10, 13, 15, 16, 17, 18, 23, 24–5, 31, 37, 38, 41, 45, 48, 53, 54–5, 83, 91, 92, 95, 96, 97, 98–9, 100, 101, 102, 106, 109 bottom, 111, 112–13, 116, 117, 118, 119, 121, 122–3, 124, 129, 134, 138–9, 140, 147, 148, 150, 152–3, 167, 171, 172, 188, 210–11, 216, 220–1, 238, 241, 242, 245, 247, 249, 251, 255, 256, 257, 259, 261, 265 border **Luis Escobar**

8, 56, 59, 65, 89, 127, 145, 156, 174, 175, 176, 177, 182, 195, 205, 208, 214–15, 226, 270–1 **Mahinahokukauikamoana Choy-Ellis**

20, 27, 213 **Jo Savage**

28, 32, 33, 42, 46, 47, 49, 50, 51, 52, 103, 104–5, 161, 163, 253 **Julie Angel**

35 Mural artist: **Griselda Madrigal**/Photo: **Devin Whetstone**

67 **Callie Vinson**

71 top **Brittany Gilbert**

71 bottom **Mikey Brown**

73, 190 **Alyx Barnett**

75, 224–5 **Eric Orton**

76 **Joshua Lynotte**

77 **Courtesy of Lucy Bartholomew**

79 **Max Romey**

85, 115 **Christopher McDougall**

109 top **Courtesy of Ted McDonald**

164 **Sheridan Marie Park**

168 **Tyler Tomasello**

185 **Elam King**

186, 229 **Kaimana Ramos**

188 **Jeff Davis**

191 **Anna Albrecht**

197 **Emily Osuna**

199, 200, 272 **Zach Hetrick**

230, 237, 265 centre **Gini Woy**

First published in Great Britain in 2022 by
Souvenir Press
an imprint of Profile Books Ltd
29 Cloth Fair
London
EC1A 7JQ
www.souvenirpress.co.uk

The excerpt on p. 179 is taken from 'I'm a Runner: Flea' by Monique Savin, which originally appeared in the September 2011 issue of *Runner's World*, a publication of Hearst Magazines, Inc.

A version of Chapter 15 first appeared on Outsideonline.com, 12 April 2012.

1 3 5 7 9 10 8 6 4 2

Designed by Louise Leffler
Illustrations in Chapter 15 by Sarah Leuzzi
Printed and bound in Italy by L.E.G.O. Spa

The information given within this book has been compiled to offer general guidance on its subject and is not meant to be treated as a substitute for qualified medical advice. Always consult a medical practitioner before stopping, starting or changing any medical care.

A CIP catalogue record for this book is available from the British Library.

ISBN 978 1 78816 581 5
eISBN 978 1 78283 734 3

Get 'Run Free' on your phone

You can download the full 90-Day programme, including daily workout schedules, weekly performance-trackers and how-to videos. Simply scan the QR code to get started.